Hunger 1995

Causes of Hunger

Fifth Annual Report on the State of World Hunger

BREAD FOR THE WORLD
INSTITUTE
1100 WAYNE AVENUE, STE. 1000
SILVER SPRING, MD 20910
USA

Cover and text
printed on recycled paper

Bread for the World Institute

President
David Beckmann

President Emeritus
Arthur Simon

Director
Richard A. Hoehn

Editor
Marc J. Cohen

Art Director
Timothy Achor-Hoch

Printer: Communications Graphics, Baltimore, MD

Cover photo: NASA

Manufactured in the United States of America

First edition published October 1994

ISBN 1-884361-50-1

Table of Contents

Foreword
by David Beckmann 1

Introduction: The Courage to Choose
by Richard A. Hoehn 2

Overview of World Hunger
by Peter Uvin, Marc J. Cohen,
A. Cecilia Snyder, Richard A. Hoehn,
and Maureen Harris..9

Causes of Hunger

Cause 1: Powerlessness and Politics
by Marc J. Cohen...21

Cause 2: Violence and Militarism
by Daniel U.B.P. Chelliah 35

Cause 3: Poverty in a Global Economy
by Don Reeves..47

**Cause 4: Population, Consumption, and
Environment**
by Nancy Wright, A. Cecilia Snyder,
and Don Reeves..61

Cause 5: Racism and Ethnocentrism
International by Sarita Wardlaw Henry..........72
The United States by Billy J. Tidwell 79

Cause 6: Gender Discrimination
by A. Cecilia Snyder 85

Cause 7: Vulnerability and Age
Children by Urban Jonsson 94
Elderly People by Jashinta D'Costa 100

Appendix
Tables
Global Demographic Indicators 105
Global Health, Nutrition,
and Welfare Statistics..................................109
Global Economic Indicators 113
Poverty and Hunger Statistics –
Developing Countries.................................117
United States Poverty Trends.......................120
United States – State Poverty Conditions 120
Sources for Tables 122
Abbreviations 123
Glossary...124
Notes and Bibliography..................................126
Sponsors and Cosponsors 135

Foreword

CAUSES OF HUNGER shows how hunger is interrelated with other social ills – powerlessness, violence, poverty, environmental destruction, and discrimination. All these ills have roots in distorted values. Tackling hunger and related social problems starts with ethical choices.

We have the means to end hunger. Eliminating widespread hunger in the United States is feasible and affordable. Changed U.S. policies could also give a huge boost to progress against world hunger. But we need to choose, as individuals and as a society.

Our hunger report last year urged that some of the effort already devoted to helping hungry people be shifted toward transforming the politics of hunger. This year's report is a more fundamental call to choose what is good and right.

Bread for the World Institute is associated with Bread for the World, a Christian citizens' movement against hunger. Bread for the World's members account for much of U.S. citizen action on behalf of poor and hungry people in other countries. We also make a difference on issues that are important to hungry people within the United States. A key to the effectiveness and persistence of this grassroots movement is its grounding in Christian moral teaching and faith.

Guilt is not a good motivator. Those who do not grow weary in well doing are often nourished by an inner, spiritual feast – for Christians, joy in response to God's grace; for others, according to their own traditions.

With only a mustard seed of faith great things are possible. We can end mass hunger, and that would be a giant step toward a more wholesome, sustainable society and world.

David Beckmann
President
Bread for the World Institute

Introduction:
The Courage to Choose

by Richard A. Hoehn

CAUSES OF HUNGER probes the most profound moral and spiritual contradiction of our age – the persistence of hunger in a world of plenty.

Twenty percent of people in the developing world suffer chronic undernutrition. More than a billion people are too poor to afford an adequate diet and other essentials of life such as health care, housing, sanitation, safe water, and education. More than one-third of the people in the world lack the vitamins and minerals they need to learn, work, and achieve full potential.

In the United States, an estimated 30 million people cannot afford to buy enough food to maintain good health. One of every five children lives in poverty and sometimes goes hungry. More than 10 percent of the population depends on food stamps for part of their diet.

Bread for the World, other public and private agencies, and thousands of committed individuals have helped reduce world malnutrition rates over the past 20 years (see "Overview of World Hunger"). But massive hunger persists in most parts of the world. There is still a wide gap between humanity's professed moral values and our collective action. We have allowed hunger to spread in some places, notably Africa, some countries that are struggling through the transition from communism, and the United States.

Our previous report, *Hunger 1994: Transforming the Politics of Hunger*, showed how the thousands of private organizations and millions of individuals who are helping hungry people could actually bring hunger in the United States to an end and make dramatic strides against hunger worldwide. To do this, the anti-hunger movement must become more political.

The world community has the knowledge and resources to eliminate hunger. In the United States, we clearly need an expansion of federal food programs and other domestic anti-poverty programs, and a reform of foreign aid and other policies toward developing countries. Reforms along these lines are spelled out in the 1989 Bellagio Declaration on world hunger and the 1991 Medford Declaration on U.S. hunger, endorsed by scores of experts and by organizations representing millions of people.[1] But despite the educational and organizing efforts that have brought incremental progress in recent years, we still lack sufficient political will to take even obvious and relatively uncontroversial actions that would reduce hunger.

This report shows how hunger is one piece of a complex of interrelated social ills. Hungry people in the United States depend on food stamps, but many would not need food stamps if they had access to good jobs. Hungry people in Sudan need food aid, but if they were not living in a war zone, they would be able to plant and harvest crops needed to survive.

Just as providing jobs or ending wars could reduce world hunger, progress in reducing hunger can lead to progress on other fronts. For example, less hunger and poverty would surely mean that social tensions that often lead to violent conflicts would recede.

Thus, people who are moved to end hunger find themselves united with people who are working against war, communal violence, racism, poverty, human rights abuses, gender discrimination, and despoliation of the planet. Ending hunger is part of a larger vision for society, a vision exemplified in this excerpt from the biblical book of Isaiah:

> For behold, I create new heavens and a new earth . . .
> Jerusalem to be a delight and her people a joy . . .
> weeping and cries for help shall never again be heard
> in her.
> There no child shall ever again die an infant,
> no old person fail to live out life;
> every child shall live a hundred years before dying. . . .
> People shall build houses and live to inhabit them,
> plant vineyards and eat their fruit. . . .
> My people shall live the long life of a tree,
> and my chosen shall enjoy the fruit of their labor.
> They shall not toil in vain or raise children for
> misfortune.
> For they are offspring of the blessed of the Lord
> and their issue after them;
> before they call me, I will answer,
> and while they are still speaking I will listen.
> The wolf and the lamb shall feed together
> and the lion shall eat straw like other cattle.
> They shall not hurt or destroy in all my holy moun-
> tain, says the Lord.
>
> – Isaiah 65:17-25 (adapted from New English Bible)

Introduction

The Importance of Choices

Causes of Hunger is about the conscious and often unconscious choices we make – choices we make as individuals, and collective choices we make as consumers and as voters; choices that may appear innocuous in their own right but may contribute to the perpetuation of hunger, poverty, racism, and violence.

For example, in 1991, U.S. citizen-consumers chose to spend:

- More on jewelry and watches ($30.1 billion) than on federal food and nutrition assistance ($28.5 billion), or the entire Gross Domestic Product of 20 low-income countries in the world;

- More than three times as much on tobacco products ($47.8 billion) as on foreign aid ($15.9 billion);

- Almost twice as much on toys and sporting goods ($32.2 billion) as federal housing assistance ($17.2 billion); and

- More on household cleaning and polishing preparations ($52.8 billion) than on federal contributions to education, training, and employment services ($43.4 billion).[2]

No one consciously decides to buy a can of beer instead of a can of baby milk. Yet it is easy to make what appear to be small, individual choices without being quite aware of their cumulative consequences and the tradeoffs that are being made. The fact is that choices, just like votes in an election, do finally add up to outcomes.

A volunteer who served in Iraq during the Gulf War reported, "Twenty years of work by my [development organization] was wiped out by a single surgical air strike." The choices made by governments – which in democratic countries reflect individual voters' choices – can make important differences to hungry people.

What choices would bring historical reality closer to religious and humane visions such as Isaiah's new Jerusalem?

Causes of Hunger outlines broad changes in politics and economics to empower poor people, and changes in attitudes to protect vulnerable groups and nature. It offers a critique of the attitudes that contribute to powerlessness among hungry people, racial and ethnic conflict, poverty, environmental damage, war and violence, discrimination, and neglect of vulnerable people. These are the sins that conspire to foment mass hunger in a world of plenty.

Causes of Hunger urges that we ground our choices – small and large, individual and collective, political and economic – in ethical values. These include empowerment and justice, stewardship of common resources for the common good, and affirmation of diversity and community. The persistence of mass hunger is, at its root, a moral and religious challenge.

Empowerment and Justice

People are poor and hungry because they lack the power to be otherwise, in part because they are dominated by others who are more powerful.

Power can be used for good or ill. It is good to have some control over one's life and environment, to be protected from the whims of nature and other people, to express and develop one's own potential. But people often use power to dehumanize others and destroy nature.

The struggle for power can foster a culture of violence, manifested in hunger, rape, child abuse, murder on street corners, ethnic conflict, militarism, and war. It also fosters acceptance of the idea that problems are solved by attacking and destroying rather than supporting and nurturing.

"Powerlessness and Politics" (Cause 1) examines the uses and misuses of political and economic power, and advocates empowerment of marginalized peoples, particularly through grassroots organizations. It shows that by feeding hungry people and changing public policies, mainstream society can help vulnerable people transform the politics of hunger.

The history of the 20th century has to a large extent been a history of wars – first of "world wars" and now of many "small" wars. "Violence and Militarism" (Cause 2) points out that war, civil strife, and militarism lead to hunger, uprooting people from their homes and families, creating refugees, draining resources into military budgets, and destroying the environment and infrastructure that people need to survive. This chapter suggests that, in situations where power and interests clash, opposing parties should pursue conflict resolution and peace making as alternatives to violence.

Causes of Hunger

Despite the crises in Bosnia and Rwanda, fresh winds are breathing hope across some parts of the globe. The fearsome Berlin Wall is rubble. Positive change is occurring in South Africa and the Middle East. The civil and human rights, women's, peace, environmental, and related movements have empowered hundreds of millions of people. People are no longer content to have others decide things for them.

In a world where power is broadly shared, all citizens, especially those traditionally excluded, would be able to assert their concerns and interests in the life of political community. Civic culture and democracy would flourish. Justice, not "just us," would be the political norm. No one would have to fear for the next day's bread.

Stewardship and the Common Good

"Poverty in a Global Economy" (Cause 3) and "Population, Consumption, and Environment" (Cause 4) discuss a complex web of factors that shape the context in which humans live and struggle to survive.

Lack of money to buy food and lack of land to grow crops are the immediate causes of most hunger. Three quarters of a billion of the earth's people are desperately poor; they are also undernourished. Their misery exposes our collective failure to practice sound "economics" – a term that has its origins in the concept of "household management," referring to the stewardship of acquiring and managing property in order to support the family. These two chapters suggest that the human household is not being well managed, that the present generation is robbing Old Mother Hubbard's garden as well as her cupboard. If we continue to let this happen, what will be left to meet her grandchildren's needs?

Human beings must consume natural resources to have food, shelter, and safety; and these, in turn, are prerequisites to life's higher goals. But in wealthy societies, the means (money, wealth) sometimes replace the ends (human fulfillment) for which they exist. "Good" in "the good life" is reduced to "goods." Pursuit of material goods and private consumption replace spiritual, artistic, and intellectual pursuits; family and civic mindedness.

The $341 billion spent in the United States in 1993 on recreation and entertainment, for example, is 100 times the amount spent on the Special Supplemental Food Program for Women, Infants, and Children.[3] Our individ-ual decisions about entertainment and politics contribute to this scandal.

The crisis of spirit in industrialized countries and the deterioration of family and communal values are interrelated with a culture that thinks first in terms of financial goods rather than the good of humanity or nature as a whole. Excessive individualism and the high failure rate among marriages and families have other causes, too.

But a culture dominated by commercial values erodes family and community values. Family-oriented systems treasure familial and community ties and encourage shared activities, stability, and loyalty.[4] In contrast, a culture oriented toward production and "success" spawns mobility, prosperity, and segmented relationships. It tends to look upon people and nature in terms of their use and consumption value.

> Over time the market system shapes the values that govern the choices we make. . . . It is no wonder that a great many parents in our country sacrifice family values for greater riches, even in families that are already living like royalty – in material terms – by the standards of human history. It is no wonder that men in America typically channel the best of their energies into the pursuit of professional advancement and choose to allocate little time for friendship. It is no wonder that shopping centers, not parks or sacred groves, become centers of our communities.
>
> – Andrew Bard Schmookler[5]

Choice needs to regain its moral content. We must be willing to make hard choices on behalf of the common good, to ask which individual and collective decisions enhance the human community and nature and which contribute to the community's impoverishment. We need to fashion a society that encourages and supports good moral choices – both private and public.

A good steward exercises responsible care over that which has been entrusted. In today's interdependent world, that is just about everything, everywhere, and everyone. Tuberculosis and trade, refugees and refuse,

Introduction

cash and conflict, all flow across national borders. The wind does not stop at dotted lines on a map. The globe is not so much shrinking as our consciousness and ability to act transnationally are enlarging. The fate of humanity and nature are also vitally linked.

Our world cries out for public, as well as private stewardship of people and nature. As we decide to put first things first in our economic life, we will change economic policies and institutions as well as lifestyle choices. We will invest in people, because of the immediate benefits and to enhance their productivity. We will seek economic policies that foster decent jobs for everyone who can work – a daunting goal in a world that must generate some 2 billion new jobs over the next 30 years to keep up with an expanding population. We will grapple with the problems of rapid population growth among many of the world's poor people, unsustainable patterns of consumption among the world's affluent people, and food and agriculture systems which strain their environmental underpinnings.

Economics, population, and environment are complex matters. Well-meaning people will disagree about the likely effects of policies. But the policy debate now is dominated more by special interests than different views of how best to reduce poverty, hunger, and environmental destruction.

Fundamentally, we must shift from preoccupation with getting and spending – economic growth – to the goal of sustainable development. This concept emphasizes poverty reduction, environmental protection, and democratic participation rather than expansion of gross economic activity as an end in itself. Economic growth is often important to reducing poverty and improving general well-being, especially in poor countries. But GNP growth is inadequate as a measure and profoundly misleading as a vision of progress.

We want a world rich with the beauty of healthy, happy people and a bountiful nature. And basic to attaining and living the good life is moral choice, the pursuit of the common good, and spiritual depth.

Diversity and Community

Many people go hungry because of discrimination or neglect, on the basis of race and ethnicity (Cause 5), gender (Cause 6), or age (Cause 7). Discrimination can seize your job, beat you up, and steal your meal. It determines who suffers the most; who is allowed to survive; who may share food at the world's table.

> We must design a new paradigm of sustainable human development that not only generates economic growth but distributes its benefits equitably; that regenerates the environment instead of destroying it; that empowers people rather than marginalizing them. It is development that gives priority to the poor, that enlarges their choices and opportunities, and that provides for their participation in events and decisions that shape their lives. It is development that is pro-people, pro-poor, pro-nature, pro-jobs, and pro-women.
>
> In the final analysis, sustainable human development is the famine that didn't happen, the refugees that didn't march, the ethnic violence that didn't explode, the human rights that weren't violated, the environment that wasn't degraded. . . . And it must be sustainable from one generation to the next.
>
> – James Gustave Speth,
> Administrator, United Nations
> Development Program

Discrimination distorts the natural process of establishing personal and collective identity. Early socialization records "tapes" deep in consciousness which teach thoughts, feelings, and practices for effective action in a complex world. These tapes shape individual identity – me, my gender, my race, us, my family, my community, my tribe, my religion. Sympathy goes first to groups with which we identify. The tapes also teach about "the other," the stranger, the alien, the foreigner, "them;" and are a basis of tribalisms, nationalisms, ethnocentrisms, and religious intolerance.

Causes of Hunger

Discrimination takes many forms. But its core is dehumanization – treating people as less than fully human. Discriminatory beliefs, feelings, and practices make people just like us – humans with hopes and fears, failures and successes – into objects rather than living, breathing subjects.

When those suffering discrimination do not have the power to mount an effective challenge, society, through coercion, institutionalizes discrimination in customs, policies, and law. The coercion may take the form of brute physical force, economic clout, or cultural traditions so weighty that even those who are discriminated against may come to think their situation is natural, good, and fair. They may even adopt and act out stereotypes which have been forced on them.

In many cases, whole groups of people who are relatively weak – children, for example, or elderly people – suffer neglect from groups of people who are better able to fend for themselves.

People are discriminated against when they do not receive a fair share of what life has to offer. They are born in the "wrong place" or with the "wrong body," and are excluded from food, health care, education, and other necessities and graces of life.

In a world without discrimination, everyone would truly have an equal opportunity for a good life. Communities would be composed of a diversity of colors and styles that mirror the diversity of nature. People less able to take care of themselves would be cared for. One way to make that vision a reality may be to build on common experiences to create alliances of women and men, young and old, and people of every hue in common cause: the affirmation of life-giving, life-nurturing community.

The Courage to Choose

Imagine you were given a menu at birth from which to choose family, nation, and physical characteristics. Among the choices you must make are:

- Rwanda – with 40,610 persons per physician (before the 1994 genocide) or Austria, where the figure is 230 per physician.

- Burkina Faso – where there is a 91 percent chance your mother will be illiterate or Switzerland, where everyone can read and write.

- Guinea-Bissau – where you are likely to die by age 39 or Japan, where you will live to age 79.5[6]

- Any racial/ethnic mix and your choice of gender, with the implications that accrue.

Whether a person is born in one nation or another, with an IQ of 55 or 155, blind or sighted, to one family or another, rich or poor makes all the difference. Children born at ground zero at zero hour in Hiroshima in 1945 lived five-minute lives. The lottery of birth is the single greatest influence on the quality of life, including whether a person will be poor, hungry, or powerless.

Many people would choose to be part of a minority racial/ethnic group and/or female in spite of disadvantages. None would choose hunger, illiteracy, impoverishment, or a short life span. Yet, we sometimes blame or ignore disadvantaged people for the accidents of their birth.

The other side of the story is that choice can overcome many of the effects of chance. After the lottery of birth, choice is the second most important ingredient in life. Families can provide nurture, care, and mentoring for their children – or make choices that result in the neglect of children. Adults can make powerful choices that improve themselves and society. I have watched as a blind, professionally-dressed African American tapped his white cane to negotiate a busy street crossing in a dangerous, drug-infested neighborhood, while carrying a tiny infant on his back. Courageous choices can overcome physical limitations and social stigmas. It's just harder.

Thousands, if not millions, of people pray the serenity prayer each day:

God grant me the serenity to accept
the things I cannot change,
the courage to change the things I can,
and the wisdom to know the difference.

Anti-hunger activists can think of it as the courage-to-choose prayer, because hunger is something we certainly do not feel serene about, nor have to accept. We can bequeath a better world to the future. All we need is the courage, the determination, and the political will to achieve a world that is more just, peaceful, and respectful of the integrity and diversity of creation. This choice, however, requires changes in the way we think and act. Not

Introduction

guilt; just responsible action.

Morality is about redressing the accidents of birth and upbringing. Life is not fair, but civilization should try to make it fairer. In our personal lives, we can care for the children and elderly people around us, and reach out to disadvantaged people in our own communities. And as citizens, we can join together to influence policy decisions that affect us all.

Hunger in a world of plenty is an indictment of the moral condition of modern society. Public morality is about building a society that encourages and supports good decisions; about building the structures that enable others as well as ourselves to have the good life; about doing unto others as we would have them do unto us, whether they live next door or far away.

The spiritual crisis of society is a loss of meaning, transcendent values, and constructive action. People who lack meaning are looking for it in all the wrong places; or not even looking.

The sharing of food is one of the most central experiences of human life in family and community, ritualized in religious meals and feast days. Food connects people with nature, one another, and God. By working to end hunger and its interrelated causes, such as racism and gender bias, we affirm our community with all people, particularly those in need.

Eating and sharing food can be an occasion for thanksgiving. Many of us have enough, and more than enough.

Part of the lure of the anti-hunger movement is its feasibility. The United States could certainly eliminate mass hunger in its midst within a couple of years and at a very affordable cost. The program is clear: continued and expanded private charitable action, combined with expansion of the federal food programs and other anti-poverty programs. We also know a lot about reducing hunger worldwide. Revamping U.S. foreign assistance and other U.S. policies toward the developing countries would dramatically accelerate global progress against hunger. The small step of ending hunger would be a giant moral leap for humankind.

Economic, social, and political forces can block the achievement of a hunger-free world. We may not eliminate domination, impoverishment, and discrimination in our lifetime. But, no matter what the end result or shape of the future, we are called to be merciful in a merciless world, to do justice in an unjust world.

People who are active in such efforts come to find the work profoundly satisfying. It is meaningful to know that the gifts one has received are being shared; to alleviate human distress and protect the environment; to be among those who help make a future that is more peaceful, humane, and beautiful. The entire anti-hunger movement is a deeply spiritual endeavor.

As I disembarked from a bus in Indonesia, I asked the tour guide whether his job paid enough to live.

"Oh yes," he assured me, "It pays quite well. After I have worked a couple of months as a tour guide, I have enough

> During the terror of the 1980s, I had occasion to travel with Bishop Medardo Gomez in his homeland of El Salvador. We North Americans acted as a protective international shield.
>
> His favorite term for us was "compañeros" (companions) from the Latin "cum" (with) and "panis" (bread). "Compañeros," he would say, "you are the ones who break bread with me. You share with me the bread of suffering and the bread of hope in adversity."
>
> – Rev. John F. Steinbruck, Pastor, Luther Place Memorial Church and N Street Village, Washington, D.C.

money to go work for two or three months on an ecological project to save the jungles of Kalimantan (Borneo)."

I am Christian; he is probably Muslim. Our skin color, income, family arrangements, and cultures differ. My activism is focused on justice for hungry people, his on protecting the environment. Yet this stranger serves as an inspiration and reminder of the community of people of every race and clan who share in the spiritual work of contributing, each in their own way, toward freedom, justice, and sustainability.

The goal is clear. The resources are available. The opportunity is ours to give as we have received and love as we are loved. ∎

Dr. Richard A. Hoehn is director of BFW Institute.

Causes of Hunger

Acknowledgments

We are deeply grateful for the valuable insights provided by sponsors, cosponsors, and colleagues at a May 1994 consultation and in response to drafts of this report. The diverse list of sponsors – European and U.S., domestic and international, secular and a wide cross section of religious organizations, vividly illustrates that concern for, and action to end, hunger transcends many social divisions.

The following people participated in the May consultation: John Lapp, Mennonite Central Committee; Cheryl Bartz, National Peace Corps Association; John Coonrod, The Hunger Project; Peter Mikuliak, Church World Service; Patricia Young, U.S. National Committee for World Food Day; Jud Dolphin, Food Research and Action Center; Lisa Carr, Catholic Charities; Carol Capps, Church World Service/Lutheran World Relief; David Karns, Christian Children's Fund; Jennifer Urff, World Hunger Year; Lindsey Ford, Share Our Strength; Nelle Temple Brown, House Banking Committee; Janet Green, InterAction; Augusta Hammill, Second Harvest; Susan Van Lopik, Christian Reformed Church Committee on Relief; and Mike Rock and Richard Cobb, Winrock International.

We also received comments and assistance from: Charles D. Paolillo, Society for International Development; Jayne Wood, Devres, Inc.; Ellen Messer, Alan Shawn Feinstein World Hunger Program, Brown University; Robin Shell and Karen Randau, Food for the Hungry International; Father William Byron, Georgetown University; Nancy Wright, Coordination in Development, Inc.; Suzanne Gervais, Cornell University; Patricia L. Kutzner, World Hunger Education Service; Suleiyman Nyang, Howard University; Remy Jurenas, Congressional Research Service; and John Halvorson and colleagues on the national staff of the Evangelical Lutheran Church in America.

The following BFW/BFW Institute activists, board members, and staff provided comments and assistance: Lindsey March, Maria Otero, Sheena Pappalardo, William Whitaker, Bowyer Freeman, Frank Hoffman, Larry Hollar, Julie Jarvis, Ellen Jennings, Christine Matthews, Susan Park, Sharon Pauling, Phoebe de Reynier, Kathleen Selvaggio, Lucilla Tan, and Carole Zimmerman.

We appreciate the editorial assistance provided by Ellen Hoffman, Don Reeves, A. Cecilia Snyder, Aaron Johnson, and Newman Fair. Jashinta D'Costa and Beth Morilla prepared the statistical tables.

Overview of World Hunger

Nearly 800 million people are chronically undernourished.

by Peter Uvin, Marc J. Cohen,
A. Cecilia Snyder, Richard A. Hoehn,
and Maureen Harris

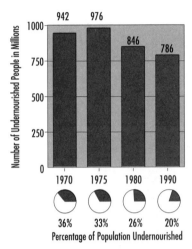

Figure 0.1:
Chronically Undernourished –
Developing Countries

Source: U.N. Administrative Committee on
Coordination/Subcommittee on Nutrition (ACC/SCN).

TWO DECADES AGO, the 1974 World Food Conference in Rome expressed alarm at the prospect of long-term food shortages and massive starvation in developing countries. However, every year since then, the world has had more than adequate food supplies for everyone to enjoy a minimally adequate diet (2,350 calories per person per day). Since 1974, the number and proportion of chronically undernourished people (i.e., people who do not consume enough protein and calories) in the developing world has fallen significantly.

But global food supplies are not evenly distributed. Nearly 800 million people (20 percent of the developing world's population) remained undernourished in 1990, the last year for which complete information is available. At least two billion faced vitamin and mineral deficiencies that posed serious health threats.

Seventy percent of the world's hungry people live in the Asia-Pacific region, but both the number and proportion of hungry people has fallen there since 1970. In contrast, the absolute number and percentage of hungry people has increased in sub-Saharan Africa. Persistent, growing poverty has contributed to the continent's food problems, along with debt, economic decline, poor terms of trade, unfavorable weather for agriculture, war, and governmental collapse. Poor economic conditions during the 1980s also led to increased hunger in Latin America and the Caribbean. Hunger has declined substantially in the Middle East, but 12 million people there remain undernourished.

Though many people are likely to think of famine when they hear the word "hunger," famine actually affects relatively few people and the amount of food needed to prevent it is relatively small. Famines can be caused by drought and other natural catastrophes, such as floods and earthquakes, or by human actions such as war, civil conflict, and the use of food as a weapon. The Alan Shawn Feinstein World Hunger Program at Brown University estimates that in 1992, 157 million people, or 3 percent of the world's population, lived in countries affected by famine or food shortage (though not everyone in these countries actually suffered from hunger).

In the industrial world, economic changes have reduced wages among low-skill workers (see Cause 3). Governments face political and financial constraints on their ability to fund social welfare programs. These trends have contributed to growing food insecurity. In the United States, many low-income people find that they run out of food at the end of the month. But hunger in wealthy nations is neither as severe nor as widespread as in developing countries.

Overall Trends in Developing Country Hunger

According to the Food and Agriculture Organization of the United Nations (FAO), the number of chronically undernourished people ("people who on average during the course of a year did not consume enough food" to maintain their weight and engage in "light activity"[1]) in the developing world began declining in 1975, from 976 million, to 786 million in 1990. During the same period, total population in the developing world increased by 1.1

Table 0.1: Number of People Affected by Micronutrient Malnutrition (Millions),[2] 1988-1991

| Region | Iodine Deficiency | | Vitamin A Deficiency | | Iron Deficiency |
	At Risk	Goiter	At Risk	Blindness	Anemia
Africa	181	86	18	1.3	206
Asia & Oceania	909	317	157	11.4	1,674
Americas	168	63	2	0.1	94
Europe	141	97	0	0.0	27
Eastern Mediterranean	173	93	13	1.0	149
World	1,572	655	190	13.8	2,150

Source: FAO and World Health Organization.

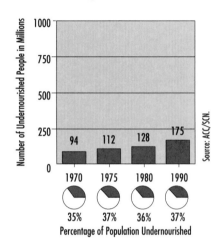

Figure 0.2: Africa

Number of Undernourished People in Millions

| 1970 | 1975 | 1980 | 1990 |
| 94 | 112 | 128 | 175 |

Percentage of Population Undernourished
35%   37%   36%   37%

Source: ACC/SCN.

billion. As a result, the proportion of undernourished people dropped from 36 percent in 1970 to 20 percent in 1990.

Micronutrient deficiencies (e.g., inadequate intake of iron, iodine, or other minerals and vitamins) are a less obvious form of malnutrition than simple lack of sufficient calories and protein. Lack of iodine can lead to goiter (an enlargement of the thyroid gland) and mental retardation. Vitamin A deficiency can cause blindness and death. Iron deficiency causes anemia, which reduces work and school performance and increases susceptibility to disease. These problems of "hidden hunger" are more widespread and have deeper consequences than is generally appreciated (see Table 0.1). Yet prevention or treatment is quite inexpensive and can be done without threatening "the existing economic and political structures."[3] The essays on Causes 6 and 7 discuss the health effects of hidden hunger among women, children, and elderly people.

Africa

Hunger is widespread and getting worse in sub-Saharan Africa. Long-term economic decline, international debt, low commodity prices, poor results from the structural adjustment policies supported by the World Bank and the International Monetary Fund, and civil strife all contributed to growing poverty and hunger in Africa in the 1980s.

One of every five African women of childbearing age is underweight (weighing less than 100 pounds) and likely to be malnourished. This heightens obstetric risks and increases the chance of bearing low birthweight babies.

Almost a third of African children under age five are undernourished, about the same proportion as in 1970.

The growth of food output has not kept pace with population growth. Average food availability per person is below minimum daily requirements, with

1,500 fewer calories available per person per day than in the United States or Canada.

In 1992, drought and crop failures left 23 million Southern and East Africans dependent on emergency food aid. Africa accounted for over half of the emergency food deliveries to victims of war and civil unrest carried out by the United Nations (U.N.) World Food Program that year. Early warning systems set up in the mid-1980s and rigorous action by local communities, African governments, and international donors avoided what could have been a massive famine.

By the end of 1993, African countries hosted 6 million refugees, more than any other world region. Millions more Africans are displaced within their own countries. Most uprooted Africans are extremely vulnerable to hunger and depend on food aid for survival.

In 1993-1994, the devastating combination of war, mass migration, and poor weather again left millions of East Africans facing a food crisis. Violence in Rwanda may have left 1 million people dead and nearly 5 million displaced out of a total population of 8 million. Ongoing civil strife in Angola, Liberia, Sudan, and Burundi disrupted local food systems. The international community was relatively responsive to relief needs, but hesitant in supporting mediation efforts and peace-keeping forces.

Asia-Pacific[4]

Hunger in the Asia-Pacific region has declined dramatically over the past 20 years. The undernourished proportion of the population has dropped from one-third in South and Southeast Asia and nearly half in China to 24 percent in South Asia, 17 percent in Southeast Asia, and 16 percent in China. This impressive achievement

Figure 0.3: Asia-Pacific

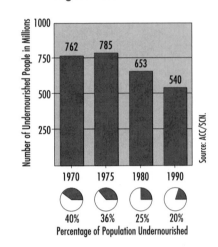

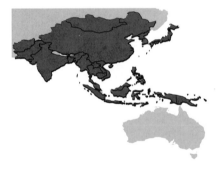

resulted from strong economic growth in much of the region, complemented by large-scale public investments in nutrition, health, and education (see Cause 3). High

Table 0.2: Malnutrition Rates for Children Under Five, Asia and the Pacific, 1975 and 1990

Sub-Region	Child Malnutrition Rate 1975	1990
South Asia	68%	59%
Southeast Asia	44%	31%
China	26%	22%

Source: ACC/SCN.

Table 0.3: Incidence of Anemia among Women of Childbearing Age, 1980s

Region	All Women	Pregnant Women
South Asia	64	64
Southeast Asia	48	56
Developing World Average	42	51

Source: ACC/SCN.

rates of population growth meant that the absolute number of chronically undernourished South Asians increased from 255 million in 1970 to 277 million in 1990. During this same period, however, the absolute number of hungry people declined in Southeast Asia (from 101 million to 74 million) and China (from 406 million to 189 million).

The scale of the decline in Asian-Pacific hunger since 1975 more than offset the worsening picture in Africa and Latin America, and accounts for much of the total decrease in world hunger.

Average caloric availability per person is below minimum requirements in South Asia. In the rest of the region, it is adequate or better.

Despite the gains, Asia and the Pacific continue to face major hunger problems, especially among women of childbearing age and children. South Asia has the highest proportion of underweight women of childbearing age in the world (60 percent), and Southeast Asia ranks second (44 percent).

South Asia also has the world's highest incidence of malnutrition among children under five; Southeast Asia ranks second (see Table 0.2). Similarly, Asian children are more likely to suffer chronic undernutrition: during the 1980s, the proportion of chronically undernourished (or "stunted,"

i.e., below the expected heights for their age) children between two and five years old was 65 percent in India, 41 percent in China, and 53 percent in the rest of Asia. All other developing regions have lower rates of stunting.

Children who lose weight because of short term undernutrition can catch up later, approximately regaining their normal weight, provided they receive adequate food. Stunting, however is largely irreparable. Stunted children are likely to remain below the average weight for their age throughout their lives.

The proportion of undernourished preschool children (and of stunting) in South Asia, and to a lesser extent in Southeast Asia, is striking. It is double the rate in sub-Saharan Africa, although all other indicators of poverty, food availability per person, and child mortality are much worse in sub-Saharan Africa than in South Asia.

The numbers on childhood malnutrition are subject to much dispute. Some experts argue that South Asian children actually need fewer calories than children in the United States (whose growth rates are the basis for international standards) and are "small but healthy." However, FAO and others insist that when Asian children are fed better, their growth resembles that of U.S. children.

Micronutrient deficiencies are especially serious in the region. Lack of vitamin A among preschool children is particularly severe in India, Indonesia, Bangladesh, and the Philippines. Thirty-six percent of Asians are at risk of goiter. The region's women are more likely to suffer from iron deficiency anemia during their childbearing years than the average developing country woman (see table 0.3).

Figure 0.4: Latin America

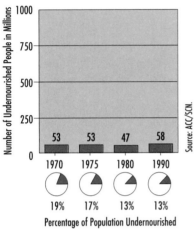

Figure 0.5: Middle East

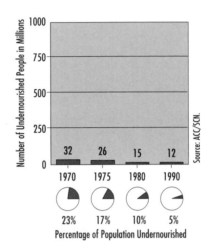

Latin America and the Caribbean

The international debt crisis and ensuing austerity policies caused an increase in hunger in Latin American and the Caribbean during the 1980s. The proportion and number of hungry people declined between 1970 and 1980. But the proportion stagnated and the number of hungry people increased during the 1980s.

Between 1975 and 1990, malnutrition rates for children under five declined – from 19 percent to 15 percent in Central America, and from 16 percent to 8 percent in South America. Families and some governments made special efforts to protect children from the hardships provoked by the debt crisis.

Income inequality in the region is a long-standing cause of hunger. Hunger is usually worse in rural areas and especially among indigenous people.

Middle East

Between 1970 and 1990, hunger declined dramatically in both relative and absolute terms in the Middle East, from 23 percent of the population (32 million people) to 5 percent (12 million). Higher oil prices made some countries rich and brought a degree of prosperity to most of the region, allowing increased food imports.

Food availability per person increased 28 percent from 1970 to 1990. Undernutrition in preschool children fell from 20 percent in 1975 to 13 percent in 1990.

There are major variations among countries in the region, however, and the Gulf war of 1990-1991 created serious food problems. People in Iraq have been hard-hit by the international embargo, and countries such as Yemen, which depended on labor migration to the Gulf, have also suffered.

Figure 0.6: Average Unemployment Rate in Member Countries of the European Union, 1985-1994

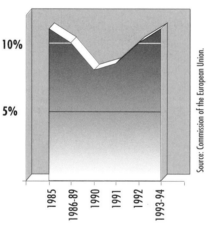

Source: Commission of the European Union.

Western Europe

The member countries of the European Union (EU) have faced slow economic growth and high unemployment during the 1990s. There is a trend of reduced social spending, often defended as the key to renewed economic vigor. All this increases the potential for food insecurity among low-income people.

In 1993, almost a quarter of the labor force was without work in Spain, along with 12 percent in France, Denmark, and Italy; 10 percent in the United Kingdom and Belgium; 9 percent in Germany; and 6 percent in the Netherlands. Unemployment rates for youth aged 16 to 24 are especially worrisome: 23 percent in France, 28 percent in Italy, and 33 percent in Spain.

In mid-1993, the EU poverty rate (defined as those receiving incomes below half the EU average) was nearly 23 percent. Homelessness affected an estimated 5 million people, about 1.5 percent of the EU population. The number of food banks in the region has grown rapidly since the first one opened in Paris in 1984.

Twenty-seven percent of Europe's population is at risk of iodine deficiency, including 10 million people in Germany.

At the end of 1993, Western Europe hosted about 900,000 refugees, largely as a result of fighting in former Yugoslavia.

North America

The United States

U.S. hunger decreased significantly between the late 1960s and mid-1970s. This was partly because the federal government substantially expanded its food and nutrition programs, and partly because of broad-based economic growth.

But hunger increased in the 1980s because of cutbacks in social welfare

Figure 0.7: United States

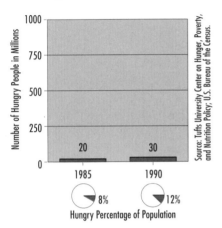

Number of Hungry People in Millions

Source: Tufts University Center on Hunger, Poverty, and Nutrition Policy; U.S. Bureau of the Census.

	20	30
	1985	1990

8%   12%

Hungry Percentage of Population

participated in the Food Stamp Program in April 1993; a year later, the figure was nearly 28 million.

Much U.S. hunger runs in cycles, appearing the last week of the month when food stamps, Social Security benefits, and paychecks run out. Unbalanced diets are also a problem. Food donated to charitable agencies may not be high in nutrition. Low-income people often do not have access to large grocery stores, and so must shop in smaller convenience stores where nutritious foods may be unavailable or expensive.

For years, anti-hunger groups such as Bread for the World have urged the establishment of a national nutrition monitoring system. The U.S. government is now finally putting it into place, so we will in the future have better information on hunger in the United States.

Growing Poverty. Poverty has increased in the United States in recent years, contributing to food insecurity. In 1992, inflation-adjusted median household income ($30,786) was $2,000 less than in 1989.

More than 40 percent of all poor people worked some time during 1992 and more than 9 percent worked full time. The federal minimum wage of $4.25 an hour – about $750 a month for full-time work before Social Security and income tax deductions – is inadequate to support a family. In 1993, the real value of the minimum wage was 22 percent below the average level in the 1970s.

Holes in the Safety Net. The maximum median monthly benefit possible from Aid to Families with Dependent Children (AFDC), the main welfare program, plus food stamps, is $647 for a family of three, 72 percent of the poverty line. AFDC provides cash assistance to needy children up to age 18 and their single

spending and long-term decline in the average worker's real wages. Between 1985 and 1990, the number of people in the United States who lacked enough to eat each month increased by 50 percent, from 20 million to 30 million – 12 percent of the total population. This included 12 million children under the age of 18.[5]

A weak economy in the early 1990s contributed to further growth in the ranks of hungry people. The unemployment rate in 1993 averaged 6.7 percent. Twenty-six million people utilized food pantries and soup kitchens affiliated with the Second Harvest national food bank network in 1992-1993. Twenty-seven million people

mothers or caretakers. In 1993, 14 million parents and children in 5 million families received benefits. The value of AFDC payments averaged 66 percent of the poverty line in 1970 but only 41 percent by 1991.

One of every six U.S. residents received food stamps or other federal food assistance in 1993. Yet cost-effective federal food programs such as the Special Supplemental Food Program for Women, Infants, and Children (WIC) are underfunded, and cannot enroll all the eligible people.

Food stamps are vouchers which can be redeemed for food at grocery stores to help poor families meet their basic nutritional needs. Eighty-seven percent of recipients are women, children, or elderly people. Food stamps provide, on average, seventy-five cents per person per meal per day. They are not much help to homeless people who lack kitchens to store and prepare food. During the early 1980s, as the poverty rate was rising, the government cut hundreds of thousands of people from the rolls and reduced the benefits of 15 million. The cuts were restored in the late 1980s.

Although the Food Stamp Program is an entitlement with funding available to all eligible people, it is estimated that only 51 to 66 percent of those eligible actually participate, due in part to poor outreach efforts. The Mickey Leland Childhood Hunger Relief Act of 1993 made important changes to update the program to reflect food needs in light of higher costs for housing and cars.

Canada

Poor people in Canada are increasingly reliant on charity to feed themselves and their families. Social and economic entitlements are declining.

In 1992, the number of people living below the poverty line grew to 4.3 million people (16.1 percent of the Canadian population). Single parent families headed by women below age 65 and children younger than 18 are those who are most often poor.

Child poverty continues to be high, though lower than in the United States. About 18 percent of all Canadian children live in poverty. According to the Canadian Association of Food Banks, 40 percent of food bank recipients are children. In 1994, an estimated 800,000 children received assistance from a food bank. More than 25 percent of homeless Canadians are children. The number of communities with food banks grew from 436 in 1993 to 463 in 1994, and most food banks served more people.

In 1993, the province of Alberta passed legislation to balance the budget by 1996.

Every fifth child in the United States faces hunger.

Photo: Joseph Czachida

In order to achieve this goal, massive cuts were made to social programs. Allowances for basic necessities such as shelter and food were slashed. Consequently, the number of needy people assisted at food banks increased. In some communities, food banks reported that demand for their services had increased by 86 percent.[6]

In Newfoundland, the collapse of the cod fishing industry has meant the loss of 30,000 jobs. A five year, $1.9 billion government program, The Atlantic Groundfish Strategy (TAGS), will provide emergency financial and job retraining assistance. Most participating fishermen have nevertheless lost 70 percent of their income. No more than a third of those who lost their jobs will ever work in fishing again.[7]

Former Soviet Union and Central and Eastern Europe

The former Soviet Union and Central and Eastern Europe have been undergoing unusually rapid and tumultuous economic and political change. Widespread violence is contributing to hunger in the former Yugoslavia and several of the newly independent states of the former Soviet Union. Poverty and weak economies have created serious food problems in former Soviet Central Asia.

In contrast, in Central and Eastern Europe, the transition from communism to market capitalism seems to be taking hold. Food prices are slowly stabilizing and there is a general trend toward purchasing less expensive vegetables and bread rather than higher priced dairy and meat products.

Central and Eastern Europe

In Poland, Hungary, and the Czech and Slovak Republics, food prices stabilized between 1991 and 1993 after initial soaring increases following the end of government subsidies. Income has fallen, but a wide range of new goods have appeared on the market, increasing the choices available.

The Slovak Republic has the weakest economy among these countries. Relatively high inflation and unemployment are expected to continue in 1994, with further declines in food intake likely.

In Albania, Romania, and Bulgaria, the development of an efficient market oriented food system has proceeded more slowly. All three countries experienced steep food price inflation in 1993.

Former Yugoslavia

The situation in former Yugoslavia remains grim. Nearly three million people in Bosnia are at risk of hunger and exposure, and are dependent on United Nations rations. Their condition is worsened by Bosnian Serb forces' systematic blocking of relief convoys. Food and medicine are clearly used as weapons in the violent struggle over Bosnia's future.

In the besieged city of Srebrenica, tens of thousands of starving Muslims have been shelled daily by the Serbs and existing on a diet of tree buds and cakes made from ground corn cobs. Disease and hunger were responsible for killing many of the 1,000 children who died in Srebrenica between October 1992 and May 1993. Air drops of food and medicine have helped, but 10 percent of the children experience scurvy, a disease caused by vitamin C deficiency. A

Table 0.4: Average Calorie Supply Per Person, Soviet Union, 1990	
Republic	**1990 Average Calorie Supply per Person**
Moldova	3,485
Turkmenistan	2,757
Ukraine	3,363
Kyrgyzstan	2,710
Belarus	3,212
Azerbaijan	2,704
Russia	3,153
Uzbekistan	2,635
Kazakhstan	3,025
Tajikistan	2,546
Armenia	2,778
Georgia	2,494

Source: FAO.

third of the city's refugees are less than three years old.

The Serb siege of Gorazde in March and April 1994 blocked food and medical supplies for the city's 65,000 people. Serbs delayed the evacuation of seriously wounded people.

Baltic States

The governments of Estonia, Latvia, and Lithuania have removed or reduced virtually all Soviet-era subsidies and regulation of production, wages, domestic commerce, and foreign trade. Incomes are declining while food prices are increasing. Non-food prices have also risen, making living conditions unduly difficult for many.

Former Soviet Union

In 1990, before the breakup of the Soviet Union, the constituent republics enjoyed average calorie supplies per person in excess of minimum requirements (see Table 0.4). The variation between Moldova, where the supply was highest, and Georgia, where it was lowest, was 40 percent, with average availability per person lower in Georgia than in South America. Since independence, the continued state of civil strife in Georgia has likely worsened the food situation.

The newly independent states' agricultural imports fell considerably in 1993-1994 compared to the year before. Crop yields rose due to partly to improved weather, but mainly because of higher prices.

In **Russia,** overall food consumption dropped in 1993, while inflation soared to an annual rate of 1,000 percent. Food prices grew more slowly, but the ratio between the incomes of the highest and lowest 10 percent of earners increased from eight to one in 1992 to 11 to one in 1993. Unemployment was estimated at 8 percent to 11 percent. There was no widespread hunger in 1992, as Russians still consumed over 2,500 calories per day on average, and most enjoyed a diet similar to that of Northern Europeans. In the United States, the average intake is 2,200 calories per day.

Ukraine's 1993 inflation rate was 2,700 percent, up from 2,500 percent in 1992. But there is no evidence of hunger, even though average wages are $10 to $30 a month, and less for people on pensions. Food prices increased by 117 times in 1993, while wages increased by 19 times. Household expenditure on food rose from 32.8 percent in 1990 to 40.4 percent in 1992, and is estimated to have exceeded 50 percent in 1993. Unemployment rates are expected to increase substantially in 1994. People subsist through black markets and informal barter networks, but unless the situation improves, food problems could loom in the future.

The economic situation in **Belarus** has deteriorated in the past several years. Between 1990 and 1993, the price index for most food items increased 500 to 700 times.

The Central Asian republics of **Turkmenistan and Uzbekistan** primarily grow cotton. Its cultivation has taken over more of the land that once produced fruit, vegetables, and meat. Rural diets have worsened. Maternal malnutrition is widespread and many newborns show signs of starvation. Turkmenistan's official infant mortality rate of 66.1 per thousand live births was the highest in the Soviet Union in 1989. The governments are now trying to diversify agriculture and increase grain production to improve the health and economy of the region. ■

Bosnian refugee in Croatia; newspaper headline reads: "Through Terror to Great Serbia."

Photo: UNHCR

Dr. Peter Uvin is affiliated with the Alan Shawn Feinstein World Hunger Program at Brown University and the Community Economic Development Program at New Hampshire College. Dr. Marc J. Cohen is senior research associate at BFW Institute and editor of *Causes of Hunger*. A. Cecilia Snyder and Dr. Richard A. Hoehn are, respectively, research associate and director at BFW Institute. Maureen Harris is a nutritionist and BFW Institute volunteer.

Powerlessness and Politics

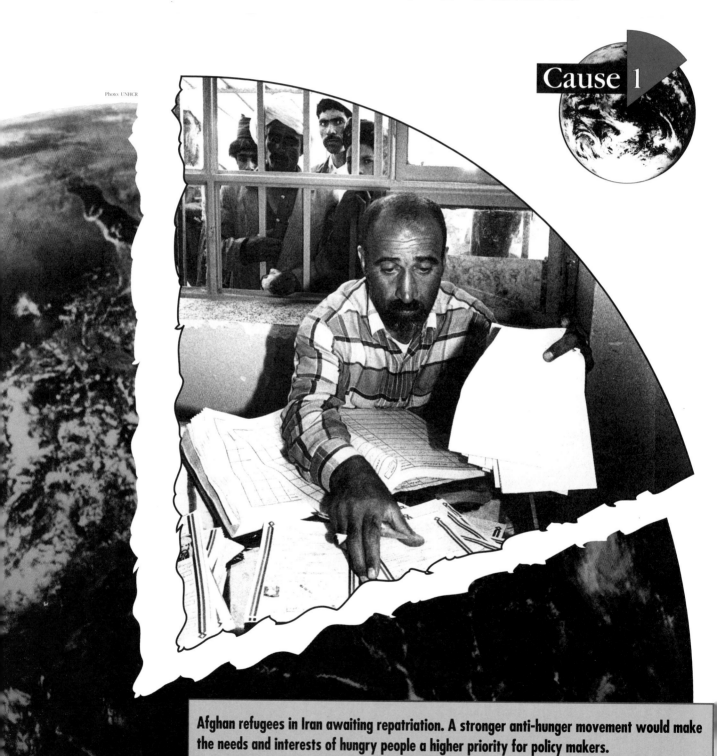

Photo: UNHCR

Cause 1

Afghan refugees in Iran awaiting repatriation. A stronger anti-hunger movement would make the needs and interests of hungry people a higher priority for policy makers.

by Marc J. Cohen

Hunger is a question of politics and power. In democracy or dictatorship, lack of political influence contributes to the persistence of hunger. Although international organizations provide assistance that can reduce hunger, they are reluctant to challenge the political structure that controls the allocation of resources. Case studies show that it is possible to overcome the powerlessness that underlies hunger. We need to strengthen political forces that favor hungry people, especially organizations that empower poor and hungry people themselves.

....

Hunger is not just about eating enough calories or having enough iodine in the diet. Fundamentally, hunger is a political question: hungry people lack the power to end their hunger. The web that connects political power and hunger manifests itself globally and within nation states and communities.

Ending hunger requires appropriate public policies. These include direct food assistance, education, sound agricultural practices, affordable health care, sanitation and safe water systems, job creation, and assuring access to productive assets. Mustering the political will to make anti-hunger policies a top government priority requires a strong public constituency.

Hungry people need to be empowered and thus require resources and organizations which they can truly call their own. People of good will who are neither poor nor hungry have an important role to play in empowering hungry people and in transforming the politics of hunger. Those affected by hunger must participate fully in devising and implementing solutions. But a wide array of individuals and organizations

(both public and private) can help by providing technical assistance, training, funds, and solidarity, and by advocating policy change.

Hungry people lack resources: they generally do not own land to grow food, and their incomes are too low to afford to provide their families an adequate diet on a regular basis. They also usually lack effective organizations to articulate their interests. As a result, governments frequently fail to enact anti-hunger programs and instead devote their attention to people with wealth and power, who can readily effect political change.

Yet policies to end hunger have a high social payoff. Improved nutrition means more productive workers, healthier people, and children who reach their full potential as members of the human family.

The Problem of Hunger and Power

The case of the Philippines illustrates well the connection between hunger and power. Most people live in rural areas, but 10 percent of the population owns 90 percent of the land. Politically prominent families and multinational companies own huge plantations. Affluent urban professionals have invested in smaller farms. Meanwhile, 70 percent of rural people earn too little to afford an adequate diet. Two-thirds of them are landless or sharecroppers. This unjust pattern has fueled 25 years of armed rebellion. Most Filipinos support land reform, but landowners dominate the Congress. The 1988 agrarian reform law covers little farmland, and few poor rural households have received any of the land that is available for redistribution.

U.S. public policies are also biased against hungry people. Between 1978 and

Hungry people lack the power to end their hunger.

Just as lack of political influence causes hunger, hunger can contribute to lack of clout.

1989, the federal minimum wage lost 25 percent of its purchasing power. By 1991, full-time minimum wage work only paid $8,840 per year. The poverty level at which a family of three might achieve bare food security was $10,723. Between 1981 and 1990, Congress refused to increase the minimum over $3.35 per hour. During this period, Congress reduced corporate, capital gains, and top personal tax rates. Between 1980 and 1990, the after-tax income *gains* of the richest one percent of income earners (2.5 million people) equalled the total income of the poorest 20 percent (50 million people). Members of Congress get most of their campaign dollars from people in the top tax brackets, along with representatives of narrow special interest groups.

The Philippines and the United States hold regular elections and enjoy open civil societies (i.e., space for voluntary associations). Under authoritarian governments, hungry people have even less influence over policy and freedom to pursue their rights and interests collectively. In the 1970s and 1980s, the military dictatorship in Sudan seized unused farm and forest land to create large mechanized farms. Often, villages received no compensation and had no avenues for legal appeal. The policy reduced the land available for fallowing and grazing and lessened access to fuel wood and wild foods. This increased the severity of famines in 1984-1985 and 1990-1991.

Just as lack of political influence causes hunger, hunger can contribute to lack of clout. It is often difficult (though not impossible, as shown below) for people who are struggling for basic survival to become effective participants in politics and policy-making. How does this complex relationship play itself out at the global level?

International Politics

During the colonial era, international economic and political power coincided. Colonialism was a system of political domination and unequal exchange, as colonies provided raw materials and farm products and bought colonizers' manufactured goods. Today, few colonies remain. Some former colonies now have per capita incomes and levels of industrialization rivaling those of some onetime colonizers (compare Singapore, Taiwan, and South Korea to Spain and Portugal). But for most former colonies – now called "developing" or "Third World" countries – the old trading patterns remain intact. Copper continues to dominate Zambia's exports, and sugar those of the Dominican Republic. The northern hemisphere still controls disproportionate wealth.

International Economic Power. Industrial countries maintain their economic power through such mechanisms as higher tariffs on processed imports from developing countries than on raw materials. These restrict sales of more profitable goods, the production of which would create jobs and help reduce hunger. Such tariffs also mean less foreign exchange for debt service and imports. Many poor countries manufacture clothing and textiles for export, but wealthy countries restrict imports of such goods. These barriers cost the developing countries $80 billion per year, more than they receive in aid from rich nations.

Industrial countries do import manufactured goods from developing countries at reduced tariffs, but this generally involves shipping parts to the Third World for assembly and re-import. A relatively small share of the profits go to developing countries. The chief beneficiaries are industrial country firms which manufacture and market the products. Poor and hungry people receive relatively little advantage, and these programs mainly involve better-off developing countries.

The power imbalance is even codified into international trade rules. The General Agreement on Tariffs and Trade (GATT) bans most import quotas and export subsidies, but the United States (the dominant power in world trade for much of the post-World War II era) pressed to exempt agriculture from both prohibitions. GATT's Multi-Fibre Arrangement – also created because of U.S. pressure – has permitted textile and garment import quotas. These exemptions have limited hunger- and poverty-reducing employment in developing countries while protecting the rich countries' declining industries and preserving their dominance of agricultural trade.

The recent agreement to tighten GATT's agricultural export subsidy rules was not a response to Third World demands. Instead, it resulted from U.S. insistence that other leading exporters, particularly France, end "unfair competition." Industrial countries also agreed to phase out textile quotas (to the benefit of some developing countries) in exchange for stronger patent protections that will profit rich countries and multinational firms.

International Political Power. The main formal institution of world politics, the United Nations, reflects power realities. China, France, Russia, the United Kingdom, and the United States each have a veto in the Security Council, which can authorize military interventions such as the multinational force which expelled Iraq from Kuwait in 1991.

The most powerful countries do not face U.N. limits on their actions. In 1984, the World Court (another U.N. body) ordered the United States to stop mining Nicaragua's ports. When the U.S.

government refused to recognize the court's jurisdiction, the court could take no further action.

In most U.N. councils and agencies, wealthy governments exercise "power of the purse" to gain policy leverage (see "Power, Hunger, and the World Bank," pp. 25-26). One symbol of this is the custom of appointing citizens of industrial countries to fill policy-making positions.

Quite a few U.N. agencies – among them the U.N. Development Program, the U.N. Children's Fund (UNICEF), the Food and Agriculture Organization, the World Food Program, the U.N. Research Institute on Social Development, and the International Fund for Agricultural Development – deal directly or indirectly with hunger by providing aid for long-term sustainable development, humanitarian relief, and technical assistance, or conducting hunger-related policy research. Some agencies have staked out a fair measure of policy autonomy for themselves. In many, however, managers are reluctant to challenge the political status quo internationally or within member countries. This is due to sensitivity to the policy preferences of donor governments and a tendency to view governments, rather than people, as constituents.

Beyond their manipulations of international institutions, the most powerful countries often intervene directly in the affairs of developing countries. Sometimes this has reduced hunger: development and humanitarian aid has helped prevent famine deaths, reduce infant mortality, boost agricultural productivity, and create jobs.

Other interventions, however, have increased hunger. During the 1960s and 1970s, for example, Belgium, France, and the United States repeatedly sent cash and military forces to bolster Zaire's dictator, Mobutu Sese Seko. Western governments

In most U.N. councils and agencies, wealthy governments exercise "power of the purse" to gain policy leverage.

Power, Hunger, and the World Bank

by Nancy C. Alexander

The world has changed enormously since the founding of the World Bank (the Bank) and International Monetary Fund (IMF) in 1945. These international financial institutions (IFIs) were established to promote economic development and financial stability after World War II. Now, many observers ask if the IFIs will adapt to the post-colonial, post-Cold War era.

The Bank lends developing countries $25 billion annually. Regional development banks for Europe, Africa, Asia, and Latin America lend another $25 billion. The total is roughly equivalent to annual development assistance grants from industrial country governments.

The Debt Problem

Developing countries owe governments and private creditors a towering $1.5 trillion, equivalent to a third of their collective gross national product.[1] Debt service is about 18 percent of their export revenues; for severely indebted, middle income countries, the figure is 33 percent.[2]

Half the debt is owed to governments and governmental institutions, such as the Bank. The Bank and IMF are owed a combined $278 billion. They now receive more in principal and interest than they lend.[3] In 1992, the Bank's net transfer to borrowing countries was about -$0.8 billion.[4] Net IMF credits were -$373 million in fiscal 1994.

Economic Reform – Is the Cure Worse than the Disease?

The IMF derives much of its power from its influence on foreign investment and commercial loans. If a country's ability to pay its debt is uncertain, many foreign investors look to the IMF for a "credit rating." The IMF offers credit when no one else will. Its approval is a carrot. The stick lies in policy prescriptions contained in most IMF credits: balanced budgets, free markets, currency devaluation, and an export emphasis. These measures are intended to restore financial stability, but often entail social hardships.

The Bank used to loan exclusively for development *projects* – construction of dams, roads, schools, and clinics. Since the debt crisis of the 1980s, the Bank has supported economic reforms ("structural adjustment programs," or SAPs) similar to those favored by the IMF. The Bank's has planned SAPs with little regard for the impact on poor people.

SAPs are controversial for environmental reasons, too. Developing

saw him as a valuable opponent of communism in a mineral-rich, strategic region. Since 1965, Mobutu has looted Zaire's natural resources, neglecting agriculture, infrastructure, health, and employment. Eighty percent of the rural population lives in poverty, with nearly 60 percent of all Zairians experiencing hunger regularly or occasionally. By unofficial estimates, Zaire has the world's highest infant mortality rate and child malnutrition rates of 42 percent to 65 percent.

Hunger and Powerlessness in Developing Countries

The dynamics of power in the developing world change dramatically as one moves from the countryside to cities.

"The Rich Eat the Poor:" Rural Power and Hunger.

Bangladesh has the world's highest malnutrition rate for children under five, 65 percent. A quarter of its people consume less than 1,800 calories a day. Eighty-seven percent live in rural areas, where the poverty rate is 86 percent. As one analyst notes, "Bangladesh's development strategy is not peasant based, but rests on the support of rural and urban elites. . . ."[1] Rural development efforts tend to benefit landlords and reinforce their power, often leaving the hungry worse off.

A study of a village in Bangladesh in the 1970s found that one of the largest landlords was also a ruling party activist and had won a local government council post. He used his influence to gain control of a World Bank-financed irrigation system. This not only increased his farm's productivity, but gave him an irrigation water monopoly.[2]

This drama of landlords gaining political influence, capturing rural development's benefits, and reinforcing their power is played out in thousands of villages throughout the developing world. It leads to sentiments such as those expressed by an elderly female farmworker on an absentee French landlord's plantation in Morocco: "The rich eat the poor."[3]

Landlords often control credit and commercial networks as well; this frequently directly causes hunger:

> Even with more than adequate food supplies and incomes, people starve either because of parasites in their stomachs or because parasitic landlords/moneylenders . . . deprive them of access to the nutritional benefits of food.[4]

Shantytowns and Shadow Economies: Urban Power and Hunger.

Eighty percent of poor, hunger-vulnerable people in developing countries – a billion souls – live in rural areas. The number of hungry poor urban dwellers is growing rapidly, though, especially in Latin America. According to the U.N. Fund for Population Activities:

> By the year 2000, some 90 percent of the absolute poor in Latin America and the Caribbean will be city-dwellers, along with 40 percent in Africa and 45 percent in Asia. World Bank estimates suggest that by 2000 the number of urban households living in conditions of poverty will have more than doubled from 1975 levels of 33.5 million persons to some 74.3 million.[5]

Many poor urban folk live in low quality housing that lacks proper sanitation and safe water, and is located in hazardous environments.

The more fortunate among poor city people have low, but relatively stable incomes from wage employment or small

countries export food and natural resources to earn hard currency for debt service and imports. Ninety percent of Africa's exports are primary commodities. Their value has dropped precipitously for over a decade. SAPs have encouraged increased exports, sometimes at great environmental cost.

IFIs and Sustainable Development

"Poverty reduction," according to Bank President Lewis Preston, "must be the benchmark against which [the Bank's] performance as a development institution is judged." Eighty percent of the world's people receive 15 percent of income, so poverty reduction is a moral imperative. However, IFIs, including the Bank, are owned by and accountable to *governments*, not citizens. Member governments may or may not care about reducing poverty and hunger; many are undemocratic. The Bank's board gives mixed messages to the 7,000-member staff about the importance of sustainable development, especially environmentally sound reduction of hunger and poverty. Economic rate of return remains the Bank's prime measure for project success and failure.

Undemocratic Governance

The IFIs' governance structure is frankly undemocratic. Instead of each member government receiving one vote, power is proportional to monetary contributions. Five of the Bank's 24 executive directors control 39 percent of the votes (the United States has 17 percent; Japan, 7 percent; and France, Germany, and the United Kingdom, 5 percent each). Nineteen directors representing 171 countries have 61 percent of the votes.

Even if this structure were changed, the IFIs would pay attention to rich country governments. They provide the institutions' financial backing.

IFIs and "Grassroots Democracy"

IFI projects and SAPs are often designed in Washington or a borrowing government's finance ministry and imposed on populations with little prior consultation. The Bank is realizing that this top-down approach often has negative environmental, social, and economic consequences. It is exploring whether or how, as a large institution with an average project size of $100 million, it can engage stakeholders in decisions.

In 1994, BFW Institute launched a project to make the IFIs more accountable, especially to poor and hungry people. The project encourages partnerships among citizens' groups worldwide and between citizens' groups and their governments, in order to strengthen popular influence on IFIs. ∎

Nancy C. Alexander leads BFW Institute's IFI Accountability Project.

Rural development projects in Bangladesh tend to benefit landlords, and reinforce their power, but landless laborers have gained new employment opportunities.

businesses. But many depend on the "informal sector" for survival: casual labor in construction, marginally viable petty commerce, prostitution, and theft.

Poor urban families frequently need credit to afford food, medicine, clothing, transportation, and education. They become highly dependent on landlords, labor brokers, shopkeepers, wholesalers, and usurers. Frequently, these patrons control local political offices and civic organizations, and broker the distribution of government and charitable welfare services. As in the countryside, aid sometimes reinforces existing economic and political power relationships.

But another element of city life changes the equation. As a leading developing country scholar has pointed out, rural poor people are usually "dispersed and disorganized," and hence politically "voiceless."[6] City folk,

in contrast, live close together, often in crowded multifamily dwellings. They are frequently better educated (since schooling is more accessible in cities) and more politically savvy than their country cousins, making them easier to organize into labor unions or community associations. Urban discontent can mean considerable disruption; in capital cities, it can topple national governments. This gives urban poor people power relative to the government that rural poor people do not enjoy. So cheap urban food policies may be bad economics, especially in relation to local farm output, but they are usually excellent politics.

This urban clout transcends the divide between relatively democratic and highly authoritarian regimes. The repressive, market-oriented Pinochet government in Chile maintained social spending, including nutrition programs for poor children and public health services. This resulted from pressure from labor unions and other nongovernmental organizations. Hunger analysts Jean Drèze and Amartya Sen conclude that authoritarian governments "may have strong incentive to respond to popular demands" for anti-hunger policies.[7] One incentive in Chile was that 83 percent of the people live in cities.

Finding Common Ground. The Pinochet regime's responsiveness to urban poor people is just one example of how poor and hungry people can sometimes gain political power. This depends upon organization, and often on coalitions and bargaining. Even in situations of opposed interests, e.g., between landlords on the one hand and tenant farmers or landless agricultural workers on the other, there exists some common ground.

Bangladesh offers several examples. Rural development projects and new agricultural technology have benefitted landlords, but landless laborers have gained new employment opportunities. Cheap food policies can hurt producers, but landless people and even some small farmers purchase all or most of their food in markets and have a stake in affordable prices. It would be very expensive for the government to subsidize prices for both consumers and producers, but it could do so if it cut the budget of the politically influential military. A coalition among farmers and food consumers (who include some politically influential groups, such as civil servants and professional people) could demand such a policy and wield countervailing power.

A segment of Bangladesh's poor rural populace benefits from the Public Food Distribution System (PFDS), which makes food available at reduced prices. The system mainly serves bureaucrats, the military,

teachers, employees of large enterprises, and city residents (without regard to income), all groups with political sway. The part which serves poor rural dwellers is known for corruption, and is highly dependent on external food aid. When resources are tight, it is always the lowest priority. But there are real benefits to hungry people. Programs such as PFDS that have a broad constituency of hungry and non-hungry people are usually less fragile politically than programs that help only very poor people.

The Politics of Hunger in the United States

As in the developing world, the needs and interests of poor and hungry people are seldom a high priority on U.S. policymakers' agenda. The federal government still spends hundreds of billions of dollars annually on the military, despite the end of the Cold War. Billions more go to:

- intelligence agencies;

- the space program;

- farm programs;

- subsidies for water use, mining, and the merchant fleet;

- the savings and loan bailout;

- pork barrel projects that benefit well-placed communities and firms; and

- home mortgage tax breaks.

Unlike supporters of these programs and their well-heeled lobbyists, low-income people seldom contribute to or work in political campaigns, and they account for many of the unregistered eligible voters. In contrast to most other industrial countries, the United States puts the burden of voter registration on citizens rather than the government. Often, registration conditions

Hunger 1994: Transforming the Politics of Hunger recommends seven priority areas for transformative action against hunger:

1. Individuals and agencies assisting hungry people can expand what they do to influence government policies.

2. Religious communities can teach how social concern flows from a relationship with God and help motivate involvement in effective political action.

3. Low-income people's organizations can be strengthened, especially in their capacity to influence government policies that affect them.

4. Organizations which help low-income people can more fully engage people of color, especially in decision making.

5. The media can move beyond stories of pity and charity to explain the causes of hunger, and people and organizations concerned about hunger can make a bigger effort to influence the media.

6. People can expand and strengthen anti-hunger advocacy organizations.

7. People and organizations working against poverty and hunger can become more aware of themselves as parts of a large, potentially dynamic movement.

(such as inconvenient locations, short hours, and even hostile personnel) lead poor people to drop out of the electoral system. Recent federal legislation has sought to ease access to registration, but up to now politicians have seldom felt the need to appeal to hungry people for votes.[8]

Transforming the Politics of Hunger

In *Hunger 1994: Transforming the Politics of Hunger* BFW Institute showed how the thousands of private organizations and millions of individuals in the United States who are helping hungry people at home and abroad could actually end hunger in the United States and make dramatic strides against hunger worldwide by becoming more political (see box at left). Mainstream society can help empower vulnerable people and support constructive changes in public policies.

Feeding hungry people can be part of such a strategy. Hunger service agencies can facilitate the creation of poor people's organizations, assist in voter registration, and encourage clients and their own staff and boards to advocate public policies that contribute to hunger reduction. These policies include full funding of federal food programs, aid to sustainable development, and changes in economic policies to foster income-earning opportunities for poor people at home and abroad.

Similarly, in developing countries, intellectuals committed to social change, foreign nongovernmental development organizations, and other organizations of non-hungry people can provide vital services to poor people's organizations and work to change public policies. This is happening in many places:

- The Bangladesh Rural Advancement Committee, in collaboration with Oxfam America, offers credit and training to rural poor people and helps them create viable organizations.

- In India, the media have played an essential role in pressing the central government to implement famine relief policies that have greatly reduced emergency food needs in that country.

- Kenya's National Council of Women took the lead in encouraging local communities to plant trees to combat land degradation.

- In Brazil, hundreds of nongovernmental organizations (NGOs) representing a tremendous variety of social sectors have formed coalitions on such issues as hunger, public health, ethical government, environmental policy, urban development, and land reform.

The empowerment of hungry people is an essential element of any strategy to overcome hunger.

Toward Solutions: Empowering Hungry People

Sometimes, as in El Salvador and South Africa until quite recently, efforts to empower hungry people lead to violent repression. But hungry people sometimes decide that resisting oppression is preferable to the "quiet violence" of hunger.[9]

Involving hungry people in planning, administering, and evaluating policies and programs which affect them – in other words, treating people as subjects rather than objects – is a matter of human rights and dignity. The 1992 "World Declaration on Nutrition," issued at the International Conference on Nutrition, recognizes this, calling "access to nutritionally adequate and safe food . . . a right of each individual"[10] (for more information, see "The Right to Food," 31-32). It also states:

> Policies and programs must be directed toward those most in need. Our priority should be to implement people-focused policies and programs that increase access to and control of resources by the rural and urban poor, raise their productive capacity and incomes, and strengthen their capacity to care for themselves. We must support and promote initiatives by people and communities and ensure that the poor participate in decisions that affect their lives.[11]

When once powerless people participate in politics and the policy-making process,

they are more likely to see programs that serve their own interests enacted. Poor people may well make mistakes, perhaps pushing for policies that will help them in the short-term but hurt over the long haul. But participation allows poor people to learn from mistakes. They can also better articulate how power sharing and reduced hunger benefit everyone.

All this requires organization. One development theorist defines genuine "people's organizations" as those set up to pursue mutual benefits, with leaders accountable to the members. Poor people's organizations are most effective when they are, in the main, self-reliant, though they may work in alliance with other groups.[12]

People's organizations have the best chance of developing where government respects freedom of association, an independent judiciary prevents powerholders from interfering with this right, and foreign intervention does not nullify people's efforts to define and control their situations.

Even under very restrictive conditions, poor and hungry people often organize to address immediate concerns, such as improved government services or more equitable distribution of resources. Such people's organizations sometimes go on to help promote democracy at the national level.

It is no accident that the trend toward political pluralism and representative government in Africa, Asia, Latin America, the former Soviet Union, and Central and Eastern Europe has gone hand in hand with the proliferation of popular organizations. Today there are 18,000 registered NGOs in the Philippines and 3,000 in Brazil.

In Zambia, labor unions which had agitated for improved living conditions led the fight to restore multi-party democracy. In 1991, the head of the labor movement was elected president, defeating the country's independence leader and only previous

The empowerment of hungry people is an essential element of any strategy to overcome hunger.

The Right to Food

by Richard A. Hoehn

It is paradoxical, but hardly surprising, that the right to food has been endorsed more often and with greater unanimity and urgency than most other human rights, while at the same time being violated more comprehensively and system-atically than probably any other right.[1]

The field of human rights is littered with abuse and paradoxes. Governments boycott each other over violations of civil and politi-cal rights while neglecting the violence of hunger among their own children. They are oblivious to the contradiction. Civil and political rights – freedom of expression and association, the right to vote and due process of law – often have little meaning to those who lack food.

The Hague and Geneva Conventions promise enough nutri-tious food for good health for prisoners in time of war, but few nations guarantee food for families in time of peace. All should.

The 1974 World Food Conference produced a Universal Decla-ration on the Eradication of Hunger and Malnutrition which names social inequalities, conflict, neo-colonialism, and racial discrimination among the causes of hunger. It asserts that each "man, woman, and child has the inalienable right to be free from hunger and malnutrition in order to develop fully and maintain their physical and mental faculties."

The United Nations has undertaken peacekeeping efforts, passed resolutions, and established anti-hunger agencies. The General Assembly adopted the Universal Declaration of Human Rights, later elaborated in the International Covenant on Econom-ic, Social, and Cultural Rights:

Everyone has the right to a standard of living adequate for the health and well-being of himself and his family, includ-ing food, clothing, housing and medical care, and necessary social services, and the right to security in the event of unem-ployment, sickness, disability, widowhood, old age, or other lack of livelihood in circumstances beyond his control.

More than 120 international declarations, conventions, and "right to food" related resolutions address: the rights of children; elimination of racial, ethnic, and gender discrimination; popula-tion policy and natural resource use; minimum wages; and the rights of indigenous people.[2]

The preamble to the U.S. Constitution seeks "to form a more

president in free and fair balloting.

NGOs from developing and industrial countries are increasingly working together (though they sometimes differ on both strategy and substantive positions). Such a coalition challenged international policies and power structures at the 1992 U.N. Con-ference on Environment and Development, for example.

Citizens' movements in the industrial world have an important role to play in opposing their governments' harmful inter-ventions in developing countries (e.g., the broad movement in the United States which opposed U.S. military involvement in Central America in the 1980s) and in seeking a fairer international economic system. A coalition of U.S. religious, labor, and human rights groups has sought to make respect for workers' rights a part of U.S. trade policy.

Other examples illustrate how empower-ment leads to sustainable progress against hunger.

Case Studies

Kerala[13]

The people of the Indian state of Kerala have shown how to reduce hunger and improve well-being even under conditions of general poverty and little economic growth. The state has a higher literacy rate and lower infant mortality and birth rates than the rest of India. Nutritional standards equal or exceed those of other states. Health, food, and education are available without regard to gender, caste, or urban vs. rural residence. Only 35 percent of India's rural villages have ready access to health centers and subsidized food shops, but in Kerala the figure is 99 percent. Most children participate in nutrition programs.

Strong and persistent organizations of peasants, workers, women, and low status castes explain these successes. A tradition of widespread education and literacy dating to the 19th century has helped political mobilization. These organizations have enjoyed dedicated, honest leaders, and have pressed to maintain high quality services for all Keralites. So even though parties supporting their demands have alternated in office with more conservative forces, the state has continued to offer social service programs. Kerala still faces many problems, including high unemployment, but it shows how well-organized and determined people can transform their lives.

ORAP in Zimbabwe[14]

The Organization of Rural Associations for Progress (ORAP) has sought to help poor rural people in the southern African nation of Zimbabwe draw on the strength of their own culture to achieve sustainable livelihoods. In Matabelaland, one of three provinces in which ORAP works, there is a long tradition of *amalima*, or collective self-help, as well as an extended family structure. ORAP also draws on village organizations which grew out of the country's struggle to end white minority rule.

ORAP provides funds and technical assistance to groups of five to 30 families who pool their resources for mutual aid. The organization does not approach communities, but rather responds to their requests.

ORAP seeks to engage villagers in a process of educational dialogue, through which they gain a clearer sense of their problems and how development projects (such as recreating traditional village granaries, raising livestock or cash crops, education, sanitation systems, promoting stoves that use less wood, and starting sewing clubs) address them. The dialogue also involves how to relate to the government, e.g., whether to undertake activities requiring government permits.

According to ORAP staffer Cornelia Nkomo, projects are a vehicle for development, not development itself, which is "help-

perfect Union, establish Justice, insure domestic Tranquility, provide for the common defense, promote the general welfare, and secure the blessings of Liberty. . . ." But where basic needs are not met, justice has not been established, domestic tranquility is threatened, a nation is more difficult to defend, the general welfare has not been achieved, and the most basic freedom – to live – has not been secured.

In 1976, prompted by Bread for the World, the U.S. Congress passed the Right to Food Resolution. It affirms that all people "have a right to a nutritionally adequate diet." More recent statements call for the "right to food security" – assured access for every person, primarily by production or purchase, to enough nutritious food to sustain productive human life.

John Haughey, ethicist at Loyola University, argues that a more formal official commitment to the right to food would help to change U.S. politics and culture. The public usually supports measures to protect the civil rights spelled out in the Bill of Rights, but relatively few U.S. citizens or public officials believe that everyone has a right to eat.

The human rights movement has made great strides. Even some totalitarian governments feel a need to show that they are not abusing civil rights. International moral sentiment has consequences.

However, in the 20 years since the adoption of the Universal Declaration on the Elimination of Hunger and Malnutrition, millions of people have died or been physically or mentally impaired due to malnutrition.

No one is against the right to food. But we must transform the politics of hunger to translate the emerging human consciousness of the right to food into day-to-day food security for all people. One effort to achieve this is the campaign for a global Food Security Treaty, launched in 1994. It seeks to create U.N. enforcement mechanisms – akin to peacekeeping forces – to prevent the use of food as a weapon and assure that everyone actually does enjoy an adequate diet.[3] ∎

Dr. Richard A. Hoehn is director of BFW Institute.

ing people become what they want to be." Most ORAP staff are recruited from the villages, so the organization is primarily a "cultural grassroots movement." How has this affected hunger? Nkomo says that since 1984, no one living in the areas in which ORAP works has gone hungry, despite periodic severe droughts.

We must transform the politics of hunger to translate the emerging human consciousness of the right to food into day-to-day food security for all people.

One strong feature of ORAP is its emphasis on productive, income-earning projects. When poor people anywhere are asked what they most want, the answer often has to do with jobs and income-earning capacity. But people's organizations often lack sufficient knowledge or power to create jobs or sway national policies to create jobs, so they push instead for social services. ORAP is also unusual in its ability to deal with national policy; most organizations of poor people are local and focused on local problems.

ORAP has pressed the government for more extensive land reform, and persuaded the Ministry of Agriculture to permit direct grain sales from one village to another without going through the state grain marketing agency. This effort to ease the marketing monopoly has helped reduce the droughts' impact and strengthened economic links among the villages.

ORAP is nonpartisan and works with people from both of Zimbabwe's major ethnic groups. However, the government banned the organization from working in two provinces for a year, accusing it of partisanship in the political and ethnic struggles of the 1980s. Nkomo notes, "When you empower people, they challenge structures," and fearful reaction by powerful people is predictable. More recently, though, other Zimbabwean organizations have looked to ORAP's combination of service delivery and social mobilization as a model.

Nutrition Education and Action in Barahona, Dominican Republic[15]

In 1976, Caritas Dominica, the charity of the Dominican Republic's Roman Catholic Church, established a nutrition center in Barahona, a small port and sugar processing town located in the country's southwest, the area of the most severe malnutrition. Later, a second center opened; the two facilities focused on providing supplemental foods (mainly using foreign food aid) to severely malnourished children, improving family incomes, and nutrition education in the city and surrounding villages.

The centers trained women to work as community health promoters. Eventually, they took the initiative to reorganize the project toward increased emphasis on "self-development." They obtained new funding from Caritas Holland and other European aid agencies.

The project focused increasingly on engaging the region's women in discussions of what caused their health and nutrition problems. They identified one problem as their lack of access to clean water, while sugarcane plantations, which supply the country's main export, had plenty of water. They also explored how to use locally available foods to plan affordable, nutritious meals.

The project continued to promote income generation. It emphasized producing food (small livestock such as chickens and rabbits, as well as vegetables) which participants could both consume and sell.

In the 1980s, the world price of sugar collapsed. The Dominican government's foreign debt mounted, and it expanded the money supply so that it could continue to provide essential services. Prices rose, but wages stagnated. Malnutrition rates, which had declined in the 1970s, increased. As the price of financial assistance, the International Monetary Fund pressed the government to raise water fees to balance its budget. The new rates threatened to make clean water unaffordable for many poor people.

The Barahona nutrition project organized a non-payment campaign. The government cut off participants' water, but the project women worked with the water utility employees' union to get it restored. Researchers for Oxfam United Kingdom and Ireland comment on how the women had mastered politics as "the art of the possible":

[T]here was something which could be done within the control of the people. They could not change the price of sugar, or boycott the IMF. But they could challenge their government as mediator between the international world and their community's distress on a specific and pertinent issue.[16]

ROCC, Lexington, Mississippi[17]

The Rural Organizing and Cultural Center (ROCC) is located in Holmes County, Mississippi, the fourth poorest county in the United States. In 1978, it helped organize a boycott of white merchants in Lexington, as a protest against racially segregated facilities and police brutality against African Americans. Following the success of the boycott, ROCC surveyed 1,000 families to learn their priorities. They wanted an end to racial prejudice in the criminal justice system; quality education for children; and better access to food, housing, and public assistance.

ROCC has undertaken projects to address each of these concerns. In addition to continuing to challenge police abuses, it has organized community gardens to improve the quantity and quality of local food supplies, worked against corruption at the local water utility and sought improved water safety, and helped to enhance the school curriculum, with an emphasis on preparing students for work.

ROCC has also worked on training Holmes County residents for advocacy and political participation. Organizers brief welfare recipients on the rights and benefit levels to which they are entitled. Recipients then lobby state agencies. In addition, ROCC has registered low-income voters and worked on electoral districts so as to assure fair representation for low-income and minority people.

Conclusion

It is possible to overcome the powerlessness that underlies hunger. What is needed is the broadening and deepening of the global anti-hunger movement, and the empowerment of poor and hungry people to participate as an integral part of that movement.

These case studies show that hungry people can obtain greater power, equity, and food security short of revolution. The common elements include:

- development of literacy and other basic skills;

- creation of organizations that allow people collectively to pursue their interests as they themselves define those interests and bargain with already powerful groups; and

- willingness to engage in sometimes difficult struggles to make and keep gains.

There are no magic formulas. Specific circumstances differ in every locale and country. Still, these examples show that the Chilean poet Pablo Neruda was not dreaming an impossible dream when he spoke of a world where everyone could enjoy "the justice of eating."[18] ■

Dr. Marc J. Cohen is senior research associate at BFW Institute and editor of *Causes of Hunger*.

It is possible to overcome the powerlessness that underlies hunger.

Violence and Militarism

Cause 2

The U.N. estimates that 105 million unexploded land-mines are buried in 62 countries. Here, a U.N. staff member in Cambodia practices mine removal.

by Daniel U.B.P. Chelliah

This chapter explores violence and militarism, overt community violence, and institutional violence as causes of hunger and human suffering. It suggests a framework for overcoming violence at the individual, community, national, and international levels based on ways of managing and resolving disputes and on changes in attitudes and behavior. Hunger and poverty also contribute to violence; reducing hunger can aid in reducing violence.

Hunger and Violence

Rwanda. In just a few weeks in 1994, about 300,000 people were slaughtered in the conflict between the Tutsis and Hutu extremists in Rwanda. More than 2 million people took refuge in neighboring countries.

Without food and water, hundreds starved to death. Food supplies were plundered. Crop cycles were interrupted; seeds and breeding livestock were consumed. Markets broke down. Tens of thousands of children suffered permanent damage from too little food and related illnesses.

The conflict in Rwanda is only one of dozens of current conflicts, and countless instances throughout history, in which violent struggles over resources and privilege have resulted in fear, chaos, uprootedness, genocide, disease, malnutrition, and hunger.

The world was startled by the gruesome murders. People who watched this genocide and its after-effects on TV asked how humans could inflict such atrocities on each other.

Washington, D.C. James was a brilliant high school student. He was shot in the head and died immediately in inner-city Washington, D.C. His mistake: being in the wrong place at the wrong time, caught in the crossfire between two drug gangs. Thousands in the United States die as James did, innocent victims of street violence.

The hunger consequences of overt street violence are less obvious than those of civil or international warfare, but nonetheless real, with long-term effects. Daily nutrition suffers as families' lives are disrupted, and as energy and resources are diverted to self-protection. Crime-plagued stores must raise food prices. Children living in fear learn poorly; youth drop out of school; both are less well-equipped for the rest of their lives – less able to provide for the food and other needs of their own families.

We all continue to ask, "Why this violence?"

Chicago. Carlos, now 19, dropped out of school during the 10th grade, but reads at only a third grade level. He feels badly that he can find only occasional casual work, which does not enable him to support his girlfriend, Juanita, and their one-year-old child. They pretend they are not a family, so Juanita can qualify for Aid to Families with Dependent Children, food stamps, and Medicaid. They often run low on food at the end of the month. Carlos feels trapped. So far, he has avoided heavy drug use and turned down chances to get into drug-dealing, but the huge profits are tempting.

Over time, the consequences of institutional violence – poor education, joblessness, discrimination, poverty, hunger, powerlessness – probably outweigh those from incidents of overt violence. Many instances of overt violence are symptoms of the myriad ways that violent attitudes and behavior are woven into individual, societal, and international relationships. Denial of

Figure 2.1
Average Annual U.S. Government Research and Development Spending, 1980s and 1990s: Advanced Weapons vs. Environment

$1.4 Billion

■ Advanced Weapons R&D
□ Environmental R&D

Source: Worldwatch Institute.

Street Dogs and Food Territories

I grew up in a small town in Southern India and used to have evening discussions over coffee with my mother, who taught me many simple truths about life. One thing that irritated me in those days was the continuous barking at night of the stray street dogs, which disturbed my homework. "Why do they bark like this?," I remember asking my mother. The answer was a basic truth which has helped me understand the reason for many sociopolitical, religious, ethnic, national, and international conflicts. "They are street dogs," she said. "They fight over their food territories, the streets where they live."

Obtaining food plays a dominant role in human behavior as well. My intent in narrating this event is not to degrade humans to the level of dogs but to make the point that grabbing the sources of material goods, which include food, seems to be one cause of hatred and violence. International order, just like order in the street, often depends on who controls food and the resources to produce food. ∎

human dignity itself does mental and sometimes physical damage. Hunger, too, is often both a cause and a consequence in the cycle of institutional violence.

Common Understandings of Violence

I asked several groups of people what violence meant. Children defined it as fights in school and on the streets. They are afraid of other children carrying knives and guns to school. Youngsters defined violence as the tension growing from the old-fashioned ways of parents and teachers. Women said, "It is the male-macho attitude." African-American friends said, "It is the color of skin, my brother." White friends said, "It is the dominance of one race over another, one religion over another, one nation over another." One person said, "Violence is the absence of nonviolence."

I use the term violence here to describe any act or situation that injures the health and well-being of others (or one's self) by causing physical or emotional pain.

We usually think of violence as harmful actions against persons or property. Violence at this level is the easiest form to assess, since it usually involves direct actions with immediate consequences – violence among children in schools; within families and communities; among youth gangs in drive-by shootings and terror; and between neighbors in civil wars.

But violence is not only what we see. It also includes destructive actions that may not involve a direct relationship between the victims and the institution or persons responsible for harm.[1] Visible violence is the tip of the iceberg.

Institutionalized forms of violence are often so submerged from view as to be almost invisible. In nearly every culture, violence perpetuated by social institutions denies human dignity and human rights to many despite religious and governmental declarations of equality for all. Discrimination based on race, sex, age, or other factors are forms of institutional violence. The Rural Organizing and Cultural Center in Holmes County, Mississippi (see Cause 1) focused on reducing police violence as its top priority.

Violence at this level often results from oppressive social policies. The oppressive violence of one community over others has led to conditions of human degradation and has periodically required a Moses, a Jesus, a Mohammed, or a Gandhi to redeem the masses.

While responding to overt violence at the personal, community, and global levels is critical in the short term, longer term changes in underlying attitudes, behavior, and public policies are essential to overcoming violence and its effects on people, including hunger.

Militarism and Violence

Militarism is an institutional expression of violence. Nations, as well as individuals, use violence and the threat of violence as a means of domination and social control. Over time, ordinary citizens come to accept the tendency to look first for military solutions to issues which might be solved by other means. Violence and militarism almost inevitably lead to hunger.

Human history is littered with conflicts based on communities' need to control land and sea in order to produce or trade food. The stone, copper, bronze, and iron ages were all marked by struggles over the ownership of pasture lands by riverside and seashores. The effects of these struggles on hunger varied. Fighting itself nearly always increased hunger. Victors often secured their own food supply, but at the expense of increased hunger or other suffering for the vanquished.

The 20th century started with a major ideological conflict in Europe and Russia. Millions lost their lives. World Wars I and II killed tens of millions of people, destroyed property worth billions, and led to hunger and deprivation for millions of people. Each war left thousands homeless, without water, sanitation, electricity, and food. Starvation deaths occurred throughout Europe. Churches and many private organizations set up relief programs. After World War II, the Marshall Plan and the World Bank opened new possibilities for development and peace. The United Nations was created in an attempt to build an alternative to systems of warfare.

However, an uneasy Cold War continued between the superpowers, draining global financial, material, and human

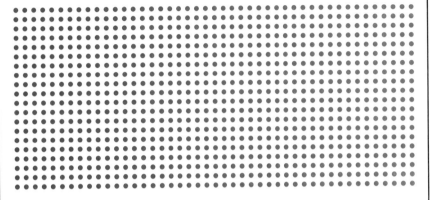

Figure 2.2: World Firepower

Each of these dots represents the quantity of firepower expended in World War II. The total above represents the size of the world's nuclear stockpiles if agreements between the United States and the former Soviet Union are honored. The total is 900 times more explosive power than that expended in World War II – including some 10,000 nuclear warheads, each far more powerful than the bombs dropped on Hiroshima and Nagasaki.

resources to build war machines.

At the same time, new movements toward independence and liberation from colonialism inspired leaders such as Gandhi in India. They challenged the ethical standards of colonial powers which had long forced people to work in mines and on plantations and farms for minimal wages, determined on the basis of color and sex. The colonial powers also adopted a "divide and rule" strategy in many parts of the world which ignited ethnic and religious conflicts (e.g., the Belgians put the Tutsi minority in Rwanda in power over the Hutu majority).

Politically derived borders often crossed ethnic community lines. For example, splitting the Ottoman Empire into several nations after World War I left Kurdish minorities in Iraq, Turkey, Iran, and Syria rather than creating a Kurdish state. This led to conflicts that continue even today.

Military expenditures mounted steadily throughout the Cold War era in many

Militarism:
Use of Resources

Despite the end of the Cold War, the world continues to devote huge resources to military preparations:

- Global military expenditures are estimated at $767 billion for 1994 – more than the total income of the poorest 45 percent of the world's population.[2]

- The "peace dividend" can be calculated from the reduction in global military spending from its peak of $1 trillion in 1987. The peace dividend has totalled $935 billion over the seven years since then. Part of it has financed social programs within countries, but none has gone to boost declining international development assistance.

- Further global military spending cuts of 3 percent per year would accumulate an additional $460 billion by the year 2000 – enough to more than double recent levels of development assistance.

- Developing countries themselves spend about $125 billion per year on military forces. One quarter of this would provide primary health care for all their citizens, reduce adult literacy by half, and provide family planning to all willing couples.

- World arms trade in 1992 totaled $18.4 billion, most of it originating with the five permanent members of the United Nations Security Council. Military assistance in 1993 totaled $4.6 billion, nearly 75 percent from the United States – most of that to Israel and Egypt.

- The United States remains the largest exporter of arms, partly in response to fear of job losses in businesses and communities dependent on arms manufacturing. But reduced military spending, coupled with increased development investment, could create more employment – and reduce tension, violence, and hunger. ∎

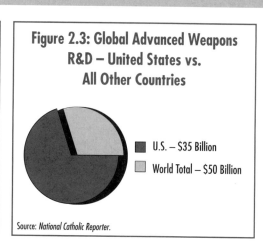

Figure 2.3: Global Advanced Weapons R&D – United States vs. All Other Countries

■ U.S. – $35 Billion
□ World Total – $50 Billion

Source: *National Catholic Reporter.*

newly independent nations as well. Some of the rising expenditures were financed by the superpowers for their own purposes, but funding also came from scarce national resources.

Effects of Militarism

Globally, and in each nation, resources spent on arms build-ups are not available for investment in food production, education, health care, or other development efforts. With rare exceptions, wherever arms are used, suffering and hunger increase. In addition to draining resources, military forces are regularly used by autocratic and military governments to prevent needed social, economic, and political changes – to perpetuate institutional violence.

The Impact of Warfare

According to the U.N. Development Program:

Global conflicts seem to be changing – from wars between states to wars within them. Of 82 armed conflicts between 1989 and 1992, only three were between states . . . although often cast in ethnic divisions, many also have a political or economic character.[3]

Civil wars are one of the most potent causes of human suffering and underdevelopment. Although the end of the Cold War has led to peace moves in those areas in which conflict had been fueled by East-West antagonism, new wars have erupted. The 1990s opened with the Persian Gulf conflict, which displaced approximately 5 million people. New and continuing civil strife are the source of severe human disasters in the former Yugoslavia, Somalia, Sudan, Mozambique, Afghanistan, Nagorno-Karabakh, Sri Lanka, and Burma. The immediate costs and negative impact on long-term development are very high.

Warfare has always resulted in hunger and suffering for ordinary citizens. But the damaging effects of the recent and current fighting has shifted even more from combatants to civilians. The proportion of civilian casualties has increased. Huge numbers of refugees have been forced from their homes and communities. Social and economic disruptions are usually more pervasive from internal fighting than from an international war. Recovery from a civil war is more difficult, since it requires cooperation with "the enemy," while international war tends to unite a population against their common outside enemy.

Frances Stewart, of the International Development Center at Oxford University, recently studied sixteen different developing countries at war. In fourteen of the countries, civilian deaths account for over two-thirds of the total. Only in Iran and Iraq were military deaths higher than those of civilians.

Civil wars generate large numbers of refugees and internally displaced persons. In 1983, there were nine countries from which more than 50,000 people had fled. A decade later, there were 31. At the end of 1993, more than 16 million refugees lived outside their own country, not including

A Global Demilitarization Fund

I would like to propose the establishment of a Global Demilitarization Fund. This fund could add dynamism to the current demilitarization trend by rewarding primarily, but not exclusively, the efforts of developing countries to:

- Disarm and demobilize their armed forces;

- Re-integrate military personnel into society through retraining and re-education programs in order to expand their range of choices and economic opportunities;

- Promote arms control and the shrinkage of arms production facilities; and

- Encourage civic education and participation in fully democratic political life.

Let the nations of the world, both rich and poor, commit themselves to at least a 3 percent a year reduction in their military spending levels over the next five years. The rich nations should agree to earmark at least one-fifth of these savings towards a demilitarization fund which is under international jurisdiction. Developing countries should also agree to contribute a fraction, perhaps one-tenth, of these savings towards such a fund.

. . . the manage[ment] of the fund [should be decided by] the 1995 U.N. Conference on Social Development.[4]
— Oscar Arias, winner of the 1987 Nobel Peace Prize

millions more who have permanently relocated. Thirty-eight African countries hosted refugees from other nations, but people had fled from all but two of these as well. More than 3 million Afghans were refugees in Pakistan and Iran.[5]

People who have fled their homes, but remained within their country, are harder to identify, but are estimated to exceed 25 million.[6] Refugees rank near the bottom on every social indicator. They are particularly vulnerable to hunger, usually having neither

TABLE 2.1
War and War-Related Deaths

Country	Deaths in thousands, 1970s	Deaths in thousands, 1980s	Percent Civilian Deaths,1970s	Percent Civilian Deaths, 1980s
Cambodia	1,156	65	75	22
Afghanistan	n/a	1,300	n/a	62
Mozambique	n/a	1,050	n/a	95
Lebanon	100	63	75	65
Angola	n/a	341	n/a	94
Sudan	n/a	506	n/a	99
Vietnam	1,000	n/a	49	n/a
Guatemala	n/a	140	n/a	75
El Salvador	n/a	75	n/a	67
Ethiopia	n/a	609	n/a	85
Somalia	n/a	55	n/a	91
Liberia	n/a	15	n/a	93

n/a= not available or applicable.

Source: Ruth Leger Sivard, *World Social and Military Expenditures 1991* (Washington: World Priorities, 1991); figures are approximate.

land to grow food nor wages from employment to buy it.

The hunger effects of warfare depend on the intensity of the fighting. Severe fighting has almost immediate consequences. If people flee for their lives, as in Rwanda, hunger is almost immediate. Without food, fuel, or safe water, illness and symptoms of hunger appear within days, especially among children. Starvation may appear within as little as two or three weeks. Places like Bosnia, Sudan, and Cambodia provide additional deadly testimony. In some of these instances, withholding food is a deliberate strategy of warfare.

Even where fighting is less severe, markets and transportation are disrupted; food and fuel supplies shrink and prices rise; utilities may be cut off; work is interrupted; and incomes stop. Countries at war in the 1980s and 1990s showed falling per capita income. The worst performances were in Mozambique, Liberia, Nicaragua, Afghanistan, and Guatemala. As always, poor people are most vulnerable.

If warfare continues, longer term effects contribute to hunger. Stewart found that per capita food production dropped in all except two of the sixteen countries she studied – by more than 15 percent in six countries, with Cambodia, Nicaragua, Sudan, Angola, and Mozambique the worst performers. Export volume (and thus, the livelihoods of numerous workers) fell sharply in Afghanistan, Mozambique, Somalia, Nicaragua, Liberia, and Uganda.

Governments at war often must reduce expenditures for social services such as health care, education, and food subsidy programs. They usually also postpone repair and investment in social infrastructure, and schools, hospitals, and clinics are often systematically destroyed in civil conflicts. For example, 40 percent of the primary schools were destroyed in Mozambique. Transportation systems and energy projects were also targeted. Forty-four percent of the rail fleet was destroyed.[7]

Another effect of war is long-term agricultural damage. Many or most farm animals were killed in Afghanistan and Cambodia. The United Nations estimates that 105 million unexploded land-mines are buried in 62 countries, more than 20 million in Angola alone.

Other long-term effects include losses of

human resources. Half the doctors and 80 percent of the pharmacists left Nicaragua and Uganda.

Perhaps worst of all is the breakdown of cultural and social relationships and institutions – trust, respect for property, law, and integrity (see table 2.2).

Stewart's study also showed that some governments of countries at war left food distribution to the market, while others intervened quite heavily. The most comprehensive interventions occurred in Nicaragua, Mozambique, Iraq, and Iran, with a varying combination of price controls, subsidies, and rations. In Iraq, a food rationing system introduced after the imposition of economic sanctions in 1990 entitled every citizen to a uniform ration at set prices. In fact, this provided people with only half of their pre-crisis calorie intake. There was widespread hunger due to the economic collapse, the breakdown of the plan, and disrupted supplies. Since the Gulf War, the ration system has provided only partial protection of nutritional standards.[8]

Responses to Militarism and Warfare

The international community copes with warfare through humanitarian assistance, U.N. peacemaking and peacekeeping agencies, and a wide variety of other contacts, agreements, and understandings.

During the Cold War, humanitarian assistance was usually granted only to friendly or strategic countries. This practice seems to be diminishing, with humanitarian need becoming the principal basis for assistance.

But delivering humanitarian aid during civil wars is often difficult. The people with the greatest need are often opposed to the prevailing government, whether or not they support armed resistance. Governments almost always resist humanitarian

Table 2.2: Development Costs of War	
Destruction of:	**Existing Capital**
Physical Infrastructure	Transportation System
	Irrigation
	Power
	Factories
Social Infrastructure	Schools
	Clinics
Human Capital	Health
	Migration
	Knowledge
Institutions	Extension
	Banks
	Health Care
	Marketing Links
	Educational
Social/Cultural	Trust
	Work Ethic
	Respect for Property

assistance that might strengthen a rebellious faction. Great tension often exists between the principle that outsiders should not intervene in the affairs of sovereign nations and widespread perception that a particular government is threatening the lives and well-being of part of its citizenry.

Calls for emergency food assistance during civil strife seem likely to increase. Strategies of response to these hunger emergencies should ensure two linkages:

- Planning and delivery of food assistance should engage all parties and enhance dispute settlement processes and the development of democratic institutions;

- Food aid should be integrated with reconstruction and longer term sustainable development.[9]

Developing new institutions for dispute resolution and the promotion of democracy

Poverty and hunger breed violence.

is proceeding, albeit slowly. The role of the United Nations as peacemaker and peacekeeper is gaining momentum. The number of U.N. peacekeeping missions has increased rapidly since 1989, as the international community has turned to the U.N. as its preferred vehicle for dealing with internal conflicts. In some instances, warring factions within a country have also turned to, or accepted, a U.N. presence in settling disputes.

In his report, "Agenda for Peace," the U.N. Secretary General, Boutros Boutros-Ghali, proposes that the world community pay greater attention to dispute resolution before the outbreak of violence through active diplomacy. He also proposes the deployment of U.N. contingents of personnel trained in preventive diplomacy, peacemaking, and peacekeeping. He calls for secure financing from the international donors, emphasizes the role of the World Court, recognizes the growing role of military and humanitarian interventions, and embraces peace enforcement efforts.

Bilateral, regional, and international agreements outside the U.N. system also play important roles in resolving disputes and in modeling attitudes and means for dispute resolution between and among nations. The United States has not seriously considered turning to war or threats of war in its dealings with Canada and Great Britain for more than a century. War between the United States and Europe, Oceania, Japan, or Mexico also seems unlikely now. Hundreds of formal conventions, agreements, and treaties, plus informal understandings, undergird most of the world's trade and much of its foreign policy – the European Union, the Organization of Petroleum Exporting Countries (OPEC), the Organization of African Unity, the Association of Southeast Asian Nations, the Arab League, postal unions, and trade and

environmental agreements, to name a few.

Each effort to resolve international or civil disputes by non-military, non-violent means increases the body of relevant information and experience, and raises the likelihood of such efforts succeeding. Probably even more important, the availability of trusted mechanisms will reinforce a shift away from first or primary reliance on military force as a means to settle disputes.

Violence and Hunger in the United States

Poverty and hunger breed violence. People who live without steady income to feed, house, and clothe their families tend to be especially prone to, and vulnerable to, violence.

In the United States, someone dies from a gunshot wound every 14 minutes. The incidence of suicide and homicide are much higher in poor communities than in middle-class neighborhoods. The homicide rate in poor African-American communities is 159 per 100,000 compared to 17 per 100,000 in middle-class white communities. The Centers for Disease Control and Prevention report that one in 25 African-American children die before the age of 18 from handgun violence.

In the District of Columbia, 11 acute-care hospitals spend more than $20 million a year treating injuries from violent crime. Follow-up care, including rehabilitation after crime victims leave the hospital, doubles the annual cost to $40 million.

This violence is closely related to discrimination and poverty. Poor people who live in the midst of an affluent society but cannot regularly obtain the basic necessities of life sometimes come to see violence, crime, and drugs as their only means of surviving.

Poverty in the United States is closely associated with family breakdown, out-ofwedlock births, declining interpersonal empathy, and a tendency to view others as means to one's own satisfaction. People are no longer viewed as fellow humans worthy of respect and dignity. According to Harvard professor Cornel West, a survey found that 42 percent of African-American youth reported having no best friend.[10] These circumstances lead to various forms of pathological behavior. The violence of poverty breeds more violence and despair, a sense that one must live for the moment, because things will not get better.

We describe wars of "low intensity conflict" in such places as El Salvador, South-Africa, and the disputed South Asian territory of Kashmir. What is happening in South Central Los Angeles, inner-city Detroit, and other urban caldrons of human suffering across the United States can be termed "low-intensity riots."

Every night, children of the inner cities of the world's only remaining superpower go to bed to the sound of gunfire. About two in five sometimes go hungry.

It takes only a spark to escalate the violence from low intensity to high intensity. When the explosion comes, it is in the form of a rebellion. The 1992 Los Angeles riots broke the long silence in both the media and the highest levels of national political leadership about the disintegration of life and society in many inner city "low-intensity" areas. Everyday stories tell us that the cause of this active volcano is young men and women living without education, jobs, health, homes, security, respect, or hope.

Increased funding for federal food programs such as the Special Supplemental Food Program for Women, Infants, and Children (WIC) and school feeding would end widespread hunger within a year or two. Other steps are needed to break the cycle of poverty and violence:

- Education that imparts basic skills and equips young people for employment;

- Assurance of decent jobs, supplemented when necessary by the Earned Income Tax Credit, to allow workers to meet their families' basic needs; and

- Support for families to remain intact and give emotional support to each other, especially to their children.

Needed even more than these programmatic approaches is a fundamental revolution in values, attitudes, and relationships. Individuals, communities, and nations must find ways to turn away from domination and violence to relationships based on dignity, respect, and love.

Overcoming Violence

Violence results from the desire of individuals and communities to dominate other people and other communities, and a refusal to share wealth, land, and political power. The struggle to dominate and control resources has polarized rich and poor, industrial and developing countries, black and white, men and women, landlords and landless, skilled and unskilled laborers, indigenous and migrant communities, believers and non-believers, church and state, industrialists and non-industrialists, and North and South. Unreconciled polarization leads to conflicts and violence.

Preventing violence and resolving conflicts, therefore, must be based on changing individuals' attitudes and assuring equal access to resources. Securing food for all, regardless of political, religious, ethnic, racial, and national identities, will help end violence. But ending violence requires spiritual as well as social and political approaches. The values held by individuals and communities are gradually woven into the formal and informal institutions by which we live and relate to each other. In most

I never intend to adjust to the madness of militarism.
– Rev. Dr. Martin Luther King, Jr.

*Nonviolence is
not the cover for
cowardice,
but it is the
supreme
virtue of
the brave.*
– Mahatma Gandhi

cultures, the values to which people aspire are derived from religious heritage or experience. Stable societies are based on wide acceptance of moral values and the development of morally grounded institutions.

Sometimes the values expressed in law, education, religion, family and work relations, the media, and the economy belie the values which we profess. We claim allegiance to the values of equality, but frequently deny dignity by personal behavior and fail to provide equality of opportunity in education or livelihood for whole groups of citizens, based on race, sex, age, or other qualities. We say we would like to meet everyone's basic needs, but fail to enact or implement requisite programs. We would be peacemakers, but rely on armed forces as the first instinct and the ultimate resort for foreign policy.

In many ways, we rely on overt and institutional violence to maintain dominance and privilege.

Genuine respect for all other people as equals and peaceful reconciliation of differences are the basic antidotes to violence. These moral truths can be learned from experience, but for many gain added power as tenets of faith. They are found in the ancient Chinese Taoist doctrine of *wu-wei,* or non-action. The ancient Indian principle of *ahisma,* or non-harming, is shared by Buddhists, traditional Hindus, and Jains. *Ahisma* was the basis for Gandhi's efforts to lead India to independence. Commitments to non-violent behavior are also found in Christian, Jewish, and Muslim traditions.

Participants in virtually every war have had the endorsement of religious leaders. Most commonly, each of the participants claim right or justice for their own position, to justify their resort to violence, warfare, or threats. Only rarely have national religious bodies spoken out against the position of their own governments – e.g., the

Serbian Orthodox Church regarding Serbian actions in Bosnia.

Within Christianity, the tradition of just wars stretches back to the fifth century. The criteria for a just war are quite rigorous. To be just, a war must have a just cause; be waged by a legitimate authority; be formally declared; be fought with peaceful intention; be a last resort; hold out a reasonable hope of success; and be waged with means proportionate to the ends sought.[11]

Some wars seem to have the weight of justice on one side. World War II is generally regarded as having been necessary, in spite of the great human suffering which resulted. Other wars are indefensible, particularly those which appear to preserve or increase dominance by one party over another.

As the international community is confronted with more calls for intervention in civil conflicts, including the possibility of armed intervention, just war arguments become more complex as they are intertwined with issues of sovereignty, legitimate authority, and self-determination.

In addition to an emphasis on preventive diplomacy, peacemaking and peacekeeping, a fresh look at nonviolence, both as technique and as philosophy, is needed.

Nonviolent action has been used at times as a political strategy. U.S. abolitionist William Lloyd Garrison preached the use of nonviolent methods in the fight against slavery. Many of the suffragettes who struggled for women's rights in Britain and North America adopted nonviolent resistance. Russian Count Leo Tolstoy advocated a pacifist rejection of war and the use of civil disobedience as an alternative to violent revolutions in *The Kingdom of God Is Within You.*

The horrors of World War I strengthened pacifist sentiments in the West. Students at

Oxford University as early as 1935 passed a resolution pledging not to fight "for king and country." In the United States during the 1950s and 1960s, the Rev. Dr. Martin Luther King, Jr., led the nonviolent civil rights movement against racial segregation and for civil rights. In the 1960s and 1970s, the war in Indochina led to widespread anti-militarism. These experiences have made nonviolence a growing moral force over the course of the century.

Conclusion

The world is not without hope. The end of the Cold War, progress toward peace between Israelis and Palestinians, and the end of *apartheid* in South Africa are indicative of new possibilities for peace.

In the United States, the Job Corps has proven that intensive training and education can reduce crime rates. A key to the success of the Job Corps and similar private programs is providing youth with a whole new environment. A year in the Job Corps costs $22,000 per youth, cheaper than $33,000 per juvenile for incarceration. Such programs could substantially reduce the cost of crime in the United States, which is now $425 billion a year.

Huge global investments in armaments during the 20th century have brought misery, disease, and hunger in unprecedented proportions, along with whatever benefits they have provided to world order. Although the end of the Cold War has led to a decline in global military expenditure, the world has a long way to go toward creating global peace and alleviating poverty and hunger.

An essential element in ending violence is to increase our own and others' awareness of the deeply-embedded, structural foundation of violence. A paradigm shift is required. We must be aware of the degree to which we have embodied dehumanizing attitudes in our behavior and our institutions.

To accomplish this paradigm shift, we must focus on our own values, attitudes, and behaviors. We have placed too much emphasis on reforming the other person, the other nation. Violence is in our minds. Let each person base his or her conduct on principles firmly rooted in ethical traditions. Faith is essential to reduce violence, poverty, disease, and hunger in this world. ∎

Let us take the risks of peace upon our lives, not impose the risks of war upon the world.
– Quaker proverb

Daniel U.B.P. Chelliah is coordinator of refugee affairs at BFW Institute.

Warfare has always resulted in hunger and suffering for ordinary citizens. Here, Eritreans tackle post-conflict reconstruction.

Poverty in a Global Economy

Cause 3

A landless widow in Bangladesh receives a loan for a milk cow from the Grameen Bank. The Bank is a pioneer in efforts to provide credit for poor people — mainly women — to start small businesses.

by Don Reeves

This chapter explores poverty as a cause of hunger. It shows why "sustainable development" is a more adequate goal than economic growth. It discusses the increasingly global economy, the role of markets, and the limits of transfers as a solution to hunger. It then outlines national and global economic policy changes to help lift people out of poverty. The most important area of policy is investment in human resources – the health and education of poor people themselves. Another major challenge is to create 2 billion new income-earning opportunities, principally in the private sectors of the poorer developing countries, by the year 2025. These tasks are awesome, but possible.

Hunger is a symptom of poverty. If we can root out poverty, we root out the systemic cause of hunger.

– Professor Mohammed Yunus, founder of Grameen Bank in Bangladesh

Poverty as a Cause of Hunger

Hungry people are almost always poor, and very poor people are chronically hungry. Economic problems and policies that contribute to poverty are among the basic causes of hunger.

Poverty, the lack of sufficient resources to provide or exchange for basic necessities – food, shelter, health care, clothing – is not an exact indicator of hunger. But its correlation with undernutrition is high.

Worldwide, more than 1.3 billion people live on the equivalent of less than one dollar per day. The majority of these (700 million) are desperately poor and chronically

hungry. The balance live so close to the edge that any emergency – illness, work layoff, drought – pushes them over, from just getting by, into hunger.

No place on the globe is immune to poverty. The people so poor that they are seriously affected by hunger are disproportionately located in Africa. The largest number are in Asia. A significant number are in Latin American and Caribbean countries. Seventy percent to 80 percent of the people are poor in sub-Saharan Africa, and nearly one-third in all developing countries together. But the United States, some European countries, and Australia also have large blocs of poor and hungry people.

With few exceptions, the incidence of poverty is higher in rural than urban areas. Nearly everywhere, women and girls suffer more from poverty than men and boys. Infants, young children, and elderly people are particularly vulnerable.

A variety of forces converge to create patterns of poverty: weak economies; inequitable access to land and other resources; unequal power in markets; and poor education and health care – nearly always exacerbated by discrimination against racial, ethnic, and religious minorities; violence and warfare; and often, environmental degradation.

Growth and Inequality

Economic growth has often been held up as the primary goal of economic policy, especially since the 1960s. At times, "development" has almost been equated with economic growth. Many economists and governments expected poverty and other social problems to be reduced as economies grew.

Many growing economies widen the gap between rich and poor people. That leads some to accept growing inequality, hoping

Figure 3.1
The Number of
Poor and
Hungry People
1980 and 1990

Sub-Saharan Africa

Latin America

Near East & N. Africa

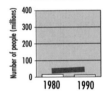

South Asia

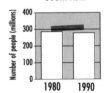

Southeast Asia

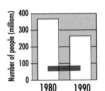

Source: ACC/SCN; Institute for Development Studies.

Measuring Inequality

The search for a vision of development that is more nuanced than economic growth has also led to increasing reliance on measures of development other than GDP and GNP, the two most often used measures for comparing income:

- **Gross Domestic Product** (GDP) – the value of all goods and services produced within an economy; and

- **Gross National Product** (GNP) – the GDP plus or minus transfers such as profit on foreign investments or remittances from people working abroad.

The World Bank counts 56 low-income economies with per capita GNP from $80 to $675 (1991). At the other end are 38 high-income economies with per capita GNP from $8,356 to $36,080. In between are 112 middle-income economies with per capita incomes between $676 and $8,355.

GNP provides a quick measure of the capacity of an economy overall to meet people's needs. It also represents the pool from which savings and public expenditures can be drawn. But GNP is seriously flawed as a measure of poverty or well-being because it gives no information about income distribution within the country.

GNP and GDP fall short even as measures of national well-being. First, they fail to distinguish among types of economic activity. Manufacturing cigarettes, making bombs, and running prisons are all scored as contributing to GNP/GDP the same as baking bread, nursing, building homes, or conducting scientific research. Second, many goods and services generate costs which are not reflected in their prices – polluted air or illness from overconsumption, for example. Third, many nurturing and creative activities – parenting, homemaking, gardening, and food preparation – are not included because they are not bought and sold.

GNP/GDP figures for various countries are usually compared after they are "translated" into another currency. After GNP has been calculated in Bangladeshi taka, for example, the result is translated into U.S. dollars at the current exchange rate – 8,833 taka equals US$220.

But 8,833 taka will buy more in Bangladesh than $220 will buy in the United States, primarily because wages are much lower. Thus the World Bank, the U.N. Development Program (UNDP), and the Food and Agriculture Organization of the U.N. have adopted a new measure – purchasing power parity (PPP) – which estimates the number of dollars required to purchase comparable goods in different countries. Bangladeshi PPP is estimated at

that growth will eventually lift greater numbers of people out of poverty.

However, studies of eight East and Southeast Asian countries show that it is possible to have both economic growth and decreasing inequality if the right policies are in place. In South Korea, for example, where per capita income has grown rapidly, the most affluent fifth of the population has about seven times as much income as the poorest fifth. The ratio has narrowed slightly over the past two decades; poor people have shared in the rapid growth. By contrast, Brazil's Gross National Product (GNP) was twice Korea's in 1970. Its economy has grown about half as fast; by 1990 Korea's GNP was twice Brazil's. But the ratio between Brazil's poorest and richest fifth is more than 30-fold. Poor Brazilians have scarcely benefitted from growth, and remain mired in deep poverty.

The Asian countries reduced, or at least did not increase, economic inequality by giving poor people the incentive and the means to improve their own earning

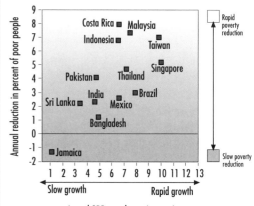

Figure 3.2
GDP Growth and Reduction of Poverty[1]

Source: Ismail Serageldin.

power: land reform and support for small farmers in Korea and Taiwan; high school education, especially for women, in Singapore; and manufacturing for export that raised the demand for unskilled factory workers in Malaysia, plus a massive affirmative action program for the poorer ethnic groups.

Declining inequality and economic growth support each other in three ways:

- As poor families' income increases, they invest more in "human capital" – more education and better health care for their own children;

- Improved health and better education, which usually accompany decreased inequality, increase the productivity of poorer workers and their communities and nations; and

- Greater equality contributes to political stability, which is essential for continued economic progress.[3]

Globally, we have accepted gross income inequality. The wealthiest one-fifth of the world's people control about 85 percent of global income. The remaining 80 percent of people share 15 percent of the world's income. The poorest one-fifth, more than a billion people, receive only about 1.4 percent. The ratio between the average incomes of the top fifth and the bottom fifth of humanity is 60 to one (see figure 3.3).

Sustainable Development

An alternative concept – "sustainable development" – has emerged as advocates of international justice, environmental protection, peace, sustainable population growth, democracy, and human rights have increasingly come to see that their goals are interlinked. Several examples:

$1,230, rather than $220.

PPP estimates make country-to-country comparisons more accurate and realistic, and somewhat narrow the apparent gap between wealthy and poor countries. Even so, vast disparities remain. PPPs of $19,000 to $21,000 per capita (United States, Switzerland, Canada, Luxembourg) are more than 50 times those of Ethiopia and Zaire, at less than $400.

GNP, GDP, and PPP are all measured as country averages. But poverty is best understood at the household and individual level.

The most used measure of inequality compares the income of the richest one-fifth, or quintile, of each population with that of the poorest quintile. In 1980, for example, the richest one-fifth of U.S. households received 39.9 percent of the total income, and the poorest one-fifth had 5.3 percent – a ratio of 7.5 to one. By 1992, the ratio had widened: the top one-fifth had 41.9 percent of all income ($48,436 per capita); the bottom one-fifth, 4.7 percent ($4,433 per capita), and the ratio was 8.9 to one.

Among industrial nations, the ratio between the rich and poor quintiles' income ranges from 4.3 in Japan up to 9.6 for Australia and the United Kingdom. Among the low-income countries with data available, the ratios range from 4.1 for Bangladesh and 5.1 for India up to 32.1 for Brazil.[2]

Differences in income distribution make a big difference to poor people. Thailand's per capita GDP is only slightly larger than Brazil's, but the poorest 20 percent of the population in Thailand has more than three times as much purchasing power. In Indonesia, with less than 60 percent of Brazil's per capita GDP, poor people have more than twice the purchasing power. Even in Bangladesh, with per capita GDP less than one-fourth that of Brazil, poor people are estimated to have as much purchasing power as in Brazil. ∎

Table 3.1: Poverty Impact of Income Distribution Selected Countries (1990)

Country	Real GDP PPP$ (1990)	Income Lowest 20%	Income Highest 20%	Ratio High 20%/ Low 20%
Thailand	$5,890	$1,796	$14,931	8.3
Brazil	5,250	551	17,719	32.1
Indonesia	2,970	1,292	6,282	4.9
Bangladesh	1,230	584	2,374	4.1

Source: World Bank.

Direct Measures of Well-Being

Sustainable development, focused on poor people, requires indicators which measure well-being even more directly than poverty rates: infant or under-five mortality, life expectancy, educational achievement, and caloric intake.

The UNDP Human Development Index (HDI) gives equal weight to three factors: life expectancy at birth; educational attainment (based on the adult literacy rate and mean years of schooling); and per capita purchasing power.

People's lives can be improved if even limited resources are focused on nutritional programs, public health, and basic education. But sustaining such improvements requires steady or improving economic performance. Both China and Sri Lanka have invested relatively heavily in education and health care since independence. They rank with industrial countries in life expectancy and educational attainment.

Three other clusters of countries rank higher on the HDI scale than other nations with comparable incomes:

- China, Cuba, Vietnam, several of the formerly communist Eastern European nations, and several of the newly independent states of the Former Soviet Union rank significantly higher on the HDI scale by virtue of educational attainment, longevity, or both;

- Several other nations rank high on the educational attainment scale by having built on educational systems established during the colonial era: Vietnam, Laos, Cambodia, and Madagascar (French); Guyana, Tanzania, Uganda, and Burma (Myanmar) (British); and the Philippines (Spanish and United States);

- Saving the rainforests of Brazil will require dealing with the land hunger of poor Brazilians;

- Reducing rapid population growth in developing countries will require improving living standards, especially for girls;

- Durable solutions to poverty and hunger in the United States will require social peace, broader democratic participation, and a shift to economic patterns that will be environmentally sustainable.

Sustainable development is defined differently by different people. Bread for the World Institute has come to define it in terms of four interconnected objectives: economic opportunity for poor people, meeting basic human needs, environmental protection, and democratic participation. An essential element is the reduction of hunger and poverty in environmentally sound ways.

Sustainable development is gaining public and political support as the prime goal for economic policy. Economic efficiency and growth often contribute substantially to sustainable development. Increases in productivity and income for African peasant farmers are certainly needed. Further improvements in the well-being of already well-off people can also be part of sustainable development, if they are not environmentally harmful.

Economic growth is one means, but not the only way, to more fundamental human ends. This is an obvious point, but the implications are far-reaching.

Four conclusions may be drawn from the discussion thus far:

- Wide disparities in income exist both between and within nations;

Figure 3.3
Distribution of Global Income, 1991

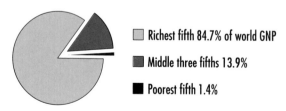

- Richest fifth 84.7% of world GNP
- Middle three fifths 13.9%
- Poorest fifth 1.4%

Source: UNDP.

- Poverty and hunger at the household level is a consequence both of national income and the way it is distributed;

- Poor nations, to reduce poverty-related hunger, need both economic growth and steps to reduce inequality; and

- Many countries have improved poor people's well-being by focused social programs, but some of these programs are threatened by poor economic performance.

A Global, Knowledge-Based, Market Economy

We live in a time of profound and rapid economic change. The well-being of billions of poor and hungry people now and in the future depends on the evolving nature of the world economy.

Three revolutions during the past two decades have transformed national markets into a truly global economy:

- The evolution of a single worldwide system of producing and exchanging money, goods, and services;

- The shift from a resource-based economy to a knowledge-based economy; and

- The acceptance of market-based economics as conventional wisdom by most political leaders throughout the world.

First, all nations are increasingly tied together into a single worldwide production and exchange system. Instantaneous electronic transfer of information and capital funds, controlled by transnational entities, permits "on-time-delivery" of components for assembly wherever labor costs are lowest or markets nearby.

The shift of manufacturing, assembly, and some service tasks to low-wage areas offers the possibility of more jobs and higher wages

- A handful of Latin American countries rate relatively high on the HDI scale, primarily because of educational attainment: Chile, Costa Rica, Colombia, and Uruguay. Cuba and Nicaragua might be added to this list by virtue of combined educational attainment and longevity.

Many of these nations have suffered recent economic downturns, or are in the midst of drastic political and economic change. In the short term, at least, they are hard pressed to maintain their education and health programs. Nonetheless, they provide evidence that direct attention to human services and relatively equitable distribution of income can improve the quality of life for most citizens.

Two groups of nations rank much lower on the HDI than on a per capita Gross Domestic Product (GDP) scale. The Middle Eastern oil-rich nations rank low in both longevity and educational attainment, particularly because of the status of women in their societies. Several African nations have extremely low educational attainment and longevity indicators, for varied reasons. Angola and Namibia have been engulfed in long independence struggles and civil war. Botswana and Gabon, although relatively rich in natural resource income, have not devoted proportional resources to education and health care services. ■

in countries or regions with abundant labor. But this same shift makes it more difficult to maintain jobs and wage levels in high-wage countries, such as the United States, where real wages have declined for most workers in recent years.

Second is the shift from a resource-based economy to a knowledge-based economy. In this new economic world, wealth and employment result less from the processing of raw materials, and more from the ability to process information, or "manipulate symbols." The new billionaires are named Gates (Microsoft) or Milken (corporate mergers); the new companies, Calgene (biogenetics) or Boston Chicken, as compared to Rockefeller (Standard Oil) or Krupp (armaments).

As assembly jobs move to low-wage areas or are robotized, semi-skilled workers must learn and re-learn new skills every few years, or face low-wage jobs in competition with poorly educated or poorly trained workers. The keys to economic stability are sound

Poor nations, to reduce poverty-related hunger, need both economic growth and steps to reduce inequality.

Nearly every proposal for sustainable development relies on a core commitment to encouraging the growth of small business.

basic education, ever-rising skill levels, and the ability to adapt.

The shift to knowledge-based economies leads to enormous gains in productivity – accomplishing more with fewer resources. These gains, if equitably shared, can greatly improve the well-being of humankind, bring relief from some menial chores, and relieve some environmental pressures. But if the gains are not shared, the new knowledge systems could be as socially destructive as monopolies and trusts were in an earlier industrial era.

The third shift in the global economy is the acceptance of market-based economics as conventional wisdom by political leaders almost everywhere. Market orientation – letting markets set most prices and guide most investments – is, or is becoming, the policy of most governments.

Countries shift to market economies because the nations that have well-developed market economies have the greatest wealth; because centrally planned economies have not been successful most places they have been tried; and because governments are persuaded by the rapid growth and dramatic reductions in poverty since the 1950s in the four "Asian Tigers" – Taiwan, South Korea, Hong Kong, and Singapore – and current similar gains in Indonesia, Malaysia, and Thailand. Some observers are ready to add China to this list because of its almost unprecedented growth since 1978, coinciding with the introduction and acceptance of market practices.

Hopes and Fears About Relying on Markets

Markets do many tasks well. Markets encourage innovations (such as smaller, faster computers) that usually benefit consumers. Markets ration goods such as clothing better than central planners, and may do as well as bureaucracies in some emergencies. Markets are sometimes fairer to poor people than governments, which are often manipulated by privileged groups. One of the major goals of ORAP in Zimbabwe (see p. 33) has been freedom from state control so that villages can sell grain to each other.

Nearly every proposal for sustainable development relies on a core commitment to encouraging the growth of small business. Most informal economic activity results from the efforts of small entrepreneurs who cannot find a place in the formal economy. If they have access to good roads, markets, and credit, small farmers and small business people can create their own new income-earning opportunities in market economies.

Large, sophisticated corporations also perform valuable market services: assembling shiploads of grain for emergency food aid, for example, or maintaining inventories of repair parts for 20-year old tractors.

But markets, by themselves, will never eliminate hunger. Poor people and their allies are often skeptical of grand claims for the "magic of the marketplace." The persistence of massive hunger in a country as wealthy as the United States demonstrates that markets must be complemented by public interventions to reduce hunger and poverty.

Markets are also subject to abuse. Wealthy landowners, private and corporate businesses, and transnational corporations sometimes fail to treat their workers, suppliers, or customers fairly. Landowners and corporations may achieve gains in collusion with one another or with their own and foreign governments. Sometimes they rely on military support for protection.

The principal defense against market failures and abuses of markets lies in widespread and well-informed participation in public policy decision-making. Corporations and wealthy individuals rely on laws and regulations for their businesses – protection of title and enforcement of contracts, for example. When society grants such protection, it should also insist that the beneficiaries behave responsibly. The importance of international, as well as national, rule-making is obvious in a global economy. As noted in the Cause 1 essay (p. 31), international associations of workers and nongovernmental organizations can play a crucial role in bringing the perspectives and interests of citizens to the process.

Businesses and other private actors in markets share an interest with anti-poverty advocates in healthy, well-educated workers, stable and crime-free communities, strong public infrastructure, and raising poor people out of poverty. The terms for sharing costs and responsibilities for these goals are decided in public policy debate.

Markets alone do not have the capacity to fairly allocate some goods and services – elementary education, health care, public safety, or passage on public streets. In actuality, everyone lives in a mixed economy. In recent years, 42 percent to 45 percent of U.S. gross domestic product has been apportioned directly by governments – federal, state, and local. This fraction ranges up to more than two-thirds in Scandinavia and below one-quarter in Japan, among industrial nations. The range is lower in developing countries: well below 20 percent in Mexico and Thailand; up to 30 percent in India and one third in Botswana.[4]

Thus, shaping a global economy that lifts people out of poverty and eradicates hunger requires a commitment to the responsible exercise of two functions:

- Collection and allocation of public resources, especially for investment in human resources; and

Needed: Two Billion Income-Earning Opportunities

As the world's population grows at least 40 percent, from 5.7 billion to 8.5 billion or more, by the year 2025, the global labor force will grow even faster, by at least 60 percent. This means an increase from 2.5 billion to more than 4 billion workers. Add today's several hundred million presently unemployed or under-employed workers, and the pressing need is to create 2 billion new economic opportunities during the next 30 years. Half these new workers have already been born, and the number of unemployed is growing annually.

Most of the new jobs will be needed in developing countries, where 95 percent of the increase in population and labor force is taking place.

Virtually all the added jobs will need to be non-farm. Governments in developing countries may increase incentives for food production, which would add some farm employment. But farmers are likely to adopt technologies which increase their productivity and reduce farm employment. While new lands have come under cultivation over the last generation, nearly all the world's cultivable land is now being farmed. Thus, farm job losses will exceed job gains over the next generation. More and more farmers, or their children, will seek non-farm employment. Whether such non-farm employment is urban or rural will depend on policy choices.

Improvements in education, health care, and public infrastructure can provide some public service jobs. But most new income-earning opportunities, if they come to pass, will be in the private sector.

Every new opportunity, whether public or private, requires savings and investment – in human resources and in creating each job or business opportunity. The rate of savings and the allocation of their investment are crucial factors in determining whether enough decent income-earning opportunities can be created. The rate of savings and the directions of investment are determined in large measure by public policies. ■

- Creating appropriate, effective guidelines for markets.

The reality, of course, is much more difficult than the assertion. Powerful political actors, as well as powerful market actors, often sway policies to their own self-interest,

On a global scale, the single most important strategy for alleviating poverty and hunger is creating opportunities to earn.

whether at the local, national, or international level. Those political forces that struggle with and on behalf of poor people are often unclear or divided on issues of national and international economic policy.

But as the global, knowledge-based, market economy extends its influence into the far corners of our planet, people of good will have only one option: to help draft and implement policies which will direct a sizeable portion of this economy toward creating income-earning opportunities for poor people.

Policy Changes to Create Income-Earning Opportunities

On a global scale, the single most important strategy for alleviating poverty and hunger is creating opportunity to earn enough – through jobs, farms, or businesses – to meet basic needs and permit human fulfillment.

Each of the following policies and policy shifts could be taken within or at the margins of the market-oriented political economies which prevail in all industrial and many other countries. Each has been part of a successful development package in one or more countries, and is an announced goal of most other countries. The key to the success of all of these policies is widespread participation in decision-making, especially by poor people and their allies.

These policies fall into the following categories:

- Investing in people;

- Agriculture and food production;

- Creating a framework for sustainable development; and

- Focusing international financing.

INVESTING IN PEOPLE

Health Care and Nutrition. Investments in basic health care and improved nutrition yield huge dividends. Healthier children learn better. Healthy adults work better.

Improved health care begins with greater attention to basic public health measures: nutrition education, clean water and adequate sanitation, vaccination against infectious diseases, prevention of AIDS, distribution of iodine and Vitamin A capsules, and simple techniques of home health care. Delivery of these services can be relatively inexpensive, especially in developing countries, employing village women with minimal training. These basic services should have priority over urban hospitals and specialized medical training.

In some instances, public health training can be delivered in conjunction with supplemental feeding programs such as the Special Supplemental Food Program for Women, Infants, and Children (WIC) in the United States, or the Integrated Child Development Services in India.

Education. Investments in basic education complement those in health care and improved nutrition, and yield huge payoffs in both developing and industrial nations. Better education for youth, especially girls, leads to improved health awareness and practice for their families on a life-long basis. Cognitive and other skills improve productivity, enable better management of resources, and permit access to new technologies. They also enhance participation in democracy.[5]

A study of 98 countries for the period from 1960 to 1985 showed GDP gains up to 20 percent from increases in elementary school enrollment, and up to 40 percent for increases in secondary enrollment. In allocating educational resources, the highest payoff is for elementary education, because

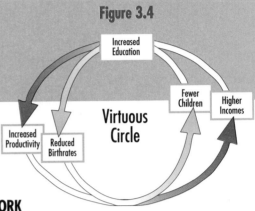

Figure 3.4

Virtuous Circle

Increased Education → Reduced Birthrates → Increased Productivity → Fewer Children → Higher Incomes

Source: Based on Birdsall and Sabot.

it reaches the most children.

In the United States, dramatic improvement has followed from investments in Head Start, which provides preschool education and meals for low-income children, and Job Corps, which provides remedial and vocational training for disadvantaged youth.

AGRICULTURE AND FOOD PRODUCTION

Access to Land. Widespread land ownership by small farmers usually contributes directly to food security and improved environmental practices. The more successful land reform programs, as in Korea and Taiwan, have provided at least minimum compensation to existing landlords.

Equitable Prices for Farm Produce. In many developing countries, state-run marketing boards have taxed agriculture by setting farm prices very low and retaining for the government a large share of the value from farm exports. Such disincentives to farmers may have been the greatest single barrier to successful development in many poor countries where agriculture is a large share of the national economy. As farmers' incomes rise, they expand their purchases of consumer goods, providing an important source of non-farm employment. In many poor nations, much of domestic savings must be accumulated within agriculture, since it is such a large share of the economy. Such savings are important for increasing agricultural productivity and to help finance rural non-farm businesses.

Eliminating Agricultural Export Subsidies. The United States and the European Union support their own farmers in ways that generate surplus crops. They also subsidize exports of these crops, driving down prices around the world. Developing country farmers, who usually are not subsidized, cannot match the low prices, even in their own country. Local agriculture falters, and with it, the whole process of development.

These agricultural export subsidies should be phased out as quickly as possible.

CREATING A FRAMEWORK FOR SUSTAINABLE DEVELOPMENT

Access to Credit. Equitable access to credit for small farmers and small businesses is probably the highest priority for allocation of domestic savings or outside investment. Training in resource and business management is often part of successful credit programs.

Adequate Physical Infrastructure. Creating and maintaining an adequate physical infrastructure is essential to a viable, expanding economy. Important elements include: for rural areas, farm-to-market roads and storage oriented to domestic production and, if appropriate, exports. For all areas, safe water, sanitation, electricity, and communications networks are needed.

Stable Legal and Institutional Framework. Sustainable development requires a stable legal framework. This includes assured property titles; enforceable contracts; equitable access to courts and administrative bodies; accessible information networks.

Stable Currency and Fiscal Policies. Neither domestic nor international investors, including small farmers and microentrepreneurs, are likely to invest in countries in which the political or economic environment is unsettled. High inflation or continuing trade deficits, which often go together, discourage needed investments and may even drive out domestic savings.

Twenty-nine African countries undertook structural adjustment programs during the 1980s. Often, these reforms fall heavily on poor people, as social service programs are frozen or cut back to help balance national government budgets. Other possible measures to reduce budget or trade deficits –

Widespread land ownership by small farmers usually contributes directly to food security and improved environmental practices.

For the first time in United States history, young adults face lower economic expectations than their parents.

more progressive taxes, cuts in military spending, or curtailing luxury imports – have not always been pursued with equal vigor. Economic reform programs, some of which will continue to be necessary, should be revamped to reduce the costs and increase benefits for poor people.

Effective, Progressive Tax Systems. Effective progressive tax structures are key to sustainable financing for investments in human resources and infrastructure. Taxes based on ability to pay are also key to stabilizing or reducing wide disparities in income distribution in both rich and poor countries. Such tax systems are difficult to enact where wealth and political power are controlled by a small minority.

Incentives for Jobs-Creating Investments. The Asian countries which have grown so rapidly have all placed emphasis on labor-intensive exports, some in joint ventures with overseas partners, some with investments solicited from abroad, but many with strong subsidies from within their own economies. This is a distinct departure from their more general commitment to following market signals.

A primary target for jobs-intensive investments will be processing operations for primary products – whether for domestic consumption or for crops or minerals now being exported.

FOCUSING INTERNATIONAL FINANCING

Direct Foreign Investment. Some developing countries are attempting to create an economy stable enough to attract direct foreign investment. They usually negotiate for investments which will create decent jobs for newly educated workers.

Loans from International Financial Institutions. For the poorest countries, a major source of outside finance will continue to be the international financial institutions – the World Bank, regional development banks, and the International Monetary Fund. The conditions which accompany their loans are a major influence on the national policies of borrowing countries. In addition, these institutions often influence private banks and foreign and domestic investors. These multilateral lenders, as well as government-to-government aid, could be a model by focusing most of their resources on human development and generating income-earning opportunities for the poorest people in poorer nations (see "Power, Hunger, and the World Bank," pp. 25-26).

Forgiveness of Unmanageable Debt. Many of the poor countries have large debts left over from the 1970s. Large payments of interest and repayment of principal severely curtail poor nations' capacity to save and invest, or even to meet current basic needs. Unpayable debts should be forgiven or dramatically rescheduled. Creditors are more likely to get part of their money back if countries that are making serious efforts to achieve economic recovery are given some debt relief.

The American Dream: Diminishing Expectations

For the first time in United States history, young adults face lower economic expectations than their parents. Real wages average the same as during the early 1970s. Total compensation per worker has climbed slowly with the increasing value of work-related benefits – retirement plans and especially health care. But higher-paid workers have garnered a larger share of this increase. Real income for the bottom 60 percent of U.S. residents has declined.

The prospects for younger and future workers are further clouded by the projected costs of future benefits for elderly people and ballooning public debt. As the average age increases, relatively fewer workers will pay for benefits for a much larger number of retirees. Promised Medicare and Social

Security benefits, plus interest on the public debt, by themselves, would require people born after 1990 to pay three-quarters of every dollar earned in federal and state taxes. This is clearly impossible, economically or politically![7]

The high expectations of U.S. citizens are based on a century of growth in worker productivity. Output per worker grew at an average rate of nearly 2 percent per year from the 1860s until the early 1970s – unprecedented in all human history. Workers shared these productivity gains, especially during the period of strong labor unions and supportive federal legislation, from 1936 until 1971.

From this perspective, the post-World War II period was an almost golden age – nearly a quarter century of increasing real wages, based on increasing productivity. Not only did the economy provide opportunity for all who wanted to work, but the country's wealth permitted the Great Society programs of the 1960s. The U.S. poverty rate dipped to an all-time low of 11 percent in 1973.

By the early 1970s, several long-developing changes matured. Since then, several new factors have developed. Among them:

- A cartel among oil-producing countries raised oil prices and maintained them at high levels throughout the 1970s;

- Europe and Japan, nurtured in part with U.S. assistance, increased their productivity and became economic competitors, even in highly sophisticated products such as electronics and automobiles;

- Four Asian economies (South Korea, Taiwan, Singapore, and Hong Kong), with a combined population of about 75 million people, and other Asian countries with much larger populations also became more competitive with the industrial countries, notably in less sophisticated manufacturing;

- Worldwide systems of production emerged, shifting some labor-intensive manufacturing and assembly jobs to low-wage regions; and

- An explosion in the ability to manipulate knowledge placed a premium on new skills and ability to adapt.

In this new setting the United States has failed to keep pace in several key respects:

- Workers performing routine manufacturing and assembly tasks, some highly skilled, lost their jobs to automation or to lower-wage workers, mostly overseas; many have been forced to take lower-wage jobs;

- Gains in output per worker have declined sharply, averaging only 0.7 percent since 1970, in contrast with productivity gains of 3.3 percent in Japan and similar increases elsewhere during the same period;

- People in the United States have failed to scale back consumption to match income – household, business, and government debt all increased rapidly during the 1980s. Response to the recession of the early 1990s has reduced the growth of private debt, but government debt continues to grow;

- The educational system has not kept pace with changes – achievement scores have declined and drop-outs and functional illiteracy have risen;

- During the 1980s, high debt and high

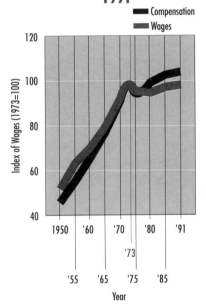

**Figure 3.5
Yearly Compensation for U.S. Workers: 1950 to 1991[6]**

Note: "Wages" means take home pay. "Compensation" includes all fringe benefits, such as health insurance.

Source: Peterson.

Transfers of Food or Money

Transfers of food and money are important to reducing hunger domestically and globally, but jobs and other income-earning opportunities are much more important.

The United States and other industrial countries could easily assure adequate food and other necessities for all their own citizens. For some groups of people – elderly and disabled people, many single mothers with young children – continuing food grants and/or equivalent cash are the only way to assure daily food. Such programs must be funded at adequate levels. An expansion of the federal food programs of less than $10 billion (one percent of the federal budget) would quickly eliminate widespread hunger in the United States.

Industrial nations could finance adequate transfers of food or money to meet global chronic hunger into the foreseeable future. The cost would be only a fraction of present arms expenditures. But there is no evidence of the political will to fund programs of this scale, even for a short period.

In low income countries, the political will to support transfers to needy people is often similarly weak. Moreover, many developing countries simply could not afford to maintain transfer programs of sufficient scale.

More fundamentally, in both industrial and developing countries, poor people themselves want and need the opportunity to meet their own needs. Jobs and opportunities to develop businesses are the primary means to overcome poverty and hunger.

Wealthy nations can and should give more. The U.N. established a goal of each industrial nation giving 0.7 percent of its GNP for development assistance. Only Norway, Sweden, Denmark, and the Netherlands have exceeded this goal. Some nations contribute much less, most notably the United States, which gives less than 0.2 percent of GNP. In addition, much of such assistance is not well-targeted.

Development assistance should be expanded, but even more important, it should be redirected toward sustainable development. Wealthy nations should help develop human resources through education and health care initiatives. They should support efforts to expand economic opportunity in ways which are environmentally sustainable, and which poor people have helped plan and implement. Transfers to meet emergencies or the needs of especially vulnerable groups – the needs of elderly and disabled people or refugees and victims of warfare and natural catastrophe – should be carried out in ways that contribute to, or do not undercut, sustainable development efforts. ■

whether in the United States or abroad. Policy changes reduced the relative share of taxes paid by wealthy individuals and businesses, and the cost of public spending for the middle class was not curtailed; and

• The United States rapidly expanded military spending in the 1980s while efforts to reduce deficit spending blocked needed investments in human resources.

The cumulative impact of these changes emerges most dramatically in the data on income and poverty; income disparity has increased. In 1992, the last year for which information is available, 15 percent of U.S. residents – 38 million people – lived below the poverty line. This is the highest proportion since 1966, and the highest number since 1962, before the Great Society programs and the peak of U.S. productivity gains.[8]

The economic changes have not all been negative. Some innovators, owners, and workers skilled in the new information-based technologies have gained from the shifts to a more knowledge-based economy. Some industries, such as steel, have been restructured to improve productivity.

Policy Dilemmas

The United States is still the wealthiest country on earth. But the burgeoning costs of debt, health care, and Social Security must be brought under control. Environmental constraints will force changes in the use of irreplaceable resources and the amount of wastes generated. The nation faces wrenching policy choices.

Politically popular visions of the future center on regaining the economic growth momentum of the 1950s and 1960s. Programs of education and training would be coupled with incentives for saving and investment in knowledge-based, globally competitive businesses. These new ventures would generate enough income-earning opportunities for all people in the United States willing and able to work. Increasing productivity and an expanding economy would also finance environmental protection and progress against social problems.

Alternative visions give higher priority to environmental sustainability. Public policies at local, national, and international levels would support individuals and communities as they reclaim influence and resources from giant corporations and central governments. Most such visions presume reduced economic activity overall and increased sharing of wealth.

Regardless of which of these two visions of the future we pursue, it makes sense to:

- Invest more in people, assuring adequate nutrition, education, health care, and opportunity for retraining as job needs change; and

- Encourage employment, including public sector jobs, to provide quality child care and expand low-income housing.

Sources of Hope and Optimism

In the face of persistent or increasing poverty and hunger in both the developing and industrial worlds, and the stubborn persistence of entrenched power and privilege, it would be easy to abandon hope or resign to cynicism.

But it is possible, although immensely difficult, to create economic opportunity for 2 billion workers in ways that also enrich family and community life and protect and enhance the environment. If we pause to look back at where we have been and at the directions we seem to be headed, we can see reasons for hope:

- After nearly a half century of attempts to improve economies and communities – including mistakes and disasters – governments and citizens, in poor and rich nations, understand better now what works to relieve poverty and hunger, and what does not;

- Due to the growth of the environmental movement across the globe – as exemplified at the 1992 U.N. Conference on the Environment and Development in Rio de Janeiro – commitment to sustainable development is growing rapidly; and

- Underlying, and most important of all, is the faith and persistence of poor people themselves. ∎

Don Reeves is economic policy analyst at BFW Institute.

In 1992, the last year for which information is available, 15 percent of U.S. residents – 38 million people – lived below the poverty line.

Population, Consumption, And Environment

Cause 4

Photo: U.N.

Industrial pollution in the wealthy countries may be causing the permanent warming of the earth – the "greenhouse effect."

by Nancy Wright, A. Cecilia Snyder, and Don Reeves

Rapid population growth contributes to poverty and environmental strain in many poor countries. Overconsumption by affluent people diverts resources that could meet basic human needs and adds to the strain on the global environment. Even optimistic scenarios require a doubling of food production within the next generation. We need improvements in social welfare (especially education for girls) and voluntary programs of family planning to reduce population growth; policies to reduce the consumption of nonrenewable resources by affluent people; and programs of sustainable agricultural development.

The world produces enough food for everyone to have 2,500 calories a day – 150 more than the basic minimum – if it were distributed equally. Over three-quarters of a billion people are chronically undernourished not because food is unavailable, but because they cannot grow or afford to buy it.

Rapid population growth among some low-income populations puts pressure on the capacity of countries to absorb the increase into their economies and on fragile ecosystems. But overconsumption of nonrenewable resources among relatively well-off people puts even more strain on the global environment than rapid population growth among poor people. The industrial countries include only 20 percent of the world's population, but consume 80 percent of its resources.

Food systems and the soil, water, and air on which they depend already show signs of stress or deterioration. Many observers doubt whether food production can match population growth on a sustainable basis, especially if poor people raise their standard of living.

Yet slowed population growth is consistently tied to improved well-being, implying at least some increases in consumption among poor people.

Sustainable development is gaining credence as an approach to resolve these dilemmas (see Cause 3, pp. 50-52). These strategies hold the potential for overcoming hunger and poverty, improving human welfare generally, and preserving the integrity of the earth.

Population

Although many countries appear to be in the early stages of declining fertility rates, the number of people in the world continues to grow at an alarming rate. Earth's population, now 5.7 billion and increasing 90 million each year, is likely to reach 8.5 billion by 2025, and exceed 10 billion by the middle of the 21st century. Virtually all the additional people will be in poorer countries. For example, sub-Saharan Africa, already troubled by periodic famine, chronic malnutrition, and civil conflict, is expected to double its population by 2020.[1]

Explosive population growth can contribute to hunger and poverty. In many areas of the world, high birth rates lower living standards for many people. There are often too few jobs and too little land for growing numbers of young workers.

For many poor people, large families are a means of survival, providing some insurance for care and protection in old age. So high infant mortality rates lead to even greater numbers of births. It is not unusual for several children in an impoverished family to die before their first birthday. In the developing world, 13 million children under the age of five die each year due to malnutrition and related preventable diseases.[2]

High fertility rates are also an indicator of women's low status. Lack of female

The world produces enough food for everyone to have 2,500 calories a day – 150 more than the basic minimum.

Five Steps to Slow Population Growth

1. Greatly expanded efforts to enable poor people to work their way out of hunger and poverty, especially by fostering grass-roots and self-sustaining development.

2. Health programs aimed at reducing infant mortality and increasing health security.

3. Policies which would improve women's low social, educational, economic, and political status.

4. Voluntary family planning methods which respect individual consciences and religious beliefs.

5. Efforts to modify the consumption of affluent people, including reforms in international trade and financial arrangements that would reduce the use of nonrenewable resources by well-off people in industrialized countries and increase incomes for poor people around the world.

– Bread for the World Institute Board of Directors, March 1, 1994

education, health care, and employment, as well as patriarchal cultural and religious traditions, all contribute to high birthrates.

Some people justify not helping hungry people by arguing that feeding people will only allow them to have more babies. But in fact, reducing hunger and poverty is crucial to reduced birth rates. Economic and social improvement is highly correlated with reduced fertility.

Education, especially of girls, is also strongly correlated with lower birthrates:

- In Bangladesh, a midday meal program designed to increase the enrollment of girls in school resulted in a 25 percent decline in birthrates over six years, in addition to significant nutritional benefits.[3]

- A study of 38 countries found that women with seven or more years of education have 1.6 to 2.9 fewer births during their childbearing years than women with no schooling.[4]

- An extra year of schooling reduces fertility rates by up to 10 percent.[5]

Effective family planning does not occur in isolation. Lower birthrates are usually the result of several factors. Education, better health care, and increased income-earning opportunities are all essential. These all contribute to a sense of improved family security and well-being, and tend to translate into an interest in spacing and limiting births.

Contraception is the easiest and most effective way to reduce birthrates, but some religious communities oppose contraception, especially if it is imposed on people. Breastfeeding and strengthening the role of fathers in parenting are other means of family planning.

The practice of breastfeeding helps to space children by delaying the return of ovulation. Studies have shown that:

- An exclusively breastfeeding mother who has not yet resumed menstruation is 98 percent protected against pregnancy for the first six months following childbirth.[6]

- Breastfeeding reduces total potential fertility in Africa by 43 percent, in Asia by 30 percent, and by 16 percent in the Americas.[7]

Breastfeeding also has multiple health benefits for both the mother and child, and is environment-friendly.

Emphasizing the male parent's accountability will encourage men to become more effective fathers and husbands, and also reinforce their role in family planning. A father's presence or absence has a tremendous impact on the well-being of the family, especially the children. In Barbados, for example, the 22 percent of children who had a father living at home performed significantly better at school. In Chile, children living with both parents tended to have higher nutrition levels and better diets.

Education and counseling of men can result in significant changes in attitude and behavior. PRO-PATER, a health organization in Brazil, has expanded men's notions of their responsibilities in caring and planning for families. PRO-PATER's television advertisements and counseling, which disseminate information and assistance, have increased male involvement in family matters.

In 1989, the National Family Planning Council of Zimbabwe ran a series of 80 radio shows, which reached about 40 percent of the country's male population. Sixty percent of the men who heard these programs reported a change in attitudes toward their families, and 40 percent agreed that family planning decisions should be made jointly by husband and wife.[8]

Consumption

Wealthy people, mostly in industrial nations, make up about one-fifth the world's population. Yet they control 85 percent of its income and consume 70 percent of its energy, 75 percent of its metals, and 85 percent of its wood. They produce two-thirds of all greenhouse gases and 90 percent of ozone-depleting chlorofluorocarbons (CFCs):[9]

- People in the United States, for example, spend more than $7 billion per year on lawn care, even though the chemicals used contribute directly to water pollution, solid-waste disposal problems, and air pollution.[10]

- High and growing worldwide use of fossil fuels may lead to a greenhouse effect – creation of a layer of carbon dioxide and other gases which trap heat in the atmosphere and permanently warm the earth. Each person in the United States uses an average of 24 barrels of oil per year, compared to 12 in Europe, and just one in Africa.[11]

- CFCs, used as refrigerants and in pressurized cans, have seriously reduced the high atmospheric ozone layer, permitting harmful radiation to reach the earth's surface.

- Pollution from autos and coal, plus other industrial emissions, have produced acid rains which have already damaged a quarter of Europe's forests and killed fish in parts of Europe and the northeast United States. Industrial and military wastes contain toxins, including radioactivity, which are for all practical purposes permanent.

If everyone now in the world lived as the richest 20 percent do, humanity would use 10 times as much fossil fuel and 200 times as many minerals – clearly impossible, even without population growth.[12]

Poorer parts of the world have been, and are still being, stripped of irreplaceable resources to support unsustainable lifestyles of a wealthy minority.

Environmental degradation does not increase in lock-step with income. For example, air pollution increases with initial increases in income, as people use more energy and transportation. The most severe air pollution from soot and suspended chemicals is in the large cities of poor countries – Mexico City, Beijing, Calcutta, and Tehran. Dust and soot in city air cause

Figure 4.1
Population and Pollution

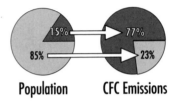

Population   CFC Emissions

■ Industrial Countries
□ Developing World

CFCs damage the earth's ozone layer and contribute to global warming.

Source: World Resources Institute.

Mrs. Kizza's Cow

In the Rakai district of Uganda, the Young Women's Christian Association gave Mr. and Mrs. Kizza a dairy cow, as part of the "Passing on the Gift" program supported by CODEL and Heifer Project International. In this program the first heifer offspring is given to another farmer. With the milk sold, a complete farming system becomes possible.

Using the waste from both the cow and the family, Mr. and Mrs. Kizza constructed a biogas system to provide power both for cooking and lighting. Meanwhile, Mr. and Mrs. Kizza and their three children developed several compost piles and an organic garden, which grows radishes the size of footballs. Mushrooms, lettuce, and root crops also thrive. Banana plants benefit from contour planting. Layers and roasters inhabit a new brick, two-storied chicken coop. In addition, Mrs. Kizza makes passion fruit, banana, pineapple, and mango wines worthy of being sold in cafes in downtown Masaka.

Under a shade veranda on what is now called St. Judy's farm, after the beneficial cow, Mrs. Kizza trains local women in her farming approach. She has spoken at international development meetings and received an award for her expertise in development. "Why would anyone want to live in the city," she asks, "when life on the farm is so good?" ■

simpler, less resource-consumptive lifestyles. Wealthy nations can also encourage and assist poor nations which choose to adopt less damaging paths of development.

Can the World Produce Enough Food?

Dramatic increases in food supplies – sufficient to provide for a world population nearly quadrupled within this century – have come in part through expanded use of nature's four major biological systems. *Oceans* have been fished and *rangeland* grazed more intensively; *forests* are rapidly disappearing; and *cropland* has expanded – mostly at the expense of forests and rangeland. Such expansions and over-harvesting are near an end; in some instances they must be scaled back.

The remainder of food gains in this century have occurred through more intensive use of resources and increased productivity. Irrigated acreage grew at more than 2 percent each year through the 1960s and 1970s. Fertilizer use grew nine-fold between 1950 and 1984, an increase of seven percent per year. Dramatic improvements in wheat and rice yields resulted from new crop varieties, which responded to both irrigation and higher fertility, introduced and adopted during the 1960s and 1970s – the Green Revolution.[14]

Sharp differences in opinion mark the debate over the severity of ecological damage to date, and whether food production can continue to increase on a sustainable basis. Without question, increased use of fertilizers, pesticides, and irrigation have resulted in environmental damage – some of it through carelessness, but probably some unavoidable. Expansion of crop production onto marginal lands has also resulted in damage – also partly due to carelessness and partly unavoidable.

But even the most optimistic scenarios

between 300,000 and 700,000 premature deaths each year.[13]

But wherever incomes continue to rise, clean air becomes both more important and more affordable. Cities in wealthier countries do a better job of cleaning their air, by requiring cleaner fuels and installing smokestack scrubbers, for example.

Consumption by poor people also contributes to environmental degradation. Indoor air pollution from burning wood, charcoal, and dung endangers the health of 400 million to 700 million people.

But affluent people can make the greatest difference by changing their lifestyles. They can actually enhance the quality of their family and community lives by choosing

regarding population growth will require a near doubling of food production before the middle of the next century. Sub-Saharan Africa will need nearly to triple its food supply. The continent, however, cannot indefinitely expand its cultivated area. This has been its principal strategy to date. By one estimate, if population in the region continues to grow at 3 percent per year, without significant gains from more intensive agriculture, the area being cultivated would have to double from its current 375 million acres to 720 million acres by 2030. Expansion by even a fraction of this amount would come at great cost to the region's forests, wildlife, and bio-diversity.[15]

Pessimists doubt that the increases of the last 30 to 40 years can continue. Potential new areas for sustainable farming are limited. Some lands now being cultivated should be returned to permanent covers of grass or forest. New irrigation projects will be more expensive, and must compete with increasing industrial, commercial, and household demands for water. Disputes, even wars, over water seem likely. Side effects from irrigation, most notably the accumulation of salts in soils – salinization – affect a number of projects. In many regions, irrigation that depends on groundwater has been over-developed, and cannot be sustained.

The practical limits to the benefits from fertilizer of current crop varieties may have been reached in many areas. Concern for damaging side-effects from fertilizers is growing. The new crop varieties of the Green Revolution have been widely planted over most of the area for which they are suited. Possible dramatic new gains from biogenetic research are years away, at best, and may carry unanticipated side effects.

Optimists, on the other hand, point out that global food production overall, and per capita, has grown steadily since 1950,

Other Environmental Gains

Optimists regarding sustainable food production also cite other recent environmental gains, including:

- Technical advances – such as solar cells and wind generation of electricity – which have become cost-competitive for some applications;

- Cleaner air – most cities in industrial nations have less air pollution than twenty years ago; and

- Reduced energy use by millions of citizens in their homes, at work, and for transportation.

In addition to these, the United Nations Conference on Environment and Development firmly fixed environmental issues on the international agenda. More concretely, it resulted in international conventions on climate change and biological diversity, as well as adoption of a Declaration of Principles and *Agenda 21*, a plan for environmental action endorsed by over one hundred governments.

Whether these agendas are implemented will depend in large part on the ability of the citizens of the world to convince governments and international organizations to provide the necessary resources. ■

while inflation-adjusted food prices have declined in all but a few areas. Some expect that the threat of food shortfalls, especially if accompanied by modest increases in food prices, would result in substantial increases in food production. They also look for continuing productivity gains from agricultural research.[16]

Optimists also point to environmental gains directly related to food production over the past decade. Conservation measures adopted in the 1985 and 1990 U.S. farm bills, when fully implemented, will have reduced soil erosion on U.S. farms by nearly two-thirds. Fertilizer and pesticide use has leveled off. Most farmers are using them more carefully. A small, but growing,

Lack of land forces small farmers to cultivate marginal soil, which quickly erodes and becomes less fertile, destroying another important part of the ecosystem.

number of farmers have switched to organic, or chemical-free, farming. Alternative agriculture and integrated pest management are gaining favor, and are the basis of major research programs at U.S., European, and Japanese universities. Sustainability is the principal goal of these approaches, and they often combine traditional, organic, and labor-intensive practices.[17]

Unjust Land Distribution

Many environmental threats have their roots in unjust social arrangements. Inequitable land distribution, most notably in Latin America, contributes to both hunger and environmental deterioration.

Colonial land appropriations, plus 19th and early 20th century land acquisitions by foreign corporations, led to ranching, mining, and export crops such as sugar, beef, coffee, and pineapple. In Venezuela, 1 percent of landowners own 67 percent of arable land. In the Dominican Republic, 92 percent of agricultural families are landless or near-landless.

Such patterns create profound human suffering for millions of the world's people, and the numbers are growing:

> *Estimated in 1981 at 167 million households . . . the landless and near-landless are expected to increase to nearly 220 million households by the turn of the century.*[18]

Without land, people have difficulty meeting their basic needs and are vulnerable to malnutrition and ill health. Lack of land forces small farmers to cultivate marginal soil, which quickly erodes and becomes less fertile, destroying another important part of the ecosystem. Anthropologist Sheldon Annis describes the differences between poor farmers who own land and those who do not:

> *In the Guatemalan village where I lived in the late 1970s, I used to marvel at the elegance with which poor farmers could optimize every available scrap of resources – every ridge of land, every surplus hour of time, every channel of water, every angle of sunlight. Though the Indians where I lived are surely poor, they do own their own plots of land. They depend upon and care for what is theirs. When I go back to the village, I always find that my friends' fields look just as I remembered them.*
>
> *Ten years ago, I also worked in Guatemala's northern Quiche province, which, for many reasons, is much poorer than the town where I lived. There, I recall watching in horrified fascination as an Indian farmer and his son planted their plot of corn on a forested slope. The land was so steep that the son had to be held in place with a rope looped around his waist. As he hopped from furrow to furrow, his father let out the slack from around a tree stump.*
>
> *When I returned to that spot recently, I was not surprised to find that the farmer and his son were no longer there. And neither was the hillside. What remained was a reddish, eroded nub – which looked just like the next and the next and the next former hillside.*[19]

In short, owning land motivates farmers to care for it.

Land Degradation

Poverty has forced farmers in many places to engage in unsustainable practices. In the Sahel region of West and Central Africa, people traditionally left land fallow for long periods. With forests nearby to provide wood for fuel, they applied manure to fertilize soil. After World War II, the human and livestock population expanded. Increasingly, farmers brought land into production before its productivity had been restored. They cleared the forests for farming and resorted to burning manure for fuel. This deprived the soil of nutrients, leaving crops more vulnerable to recurring droughts. A crisis situation, repeated many times around the world, was created.

Agenda 21, from the 1992 U.N. Conference on the Environment and Development, states, "Land degradation is the most important environmental problem affecting extensive areas of land in both developed and developing countries." Land degradation is caused by erosion, desertification, salinization, deforestation, and over-use, as well as changes in weather patterns. The United Nations estimates that one-third of the agricultural soil available in 1975 may be lost by the end of the century.

Land degradation in dryland areas deprives the world of $42 billion worth of crop and livestock production each year, with 75 percent of the losses in Africa and Asia. The creation of an inch of topsoil by natural means can take anywhere from 100 to 2,500 years, depending on the soil type.

Toward Sustainable Food Production

At least five clusters of activity or policy decisions can contribute to the immense task of doubling food production to match population growth on a sustainable basis. No one approach by itself will suffice. Three of these clusters are agricultural practices which, appropriately combined, can contribute to enhancing the food supply and the environment; the other two address the problem of creating the physical and political infrastructure necessary to

Destruction of Biodiversity

Many of the world's poor people live in tropical areas. There, rain forests and coral reefs, ecosystems that are home to the greatest number and variety of species on earth, are at risk. For survival, poor people often have no choice but to over-fish, to cut into forests for fuel, and to clear land and plant in areas that cannot sustain agriculture. The area of the world covered by tropical forests will have declined by 50 percent from 1950 to 2000.

Too often, hungry people do not have the time or resources to preserve the soil and forests by rotating crops and implementing fallow periods. Thus, poverty and population pressure reduce biological diversity. Yet biological diversity, the world's living gene bank, is the foundation for new, varied food crops resistant to old pests.

The Philippines serves as a case in point. This country was once a tropical paradise covered with virgin forests and abundant fruit, grains, and wildlife. On the southern island of Mindanao, the destruction of the forests to provide agricultural land began in the early 1950s with an influx of settlers from the northern islands. Then farmers could harvest 20 to 30 sacks of corn per acre. Now the yield is only three to five sacks. The once dark, rich soils have eroded, leaving barren hillsides, silted rivers, and oft-flooded lowlands. ■

achieve gains on a scale broad enough to affect large numbers of the world's hungry people. The most appropriate combination for each region and circumstance must be worked out by widespread participation of people at the national, regional, local, and household level.

These are the recommended agricultural practices:

- Traditional agricultural practices, the basis of stable food production for many generations. These include growing crops in rotation, with appropriate fallow periods, and interplanting several complementary crops, including trees, to provide continuous cover for fragile soils.

Water and Sanitation

At least a billion people live without safe water, and nearly twice that many lack adequate sanitation. Together, these linked causes contribute to 900 million cases of diarrheal disease and related deaths of 3 million children each year. They also contribute to widespread illness from infectious and parasitic diseases – cholera, typhoid, and paratyphoid; roundworm and hookworm.[20]

A range of technologies is available for each of the three phases of preventing water-borne diseases: a dependable supply of safe water, removal of wastes, and treatment or handling of wastes to prevent recontamination. Each phase requires an initial investment which poor families, communities, and nations often feel they cannot afford. But failure to make such investments raises economic, and especially health and social costs.

Residents in urban communities without dependable piped water pay several times as much to water vendors as a community system would cost. A 20-year demonstration in northeast Thailand and parallel research in other developing countries shows that even very poor families are willing to pay at least part of the cost of having a dependable supply of safe water (especially if they can pay for their share of the cost over several years).

In the slums of Karachi, Pakistan, the Orangi Pilot Project has provided a system of in-house sanitary latrines and simple underground sewers. Six hundred thousand people have installed a sewage removal system at a cost of less than $50 per household (not counting the trunk sewer lines). The communities were engaged in planning and contributed labor during construction, and are organized to operate and maintain the systems.[21] ■

- Organic and chemical-free agricultural practices that build on and enhance natural processes by maximizing use of crop and other plant residues, and managing insect and disease problems through natural processes; and

- High-tech agriculture, including bio-genetic advances and chemical fertilizers and pesticides. Carefully used, these can boost yields dramatically and improve insect and disease resistance through plant breeding and genetic advances. The environmental risks can be minimized through combinations with traditional and organic practices, as in integrated pest management.

Supporting these agricultural practices on a significant scale also requires:

- Institutional policies and reforms that support sustainable small-farm agriculture by ensuring secure tenancy (ownership wherever appropriate) and enhancing both basic education and extension-like education about appropriate technologies for small farmers, particularly women farmers. Markets and prices should not discriminate against local food crops as compared to export crops; and

- Both national and international policies that generate income earning opportunities for rural poor people as a major element of sustainable development. These should involve poor people in planning and execution. Policies should also provide for forgiving burdensome debts that lead to environmentally damaging production (see Cause 3, p. 57).

Conclusion

Sustainable development requires change in both public policies and personal attitudes and behavior.

It requires policy makers on all levels to shape integrated policies and programs that reflect the connections among improved lives for poor people and reduced population growth, reduced consumption of non-renewable resources, especially by affluent people, and the need to protect and enhance the environment.

To make progress toward sustainable development requires conscious, committed action on several levels:

- Citizens in all countries must press their own governments and international organizations to institute policies and programs that lead to sustainable development: economic opportunity for poor people; widespread education, especially for girls; adoption of minimum standards for air and water pollution; support for safe water and sanitation systems; and taxes or other disincentives for overconsumption.

- Industrial country governments can take the lead in: discouraging consumption, particularly of nonrenewable resources, and other environment-enhancing measures; supporting sustainable approaches to food security and job creation in poor countries; and forgiving the burdensome debts of developing countries, which may lead to exports of nonrenewable resources or ecologically unsound practices.

- On the community and personal level, in all countries, citizens can make choices that contribute to sustainable development. In poor countries, for example, more efficient stoves can reduce indoor smoke. In rich countries, most people can improve both their health and the physical environment if they adopt lifestyles that are simpler and depend less on non-renewable resources.

There is a biblical vision that can help inspire and support humanity's struggle toward sustainable approaches to the future of ourselves and the planet. The Book of Job makes clear the need to view creation in an holistic manner: "Do you know when the mountain goats give birth?/Do you observe the calving of the deer?" To begin to think and act more like God means knowing and loving our landscape.

The farmer and writer Wendell Berry suggests:

> Our present "leaders" – the people of wealth and power – do not know what it means to take a place seriously: to think it worthy, for its own sake, of life and study and careful work. . . . The right scale of work gives power to affection. . . . An adequate local culture, among other things, keeps work within the scope of love.[22]

By living sustainably – in ways that are informed, wise, and good – we, as one Indian development worker said, have the joy of recreating the Garden of Eden. ■

Rev. Nancy Wright is environment/communications director at CODEL, Inc. (Coordination in Development), and coauthor of *Ecological Healing: A Christian Vision* (Maryknoll, NY: Orbis/CODEL, 1993). A. Cecilia Snyder is research associate and Don Reeves economic policy analyst at BFW Institute.

Sustainable development requires change in both public policies and personal attitudes and behavior.

Photo: The Inter-American Foundation (IAF)

At least a billion people live without safe water, and nearly twice that many lack adequate sanitation. Here, open sewers flow in a barrio near the city of Santo Domingo.

Racism and Ethnocentrism

Photo: UNHCR

Cause 5

Fleeing ethnic violence, an estimated 250,000 Rwandans swept into Tanzania over a 24-hour period in the largest and fastest refugee exodus UNHCR has ever witnessed.

Part One: International
by Sarita Wardlaw Henry

Racism and ethnocentrism underlie many situations of unequal access to resources around the world. Hunger is a frequent result. Often ethnically-based competition for resources leads to violent conflict. Yet countries such as Zimbabwe, Jamaica, and the new South Africa offer a vision of multiracial democracy and food security.

....

It is then the strife of all honorable men of the 20th century to see that in the future competition of races the survival of the fittest shall mean the triumph of the good, the beautiful, and the true; that we may be able to preserve for future civilization all that is really fine and noble and strong, and not continue to put a premium on greed and impudence and cruelty. To bring this hope to fruition, we are compelled daily to turn more and more to a conscientious study of the phenomena of race contact – to study frank and fair, and not falsified and colored by our wishes and our fears.

— W.E.B. DuBois

Racism and ethnocentricism contribute significantly to the hunger and poverty of millions of people in the world today. Famine, war, ethnic conflict, communal violence, tribalism, and colonialism all have deep roots in racism and ethnocentrism. The case studies below demonstrate that racism and ethnocentrism cause hunger.

Historical Background

Racism and ethnocentrism have been with us since the beginning of our time on earth. Oral traditions, depicted on rock and parchment, and in stone and terra cotta, early written documents and sacred texts are clear testimony to the longstanding persistence of ethnic prejudice. It has its origin in people's first awareness of physical, cultural, religious, or economic differences between groups. Racist and ethnocentric explanations of these differences point to durable and hereditary group characteristics.

Contacts with other people – people who look different, especially in terms of skin color, or whose daily lives are conducted in a different way – have engendered reactions ranging from curiosity and wonder to contempt and violence. A Spanish chronicle translated into English in 1555 was filled with wonder in this diversity:

One of the great marvylous thynges that God useth in the composition of man, is coloure: whiche doubtlesse cannot be consydered without great admiration in beholding one to be white and another blacke, being coloures utterlye contrary. Sum lykewise to be yelowe whiche is between blacke and white; and other of other colours as it were of dyvers liveres.

Sophisticated and "scientific" theories about race developed in conjunction with European expansion and the slave trade beginning in the 16th century. Prejudice was a factor in the British American colonies when the rulers decreed in the 1660s that all "Negroes" (but no whites) who were imported should be slaves rather than indentured servants.

Racism and Ethnocentrism

In an ethnically divided society, government often intervenes in ethnic struggle by the way it distributes services.

Race, Ethnicity, and Development

Ethnic identity has both objective and subjective qualities. The objective factors are language, religion, territory, social organization, culture, race, common origin, and shared history. But ethnic identity can be manipulated for political purposes and thereby transformed.

Both racism and ethnocentrism are associated with power. They are readily apparent when one group enslaves another, but they are less apparent in other forms of domination. Many governments deny any intentionality to marginalize any group within their borders. Often only the result confirms the intention: marked disparities in income, opportunity, and rights.

Some of the most severe results of racism and ethnocentrism are primarily economic, and economic problems have great influence on ethnic relations: struggle for scarce resources, regional imbalances, infrastructural investments that disrupt indigenous economic systems, labor market conflicts, and distributional conflicts. Under the guise of development, many ethnic groups are impoverished.

Competition for scarce resources seems inherent in modern development. Sometimes this leads to the extinction of an ethnic group, the exodus of marginalized peoples (such as indigenous peoples, tribal groups, or nomads), or the destruction of local ecosystems upon which these groups depend. A dominant group may "develop" the area for its purposes, making it uninhabitable for the local population.

Access to the state is the way for a group to achieve economic development. In an ethnically divided society, government often intervenes in ethnic struggle by the way it distributes services.

Africa

Rwanda

There are two main ethnic groups in Rwanda: the Hutus (85 percent of the population) and the Tutsis. Their conflict is longstanding. It was exacerbated by German and Belgian colonial rule, which favored the Tutsis, a cattle-rearing group who had developed a position of feudal superiority over the Hutu peasants. The Tutsis were given advantages in education and employment. They were considered superior to the Hutus in other ways, notably because of their height and somewhat lighter skin. At independence in 1962, violence took the lives of between 100,000 and 200,000 people. Hutus gained control of the government and army; Tutsis fled en masse into exile in neighboring countries.

A Tutsi group undertook an armed invasion in 1990. The ensuing civil war created farm input shortages and drove farmers from their land. Fighting displaced about 900,000 people, more than 10 percent of the population. Food production and marketing were hampered.

A year-long truce began in 1993. But a plane crash in April 1994 killed the Hutu presidents of Rwanda and Burundi, and this touched off a systematic campaign of political killings in Rwanda which left an estimated 1 million Tutsi civilians and sympathetic Hutus dead. Tutsi-led rebel forces fought back and had won control of virtually the entire country by August 1994. Frightened of retaliation despite the Tutsis' conciliatory words, Hutus by the hundreds of thousands abandoned their villages and farms. More than 1 million people crossed into Zaire in less than a week in July 1994. Hundreds died by the side of the road and in squalid encampments from exhaustion, dehydration, and disease (see also Cause 2).

Agricultural production and development have been deeply disrupted. Farmers have been killed or fled, farms abandoned, and families left hungry.

Not too long ago, a particular kind of bean was successfully introduced to Rwandan farmers. The vine provided an edible leaf, and the local population accepted this new food. But the agricultural station that provided this bean was completely destroyed in the violence – just one more example of how ethnic hatred has spawned hunger in Rwanda.

Sudan

The conflict in Sudan is both racial and ethnic; the predominantly Arab Muslim north controls the government and has sought to impose its will and law on the black south, where most people are Christian or practice traditional religions. The south has fertile land and oil. Members of several of the ethnic groups from the south have launched a rebel movement. Civilians in the south find themselves the victims of the racism, neglect, and violent repression of the northern government. They have also suffered at the hands of the rebels, especially because of fighting between rebel factions. Both sides have used food as a weapon, frequently blocking relief shipments. In 1994, the United Nations estimated that 2.5 million Sudanese required food aid.

Thousands of southern refugees have fled to Khartoum, the northern capital. They have faced malnutrition, disease, and forced relocation to squatter camps which ring the city. Because of racial prejudice, the fundamentalist Islamic government has denied these black migrants the charity prescribed by the Koran. The government has forcibly relocated tens of thousands of residents from the Nuba mountains in central Sudan. Fertile agricultural land vacated by the Nuba population in 1992 and 1993 was reportedly confiscated by government supporters. The government has consistently barred relief agencies from entering the area. Human Rights Watch/Africa has characterized this as a case of "ethnic cleansing."

For 28 of its 38 years of independence, Sudan has been locked in civil war. This is a legacy of the British colonial favoritism toward the Arab north and neglect of the black south. The present civil war between the fundamentalist Islamic government and the rebels has been going on since 1983. The fighting has displaced nearly three million people, and 1.3 million people have died due to war-related famine and disease.

Malnutrition rates are the highest ever documented in the world. Among the effects of the war:

- In the so-called starvation triangle, undernutrition rates are above 80 percent and mortality rates are above 250 per 1,000 people. In parts of southern Sudan, deaths exceed births, leading to a 1.9 percent decline in population in 1993.

- Sixty-four percent of southern households surveyed in 1993 reported labor shortages or land cultivation reduced due to hunger. Forty-four percent reported seed shortages, 43 percent tool shortages. About 20 percent said their planting had been disrupted by the fighting.

- Between 1980 and 1991, per capita food production declined by 29 percent in the south.

- Agricultural lands are heavily mined.

The civil war has diverted funds from agriculture to the military, disrupted marketing activities, resulted in extensive livestock losses, and destroyed infrastructure. Inadequate rainfall has added to these disastrous developments in agriculture.

Sudan's 1993-1994 grain output is

Ethnic hatred has spawned hunger in Rwanda.

The human development disparity between blacks and whites in South Africa is four times that between blacks and whites in the United States.

expected to fall 17 percent. Starvation results from the disruption of grain shipments to deficit regions and the extreme poverty that keeps many people from buying the food which is available.

South Africa

The *apartheid* regime imposed white minority rule and racial separation; it did not want anyone to have data on disparities between blacks and whites in South Africa. But even the available data give a striking picture of inequality. According to the U.N. Development Program, if white South Africa were a separate country, it would rank 24th in the world in human development, just after Spain (see Cause 3 on the Human Development Index). Black South Africa would rank 123rd, just above Congo. These are not just two different peoples, but almost two different worlds. The major challenge for policymakers in the new era of multiracial democracy will be to promote social integration without provoking racial violence.

In addition to creating separate and unequal black "homelands," the minority government forcibly moved thousands of black farmers from land they had cultivated for hundreds of years and gave it to white farmers. They moved black families to towns and cities with no resources other than what they could carry on their backs or pack atop crowded buses. Deprived of their land and livelihoods, they became impoverished. They lacked access to employment, healthcare, housing, water and sanitation, and adequate food.

Racial violence remains a threat in the United States. But the human development disparity between blacks and whites in South Africa is four times that between blacks and whites in the United States. Yet Zimbabwe had similar racial disparities at the time of its independence, and Zimbabwe has achieved a considerable degree of social integration without substantial racial trouble.

Latin America

The Amerindian peoples of Latin America number 30 million, which is 9 percent of the population. In five countries – Bolivia, Ecuador, Guatemala, Mexico, and Peru – they are an important proportion of the total rural population. Everywhere they are among the poorest, most disadvantaged sections of society, often suffering extreme forms of deprivation.

Following the colonial conquest of the region, the original inhabitants lost control of land and natural resources to white and mixed race colonialists. An estimated 12 to 15 million Indians died during the Spanish quest for gold in the Americas.

Export agriculture has dominated since colonial days – a system that puts coffee, bananas, cotton, sugar, and beef production for export ahead of the food needs of local people. Hunger and poverty result from land use and ownership patterns designed to serve interests of a small national elite and the global economic system.

Belize is a country that imports nearly 25 percent of what it eats. The small corn farmers – mostly Indian and mixed race people – have not been given a favored place in agricultural programs. The incidence of malnutrition is 8 percent for children under a year old, and 19 percent for children one to four years old. Undernutrition and severe micronutrient deficiencies are common, especially in rural areas.

In Guatemala, Indians are the majority. Eighty-seven percent of the population is in poverty. There are enormous disparities between Indian and non-Indian health, as reflected in life expectancies:

Non-Indian men live to age......65
Non-Indian women 64
Indian men.................................48
Indian women 47

Even during the counterinsurgency campaigns of the early 1980s, more Guatemalans were dying of malnutrition and preventable diseases than from political violence. Indians are relegated to the economic margins, serving mainly as a pool of cheap labor. There is no longer enough land to support the Indian population (which continues to grow despite the persecution), and the lack of land forces relocation to urban slums.

Military-dominated governments have sought to wipe out armed resistance, threatening the cultural survival of Indian communities in the process. Only racism can explain a war which has eliminated more than 400 Indian villages.

Brazil

Children do not die in Brazil from wars or famine-induced hunger the way they do in Sudan or Bosnia. Instead they die in the midst of peace and plenty. Brazil is the world's third largest exporter of agricultural products. Yet 60 million Brazilians live in extreme poverty. Thirty-two million (equal to the population of Argentina) go hungry every day. They include 2.7 million children under two years old and 5 million under five.

Hunger is linked to the impact of racism on Brazilians of African descent. In terms of nutrition, there are two countries within the same borders. Brazil experienced rapid economic growth in the 1960s and 1970s, but only a few Brazilians benefitted. The military governments of the time allied themselves with foreign companies, state-owned businesses, Brazilian industrialists, and private banks. Public policies helped enrich these sectors by deliberately keeping workers'

earnings low. The military ceded power only after the international debt crisis had emptied their coffers and thoroughly discredited them.

In 1993, the government launched a new food subsidy program, Proalimentos, which covers 4.5 million families. So far, it has failed to reach the neediest people. For those most in need, reducing the cost of beans to 90 percent or even 70 percent of the regular price does not help much. They still have little purchasing power and go hungry.

Poverty, hunger, and malnutrition are part of the endemic deprivation which characterizes the northeast section of the country, which is predominately Afro-Brazilian. There are 7.2 million people (70 percent of the total) living in extreme poverty in the northeast. More than 60 percent of rural Brazilians whose income does not permit them to purchase enough food live in the northeast. Although food consumption is higher than in the cities (because food can be obtained outside the market-place), poor health and sanitation services lead to a higher incidence of malnutrition.

Between 1985 and 1992, Brazil produced more than enough food to meet the caloric and protein needs of its people. But food spoils in the most developed regions of the country, while people starve in the most distant corners of the poorest, more heavily Afro-Brazilian regions. This has deepened the process of exclusion and social segregation. It has provoked massive migration, with swelling numbers of underemployed workers in the cities.

Almost 90 percent of the food is produced outside the north and northeast. If the south of Brazil were a separate country, its human development would rank 42nd in the world (equal to Portugal), while the northeast would rank 111th (on a par with El salvador and Bolivia). Seventy percent of the families of the northeast have per capita incomes less

Only racism can explain a war which has eliminated more than 400 Indian villages.

than the cost of the basic food ration. The region has the worst calorie deficiencies and the poorest nutritional status in Brazil.

Seventy-eight percent of black workers and 71 percent of mixed race workers earn less than twice the minimum wage. Among white workers, the figure is 52 percent.

Slavery was abolished in Brazil in 1888. But more than a century later, Afro-Brazilians continue to experience political, social, and economic marginalization, prejudice, discrimination, and racism. Many claim that Brazil has no racial prejudice. For example, historian Gilberto Freyre says:

> With respect to race relations, the Brazilian situation is probably the rarest approach to paradise to be found anywhere in the world.

Yet the impoverished status of most Afro-Brazilians shows that paradise to be a fiction. A country-wide movement to fight hunger, poverty, and racism is gaining momentum.

Iraq

In 1988, the Iraqi government attacked the Muslim Kurds in the north of the country. Although both groups are Muslim, Kurdish culture is different. The Kurds have a long tradition of resistance and a movement for independence.

In village after village in 1988, men and boys as young as fifteen were massacred. Women, children, and elderly people were taken from their homes and relocated, sometimes several times in the course of a few months. They were repeatedly told by the Iraqi military that "the Kurds have been brought here to die." In the camps, many received no food or water for the first few days. When they did, it was unclean and insufficient. They had nothing with which to hold the water, and the food was only small chunks of bread every other day. Stress, declining nutrition, and dehydration made many pregnant women miscarry. Children weakened, and infants suffered as mothers' milk dried up.

After the 1991 Kurdish uprising, several graves were exhumed in order to corroborate the accounts of victims and other witnesses of this intentional genocide. A boy led pathologists to his sister's grave. He said that she was about one year old when she died. Her body was seven months old according to dental evidence, but only one to three months according to bone development. The difference was due to malnutrition: the teeth of malnourished children develop normally, while skeletal growth is severely retarded.

Sri Lanka

About 74 percent of Sri Lanka's 17.5 million people are Sinhalese, who are predominately Buddhist. Eighteen percent are Tamils, who are mainly Hindu. Seven percent are Tamil-speaking Muslims. Since 1983, fighting between the Sinhalese controlled government and Tamil rebels has displaced almost 800,000 people. In their efforts to push the Tamil guerrillas out of the jungle in the eastern part of the country, the military engendered violent conflict between Hindu Tamils and the Muslims. Tensions already existed because of economics. The Muslims are traders and landowners, and are generally prosperous; they have relied on the Tamils for cheap labor.

Tamils migrated from southern India, but they have lived in Sri Lanka for hundreds of years. They are still discriminated against and segregated socially and economically. Poverty and discrimination have spawned ethnic violence.

Nearly all the laborers on the tea estates in the mountains of the interior are Tamils. The estate labor population suffers unusually high infant mortality and is more prone to illness than Sinhalese Sri Lankans. Prominent causes of death among estate workers and their families include intestinal infections, infectious and parasitic diseases, and anemia and other nutritional deficiencies. Among estate children, chronic malnutrition is widespread. In one estate, 60 percent of the children aged three to 36 months suffer from severe chronic malnutrition, and 53 percent have a very low weight for age (compared to 26 and 39 percent for all rural Sri Lankan children).

Estate workers and their families are denied citizenship. They are entitled to certain benefits from the government such as health care, but access is limited. Health care workers who are Sinhalese do not want to work on the estates. Distances to hospitals or physicians are often several miles, and transportation is costly, as is taking time off from work. Fueled by centuries of racist fears of an invasion by darker-skinned people, the Sinhalese have continued to keep the Tamils in marginal and subservient positions. Even prosperous Tamils face cultural oppression by the Sinhalese majority.

East Timor

One third of the population of tiny East Timor has died or suffered enormous deprivation and famine in the last twenty years of resistance to colonization by Indonesia. Nine days after its declaration of independence in December 1975, overwhelmingly Muslim Indonesia violently annexed the former Portuguese colony, which is made up of Catholics and practitioners of other traditional religions. The Indonesian army, with U.S. arms, attempted to starve the territory's independence movement; in the process, they starved most of the population of East Timor.

When the famine reached international attention in 1979, the Indonesian government blamed it on civil strife which ensued after Portugal abandoned the territory. But independent journalists and relief workers support other evidence that starvation was a military strategy to crush the resistance. Hundreds of thousands of people fled to the mountains when Indonesia invaded. Indonesian planes sprayed defoliants, destroying the crops of the population that had always lived in the mountains. By 1978, people were forced down from the mountains. They had no buffaloes, no tools, no money to pay for labor, and their irrigation canals had fallen into disrepair. Of 75,000 refugees gathered in 13 Indonesian government camps, 60,000 were facing starvation. Twenty thousand could not be saved.

Conclusion

Romanian-born radio commentator Andrei Codrescu has said, "All you decent, peaceful, overfed citizens [are] in the throes of definitional anxiety." Definitional anxiety fosters ethnocentrism and racism. People shy away from these terms, and name these realities with words which disguise their brutality. Yet millions of people all over the world suffer terrible violence, deprivation, and daily indignities because ethnocentrism and racism persist.

There are also societies, such as Zimbabwe and Jamaica, where members of different ethnic groups live in harmony and work together on the tasks of achieving sustainable development and food security. Prophetic, moral reasoning and intentional efforts to build cultural democracies, as prescribed by those such as Harvard scholar Cornel West, are necessary to overcome the evils of ethnocentrism and racism. ∎

Sarita Wardlaw Henry is hunger educator at BFW Institute.

There are also societies, such as Zimbabwe and Jamaica, where members of different ethnic groups live in harmony and work together on the tasks of achieving sustainable development and food security.

Photo: © Sharon D'Amico

> I am talking of millions of men who have been skilfully injected with fear, inferiority complexes, trepidation, servility, despair, abasement.
>
> – Aimé Césaire,
> *Discours sur le Colonialisme*

Part 2: The United States
by Billy J. Tidwell

The evils of hunger and racism are interconnected. African Americans, Hispanics, Native Americans, and other racial and ethnic minorities control proportionately fewer resources and are more likely to need food assistance than the majority white population. Many communities and nonprofit organizations provide food assistance to those who need it. But the problem of hunger will not be fully resolved until our society makes a commitment to eradicate racism and discrimination.

Introduction

Hunger in the United States occurs disproportionately among African Americans, Hispanics, Native Americans, and other racial and ethnic minorities. The prevalence and persistence of the U.S. hunger problem is interrelated with racism and discrimination.

By virtually all definitions and measures, African Americans, Hispanics, and Native Americans are substantially worse off than the majority white population. The magnitude and persistence of these inequalities suggests that racism contributes to the hunger problem. The empirical data are compelling.

The late Michael Harrington brought visibility to "the other America" – poor, uneducated, dispirited, and voiceless people.[1] Most tellingly, this was a very hungry America – the empty bellies and hungry faces, experiencing nutritional deprivations out of public view in the preeminent land of plenty.

Hunger was then and is now the most basic, universal indicator of economic distress; a societal disease brought on and sustained by social neglect. Hunger ravages body and mind, while contradicting the precepts of civilization generally and the ideals that inform the U.S. identity in particular.

According to the Food Research and Action Center (FRAC), non-whites are disproportionately vulnerable to hunger. Whites make up the single largest racial group among both poor people in the United States and food stamp users. But a FRAC survey found that 76 percent of hungry households were non-white.[2]

The Racial Economics of Hunger

The State of Black America, published by the National Urban League, documents deep and pervasive racial inequalities in economic well-being.[3] According to the two most recent volumes:

- The poverty rate for African Americans in 1992 was 33.3 percent, nearly triple the rate for whites. About 47 percent of African-American children were poor, compared to 17 percent of white children.

- African-American workers earn less than 80 percent of the earnings of their white counterparts.

- The income of African-American families is less than 60 percent of white family income.

- The incidence of female-headed African-American families is almost 3.5 times higher than that of white families. Female-headed families suffer acute disadvantages in all areas of economic life.

The U.S. Census Bureau found that in 1992, African Americans made up just 12.6 percent of the country's population, but accounted for 28.8 percent of all poor people. In contrast, whites accounted for 75 percent of the population and about 50 percent of poor people. Only 10 percent of all whites lived in poverty.[4]

Hispanics also are more vulnerable to hunger than whites. In *State of Hispanic America,* the National Council of La Raza reports that during the 1980s, Hispanics were the only racial/ethnic group to experience an absolute decline in income. Despite high levels of work effort, they are more likely than either whites or African Americans to lack health insurance.[5]

- More than one in four Hispanics (28.7 percent) and two in five Hispanic children (40.4 percent) are poor.

- Almost half (46.1 percent) of all poor Hispanic families were headed by women in 1990.

- Hispanic children comprised only 11 percent of all children in 1990, but represented 21 percent of all children living in poverty.

According to the Census Bureau, Hispanics were less than 9 percent of the total population in 1992, but accounted for 18 percent of the people living in poverty.

Hispanics hoping to live the American dream have often been sorely disappointed. Male Hispanics have higher rates of labor force participation than non-Hispanic men, but their families are more than twice as likely as white or African-American families to live in poverty. These

Racial minorities are more likely than whites to need food assistance.

The persistence of racial and economic injustice must be attacked directly by people of all races working in concert.

Table 5.1
Percent in Poverty by Family Characteristics, 1989

	Native American, Eskimo, and Aleut	Total Population
Married-Couple Families	17.0	5.5
Male householder, no wife present	33.4	13.8
Female householder, no husband present	50.4	31.1

Source: U.S. Bureau of the Census.

Table 5.2
Race/Ethnicity of Heads of Participating Food Stamp Households, Summer 1992

Race of head	Number (thousands)	Households Percent
Total	10,238	100.0
White, Non-Hispanic	4,665	44.6
African-American, Non-Hispanic	3,621	35.4
Hispanic	1,261	12.3
Asian	222	2.2
Native American	113	1.1
Other	456	4.4

Source: U.S. Department of Agriculture.

working poor people have been unable to depend on their jobs for economic stability or security. Hispanics are over-represented in lower-skilled jobs and underrepresented in higher skilled, higher wage occupations. Hispanics must be able to acquire more education and skills to be qualified for jobs in the twenty-first century.

Native Americans likewise have a higher poverty rate – and are more likely to be hungry – than the general population (see "Native Americans"). As Table 5.1 shows, 50 percent of female-headed Native American families lived in poverty in 1989, compared to 31 percent for the general population.

Racial minorities are more likely than whites to need food assistance. Table 5.2 shows a disproportionate share of African-American households receiving food stamps, although non-Hispanic whites account for the largest proportion of those receiving benefits. African Americans made up more than 35 percent of participating food stamp households. Hispanics account for 12 percent of recipient families, again out of proportion to their share of the general population. Similar racial differences in participation rates are observable in other food aid programs, both public and private.[6] More than 27 percent of participants in the Special Supplemental Food Program for Women, Infants, and Children (WIC) are African-American, and almost 24 percent are Hispanic.[7]

Effects of Unequal Outcomes

Racial differences in economic well-being go a long way toward explaining the prevalence of hunger in the United States, and hunger further undermines the physical and emotional well-being of minority groups.

Hunger contributes to poor health. Table 5.3 shows significantly higher rates of anemia among non-white pregnant women compared to white women. Table 5.4 indicates that African-American women aged 15 to 40 are roughly twice as likely to have low birthweight babies as white women (because of a higher malnutrition rate among the mothers). The infant mortality rate among African Americans is more than double the rate among whites (Table 5.5). In addition, African Americans lag well behind whites in life expectancy.

Hunger is very much a matter of economic justice and overcoming the heritage of racism in the United States. Sociologist William Julius Wilson has succinctly summarized the African-American experience of racism:

> *Blacks were denied access to valued and scarce resources through various ingenious schemes of racial exploitation, discrimination, and segregation, schemes that were reinforced by elaborate ideologies of [explicit] racism. Racial oppression ranged from slavery to segregation, from the endeavors of [the] white economic elite to exploit black labor to the actions of the white masses to eliminate or neutralize black competition.[8]*

Hispanics suffer rigid job and residential segregation and bear much of the brunt of a rising tide of anti-immigrant sentiment. Even Asian immigrants, who as a whole enjoy higher income and educational levels than other minority groups, have suffered prejudice, violent attacks, and discrimination.

Table 5.3
Anemia Among Low-Income Women During Pregnancy, 1990

Race and Ethnicity	Second Trimester (Percent)	Third Trimester (Percent)
Non-Hispanic white	9.3	24.6
Non-Hispanic African-American	21.4	45.8
Hispanic	11.4	31.9
Native American	11.9	32.8
Asian or Pacific Islander	11.8	26.8

Source: Interagency Board for Nutrition Monitoring and Related Research, *Nutrition Monitoring in the United States, Chartbook I: Selected Findings from the National Nutrition Monitoring and Related Research Program* (Hyattsville, Maryland: Public Health Service,1993), Figure 18, p. 98.

Table 5.4
Low Birth Weight as a Percent of Total Live Births, by Age of Mother and Race of Infant, 1986-1988

Age of mother	African American	White	Afr. Am/White ratio
Less than 15 years	16.2	10.4	1.6
15-19 years	13.1	7.7	1.7
20-24 years	12.3	5.8	2.1
25-29 years	12.5	5.1	2.4
30-34 years	13.0	5.2	2.5
35-39 years	13.4	6.0	2.2
40 years and over	12.9	7.1	1.8

Source: *Nutrition Monitoring in the United States,* Figure 22, p. 99.

Table 5.5
Infant Mortality Rates, by Race and Sex: 1989 (per 1,000 live births)

	African American	White	Afr. Am/White ratio
Both sexes	18.6	8.1	2.3
Male	19.8	9.0	2.2
Female	17.2	7.1	2.4

Source: National Center for Health Statistics.

Native Americans
by Lawrence J. Goodwin

Hunger and poverty in the Native American community stem from a long history of conquest, racism, and cultural discrimination. The federal government and white society have colluded in this process over many generations.

Poverty is widespread on most Indian reservations, with a majority of adults unemployed. It forms part of a larger picture of community distress. Poor nutrition and health problems are extensive. Family breakdown and alcoholism run rampant. Residents have been forced by historical circumstances and government policy to depend heavily on food stamps and U.S. Department of Agriculture commodities. These problems contribute to, and for some justify, the discrimination Native Americans continue to endure.

The hard fact is that Native Americans are poorer – and therefore more vulnerable to hunger – than any other U.S. population. In 1989, 31 percent of Native Americans lived below the poverty level, compared to 13 percent of the total population. In Arizona, 49 percent of Native Americans live in poverty. Although they account for just 7 percent of the state population, they make up 17.5 percent of poor Arizonans.[1] In South Dakota, the Sioux Nation confronts an unemployment rate close to 90 percent.

The situation American Indians face today is rooted in a chronicle of injustice. With the arrival of Europeans 500 years ago, Native Americans suffered massacres, land theft, forced marches and relocations, enslavement, betrayal of treaty rights, destruction of food sources, and cultural oppression. Many tribes were removed from their traditional homelands so that those lands could be settled by non-indians. When tribal lands were confiscated, areas reserved for the occupancy and use of a particular tribe ("reservations") were created without regard to existing indigenous food and habitation systems or territorial claims. All means were taken, including the use of lethal force, to keep them confined.

As outsiders demanded more land and wealth, Native Americans lost control of their resources. Inevitably, they were squeezed onto smaller and smaller stretches of ever poorer farm land. In this regard, parallels with the homeland policies of the former white regimes of South Africa and Southern Rhodesia are conspicuous.

Control of food and water sources by government agents and

Responding to the Need: Programs, Policies, and Priorities

Discovery of the other America prompted serious efforts to alleviate the hunger problem. Indeed, a veritable social movement around the issue emerged, marked by intense advocacy for institutional change and numerous private initiatives to provide direct relief to those in need.

The list of food assistance activities currently conducted by nonprofit organizations in economically disadvantaged minority communities around the country is impressive. Churches and religious organizations have been particularly active:

Insofar as black churches are continuously struggling against racism they are implicitly addressing one of the root causes of hunger alongside their direct charitable and political anti-hunger activities.[9]

Paralleling the private efforts, a range of federal government food and nutrition programs have been implemented over the years, including the Food Stamp Program, WIC, the National School Lunch Program, and the School Breakfast Program.

Public and private food assistance initiatives have been critical to the well-being of poor people in general and minority poor people in particular. However, it is equally clear that these provisions cannot by themselves solve the problem over the long-term. They will not rectify the inequitable distribution of economic resources that undergirds and sustains racial inequalities. Thus, the persistence of racial and economic injustice must be attacked directly by people of all races working in concert.

Improving the relative economic position of African Americans, Hispanics,

Native Americans, and other minorities requires investment. The National Urban League's Marshall Plan for America is designed to advance the economic interests of the nation as a whole by targeting improvements in human resource and physical infrastructure development to the most needy groups and communities. The plan calls for $500 billion in new investment in education, job training, and physical infrastructure over a ten year period, based on collaboration among government, the private sector, and nonprofit organizations.[10] This is ambitious, but would it be too high a price to pay to overcome the divisive and debilitating legacy of race relations in the United States?

What is lacking is the societal commitment to complete the unfinished business of racial justice – the determination finally to eradicate racism and discrimination from American life. Those who are concerned about hunger are challenged as perhaps never before to recognize and deal with this dimension of the problem. ∎

Dr. Billy J. Tidwell is director of research and evaluation for the National Urban League.

the military weakened resistance and created dependency. The deliberate mass killing of buffalo, denial of access to hunting areas, and the imposition of food rationing schemes all conspired to undermine Indian independence.[2]

Government policy and missionary activity within the reservation system also sought to cripple Indian cultural identity. The suppression of Indian languages in government and mission schools, which only began to change in the past decade, is just one example of how native culture was under attack from state, federal, and religious sources. In addition, native people were often forced into a European agricultural life-style; and many Indian children were compelled to leave home at a very early age to be raised in a white cultural environment. This concerted policy of cultural and religious suppression sapped the strength of the community and contributed significantly to hunger and poverty.

In the face of 500 years of repression, however, Native Americans have clung tenaciously to their identity. A cultural renaissance in language, art, religion, and renewed ties with the earth is ongoing. Indian universities and colleges have mushroomed over the past 25 years. Economic initiatives like the Circle Bank project in South Dakota, which provides credit to Indian microenterprises, empower people at the local level. A heightened political activism in Congress and at state levels is evidence of a growing move for self-determination. Efforts to gain legal protection for the use of peyote in traditional rituals have engaged the support of a broad range of religious groups.

Yet racial and cultural discrimination against Native Americans persist unabated in much of society. The struggle to regain control of sacred sites such as the Black Hills, and to have traditional religion accepted on an equal footing with other faiths, is still unresolved. Justice can only come from an unflinching look at how racism, territorial conquest, cultural domination, and economic exploitation have created mass poverty and hunger for generations of Native Americans. Such an honest examination can also teach us a great deal about how exploitation is a cause of hunger and poverty elsewhere. ∎

Dr. Lawrence J. Goodwin is a BFW regional organizer.

Gender Discrimination

Photo: UNHCR

Women are more likely than men to suffer from hunger.

by A. Cecilia Snyder

Gender discrimination is one of the root causes of hunger. Most women around the world work hard, long hours in the home as well as outside it. But because their labor is not valued, women often lack the resources to support themselves and their families adequately. Development specialists have begun to focus more on programs that provide education for women and enable them to receive compensation for their work. Sustainable development will require a new perspective on hunger and poverty issues that consistently takes gender into account.

Introduction

On our planet, most women have primary responsibility to grow and gather, prepare, and distribute food. Because they bear and nourish children, they have special, additional needs for nourishment that are not shared by men. Yet women of every age have high rates of malnutrition, and women are more likely than men to suffer from hunger.

One of the root causes of hunger is gender discrimination. Because of their gender, females in almost every society, including industrial countries, do not have the same opportunities for growth – and in some cases, even for survival – as males. Societal, cultural, and governmental practices often prevent female children from reaching their full potential and their mothers from gaining access to the jobs and education that could alleviate the cycles of hunger and poverty.

According to the United Nations, 400 million women of childbearing age (about 45 percent of the total) weigh less than 100 pounds. These women are likely to be malnourished and vulnerable to obstetric complications. Nearly half the world's women suffer from iron deficiency anemia. In South Asia, for example, 64 percent of pregnant women are anemic (Figure 6.1). This increases their risk of illness, pregnancy complications, and maternal death, in addition to decreasing their productivity as workers.

Until recently, hunger and poverty data were based on the assumption that all people in a family or community were affected equally, without considering differing nutritional needs of females. In reality, pregnant and lactating women experience greater stress and demands on their bodies and must satisfy increased nutritional requirements. Micronutrient deficiencies, such as lack of vitamin A and iron, can have serious consequences for women and their babies. Death in childbirth, a leading killer of women of reproductive age in most developing countries, frequently results from malnutrition. Newer studies separate data for women and men on crucial measurements.

Women are society's mothers and caregivers, with primary responsibility for the well-being of families and communities. They are also frequently family providers, working on farms and in factories and managing natural resources. Yet women are overrepresented among poor, illiterate, and displaced people, and underrepresented in places of power. Because mothers are usually the caregivers, discrimination against them also affects their children. In 1990, there were four hungry children for every woman living in poverty.

Figure 6.1
Anemia Among Pregnant and Non-Pregnant Women by Region, 1980s

	% pregnant women anemic	% non-pregnant women anemic
South Asia	64%	63.8%
Southeast Asia	56.4%	46.8%
Sub-Saharan Africa	49.6%	40.3%
Near East / North Africa	44.4%	30.8%
Middle America	34.4%	26.9%
China	33.5%	26.3%
South America	30.5%	20.9%

Source: ACC/SCN.

Women as Workers

In 1990, Rohini was a fourteen-year-old living in India. When a development worker asked her what she did, she replied automatically, "I don't work." The worker persisted:

"Don't you do anything all day?" Looking shocked, Rohini quickly answers, "Of course I do. First, I get wood for fuel. Then I carry water in heavy buckets from a tap far from home. I clean the house, wash the clothes, milk the cows, and cook while I am looking after my little brother and sister. Then I take lunch to my mother in the fields. Sometimes I put my brother and sister to sleep in the afternoon and work in the fields with my mother." [1]

The work that girls and women perform is real and contributes to the family and society. However, women's work has consistently been undervalued and rarely recorded in official labor statistics. Despite their backbreaking labor, females are regarded in most societies as a burden, not an asset.

A recent study of Indian landless laborer households found that 86 percent of females over age 14 worked in agriculture, as opposed to 73 percent of males. In addition, more females (65 percent) tended animals and did unpaid labor than males (57 percent). The same study found that although everyone over age 14 participated in some household work, girls and women did much more, with 84 percent of females performing nine to 20 different tasks. Seventy-eight percent of males performed, at most, eight tasks (see Table 6.1).

Females work more hours at every chore except whitewashing and city shopping. Yet since housework is unpaid, women in India and many other countries are not seen as contributing economically. Indeed, since money is often the measure of a person, they are not seen as measuring up.

Valuing Women's Work

Rohini's story is far from unique. Although women are increasingly entering the formal labor force globally, most continue to do unpaid and unrecognized work at home. They care for young, sick, and elderly people; do domestic chores; and provide and prepare meals. In developing countries, environmental degradation has increased the amount of time many women spend hunting for food, fuel, and water.

Women around the world are working more than men: five hours per week more in Latin America, and 13 to 15 hours more in Asia and Africa. Many women in developing countries work 60 to 90 hours a week just to survive.

Women globally still have not attained pay equity with men. They receive on average 30 percent to 40 percent less for comparable work. In the United States, on the average, women earn about 70 percent of what men earn for comparable work (see Table 6.2). [3]

Table 6.1: Household Work During One Week, [2] Landless Indian Households

Task	Female %	Male %
Kolam*	38.5	–
Serving Spouse	40.4	17.6
Child Care	42.3	15.7
Shopping in City	44.2	47.1
Whitewashing	48.1	62.7
Collecting Firewood	65.4	47.0
Local Shopping	69.2	43.1
Wetting the Yard	78.8	5.9
Washing Clothes	82.7	25.5
Cutting/Peeling	88.5	11.8
Fetching Water	88.5	23.5
Cooking	90.1	11.8
Cleaning House	94.2	15.7
Washing Vessels	96.2	5.9

*A rice flour or chalk drawing made daily in front of the home.
Source: Mathiot.

Women account for 41 percent of the world's officially counted "economically active" population. Because of inadequate measurement, at least 10 percent to 20 percent of the world's women are not counted in the official statistics.

Women as Heads of Household

The disparity in income has even more serious consequences if a woman is a single mother. Male migration from rural to urban areas, as well as divorce and separation, have led to an increase in female-headed households. Violent conflict also contributes. In Africa, about half the women heads of household are widowed. The estimated 76 million households headed by women in 114 developing countries are responsible for securing food for 377 million people.

The global trend toward female-headed households contributes to increased poverty and malnutrition. Women-headed households usually have only one provider and must also support children, elderly, and sick family members, so they are far more likely to be poor and hungry than dual- or male-headed families.

Many women work double and triple shifts, combining child care, domestic duties, and paid labor into one exhausting schedule. The result is a fatigued mother who lacks the strength and resources to provide adequate care even for herself, let alone her family.

Women aged 16 to 49 in the east African nations of Kenya and Tanzania lose twice as many work days as men because of poor health. Female-headed households in rural Namibia in southern Africa face chronic income and food shortages due to the absence of financially supportive males and lack of access to agricultural services.

Wilkista Ajuoga, a Kenyan, married at seventeen and bore eight children. She worked a daily schedule that started at 5:00 a.m. and included such chores as cleaning, tending the farm, fetching water and firewood, and selling fish at the local market. Her husband worked for several years in Nairobi as a truck driver and was frequently absent from home, leaving her to raise their children. "It is true, women work a lot harder," muses Ajuoga:

> They feed their children. They cook. They fetch water and firewood. They farm. They were born, and it goes like that.[4]

Barriers such as rigid schedules, lack of childcare, and lack of transportation prevent entry into the formal labor market. To break the cycle of hunger and poverty, we must develop long-term strategies that enable women to enter the formal labor market at decent wage rates. In addition, support to the informal sector can allow women workers and their dependents to be fully productive and receive needed benefits.

Women Refugees

Jahan Ara was an Afghan refugee living in India with her husband and three children, ages two to six. One night in 1986, her husband did not come home. He was never heard from again.

Jahan was left to care for herself and her family. Finding work outside the home proved to be nearly impossible because she had no previous work experience and could not leave her young children unattended. Six months after the disappearance of her husband,

Table 6.2 Relative Wages in Manufacturing, Women/Men, 1990	
Country	Women's relative wage (men's = 100)
Costa Rica	74
Hong Kong	69
Singapore	57
South Korea	50
Sweden	98
Denmark	85
United Kingdom	68
United States*	61
Japan	41

*Data for United States are from 1989.
Source: International Labor Organization, U.S. Bureau of the Census.

Eighty percent of the world's 16 million refugees are women and their dependent children.

the local office of the United Nations High Commissioner for Refugees (UNHCR) reduced its level of financial assistance, based on the presumption that there was now one less mouth to feed.

Jahan was placed in a desperate situation. Unable to provide for her family, she tried to reach out to other Afghan refugees for help. Unfortunately, she did not know any other women, and she could not freely accept support from males due to cultural taboos restricting her contact with men. Jahan had no relatives in India.

About a year after her husband disappeared, Jahan was admitted to the hospital with third degree burns, possibly self-inflicted. Her last wish was for her children to be sent to live with her father in a relatively peaceful part of Afghanistan.

Eighty percent of the world's 16 million refugees are women and their dependent children. Violence against female refugees is rampant, and food is often ransomed for sex. Camps frequently do not provide sanitary napkins and diapers. Women are forced to tear the lining from tents, rendering them useless for keeping out the cold.

The men in charge of food distribution in refugee camps often make women choose between rape and starvation. Most women are responsible for feeding children or elders in addition to meeting their own food needs. Uprooted women in a foreign country may have problems with unfamiliar food, and may not know the nutritional value of such food or how to prepare it sufficiently for their families.

Pregnant and nursing mothers with extra nutritional needs suffer even more, and their babies share in this suffering. Lack of prenatal care and malnutrition increase the chances of low birthweight babies. Women who give birth in refugee camps face problems of sanitation and lack of medical attention, thus increasing the risk of infection and death.

In 1991, UNHCR issued new guidelines on the protection of women refugees. These emphasize the need to include women in planning and running camps, and recommend greater attention to the food and health needs of women.

Mother and Child Health (MCH) programs are one example of how UNHCR has focused on the health of pregnant and lactating women and their children. While this approach has been successful in improving the health of women, many experts now recognize that women must be supported in various roles. A senior UNHCR health official commented:

> *The trouble with MCH programs is that they restrict women to the role of mother. . . . This is very reductive. What about young girls who may – or may not – one day become mothers? What about women who are past childbearing age, who in many societies have enormous influence over younger women? Ignore them and you risk diluting the effectiveness of health care and health education programs.*[5]

The Feminization of Development

In the 1970s, the predominant strategy for improving the condition of women in developing countries was to integrate them into ongoing economic and social structures. The U.N. Conference on Women, in Mexico City in 1975, pointed out that women's basic needs had been ignored and marginalized. Pledges to include females in policy planning and implementation abounded.

In the 1980s, development theory emphasized general economic growth for developing countries, so integrating women into the global economy was supposed to resolve their poverty and hunger. Local people – both women and men – often had little say in the processes which so dramatically affected their lives.

By the end of the U.N.'s First Women's Decade in 1985, a global recession had worsened women's condition. Women in developing countries began to conceive alternate strategies for progress. They shifted from seeing women as marginalized pawns in men's world to recognizing women as key, albeit barely visible, players in every social and economic sphere. Funding was provided for income generation projects and farming groups. Groups like Development Alternatives with Women for a New Era (DAWN) were founded by women, mostly from the South, concerned with new ways of viewing old problems. Western development theorists shifted too, with an increasing emphasis on economic empowerment of poor women through means such as credit to start small businesses.

In 1985, the third U.N. Conference on Women in Nairobi established Forward-Looking Strategies to advance the status of women in government, employment, and education. Re-evaluated goals are to guide the Platform of Action at the fourth Conference on Women in Beijing in 1995. Eight critical areas of concern are:

- Poverty,

- Access to education,

- Power-sharing,

- Commitment to women's rights,

- Health and employment,

- Effects of armed conflict,

- Economic participation, and

- Violence against women.

Recent interest in microenterprise, community building, and empowerment has led many development workers to recognize women as the backbone of families and communities and as central to sustainable development efforts.

Approaches to Gender and Development

Improving Farms in Kenya

Women in rural Africa produce, process, and store up to 80 percent of the food for consumption. Yet development officials have repeatedly failed to include women in the planning and implementation of projects intended to alleviate hunger and improve health. For example, new technology in the form of tractors and improved animal-powered equipment were targeted at male farmers as "primary providers." While these technological advances lightened the workload for men and allowed them to acquire more land, women's work actually increased because they were forced to work more land using the same time-intensive hand labor techniques as in the past.

Patriarchal structures often prevent women from having control over resources. In Africa and many other parts of the world, a woman's access to land is determined by her marital status and the number of sons she has. Likewise, access to credit often requires permission from either a husband or adult son.

Kenya has a population of about 24 million, with a growth rate of 3.9 percent a year, one of the highest in the world. Eighty percent of Kenyans depend on their small farms to feed themselves and their family. Over the past 10 years the government has encouraged replacing sorghum and millet with corn, which can be eaten by the farm family or exported for income.

Women in rural Africa produce, process, and store up to 80 percent of the food for consumption.

Figure 6.2
Breaking Out of the Cycle of Despair

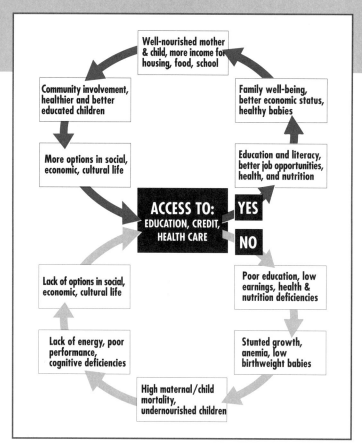

Corn is less nutritious than either millet or sorghum, and more dependent on regular rainfall. Droughts, such as the one that occurred during 1983-1984, can cause serious declines in production, increasing malnutrition. Women are often the most seriously affected when there is a shortfall.

A program in Kenya trains women farmers to make the most of their crops. The National Extension Project of the International Fund for Agricultural Development (IFAD) has an outreach system to advise hundreds of farmers about new technologies and resources. The Nandi District has more than one hundred extension workers, each responsible for several hundred farmers, including women.

As a result of such training, many women farmers in Kenya and other parts of Africa have learned to grow such crops as finger millet, cabbages, and bananas in addition to corn. This produces a surplus often sold at the market for extra income or traded for various other foods for the family.

Programs such as the National Extension Project use existing village work groups to spread knowledge. Since Kenyan women frequently form such teams for agricultural and other enterprises, the groups are a valuable vehicle for information sharing.

It pays to focus on women. The World Bank reports that crop yields in Kenya were 2.8 times higher for female than male farmers in the same program.

Empowering Women in Bolivia

Bolivia is a landlocked country in South America with a population of about 7 million people. Over 70 percent (4.7 million) of the population is made up of Indians, the Aymara and Quechua groups being the largest. More than 40 percent of the total population lacks access to running water, health care, and proper nutrition.

About 850,000 Bolivians receive donated food, mainly from the government, but provided through U.S. nongovernmental organizations (NGOs) and financed by the U.S. government. Ironically, these donations may have contributed to increased malnutrition. White bread and noodles have replaced more nutritious whole grain counterparts as staples for poor populations. Wheat, once a native crop, has now reached an annual deficit of 170,000 metric tons as a result of food donations that date back to 1954.

Saddled with the sole responsibility for providing food for the family, Bolivian wives and mothers join food clubs or do heavy manual labor in exchange for food. But many of these food aid programs have fostered dependency, promoted corruption, and undermined community development efforts. Many husbands will not allow their wives to join literacy and health programs unless they bring home food.

In 1989, more than four thousand Bolivian women traveled to the capital of La Paz to protest food aid programs that fostered dependency and corruption. Their demand to change government and food distribution agencies' policies resulted in new approaches like Pro Mujer, a private nonprofit agency. Pro Mujer addresses the needs of Bolivia's poorest women by focusing on education, maternal and child health, income generation, and empowerment. Each month, 1,300 women participate in Pro Mujer's five month training cycles.

Education of Females in Pakistan

Of 850 million adult illiterates worldwide, more than 60 percent are women. Education is an important and effective method for increasing women's status and helping them lift themselves out of poverty and hunger. Studies have shown that increases in female basic education can improve primary health care, decrease infant mortality rates, and improve crop yields.

The Primary Education Program (PEP) in Baluchistan Province, Pakistan, is a good example of an organization that offers resources to women. Surveys in 1990 and 1991 showed a desire and need for more girls' schools and female teachers in rural communities. With support from UNICEF, PEP established a mobile unit to train new women teachers. In each village, community education promoters identified prospective female teachers and formed a village education committee of parents of school-age girls. The committees agreed to take responsibility for seeing that the teachers were trained and paid, for donated land and a school building, and for monitoring the students' progress. By November 1993, 122 girls' primary schools had been established, more than 4,000 girls were studying in them, and 200 female teachers were working. In addition, a newly created local NGO had assumed responsibility for the program. More important, government policymakers were now committed to community-based girls' education.[6]

Conclusion

Gender discrimination affects poor and hungry women in various and far-reaching ways. Likewise, a new perspective on hunger and poverty issues that takes gender into account can have a variety of positive long-term and sustainable results. The recognition that women have always been and will continue to be key players at every level of society is crucial. Their work is vital to human survival.

Women worldwide need access to education and other resources. The best way to learn the specific needs of poor and hungry women is to ask them. They generally respond that their priorities relate to improved income earning capacity and developing effective organizations. African women are particularly interested in credit and land titles, as well as agricultural training and development of improved tools, which could save hours of a woman's work day. Latin America's top priorities, as cited by the region's women, are empowerment of women's grassroots organizations, employment creation, and access to credit. The main priorities for the women of Asia include employment creation and support of community organizations. The three critical needs for women in industrialized countries are: completion of at least a secondary education, opportunities for upwardly mobile employment, and affordable child care.

The injustice of gender discrimination affects every woman, man, and child on earth. By ignoring women's roles, decisionmakers seriously handicap their work and undermine progress. In order to rectify age-old social problems, such as hunger, poverty, ignorance, war, and resource mismanagement, women and men must work together as equals toward solutions. ∎

A. Cecilia Snyder is research associate at BFW Institute.

In order to rectify age-old social problems . . . women and men must work together as equals toward solutions.

Vulnerability and Age

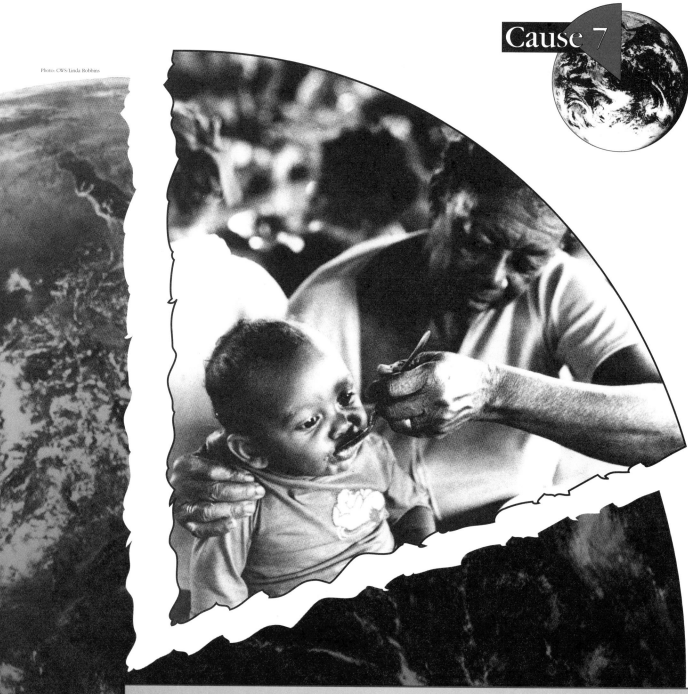

Photo: CWS/Linda Robbins

Children and elderly people are disproportionately vulnerable to hunger and malnutrition in both industrial and developing countries.

Part One: Children
by Urban Jonsson

Malnutrition causes permanent mental and physical damage to young children, limiting their potential as adults. This chapter outlines the conditions necessary for adequate nutrition, confirming that the barriers to eradicating child malnutrition are political, rather than scientific. Citizens need to urge their political leaders to commit resources to achieving the goals of the 1990 World Summit for Children.

Introduction[1]

Child malnutrition strikes silently and unnoticed – not seen on television. Yet it is the world's most profound nutritional emergency, stunting the mental and physical growth of one in three children in the developing world. Low-income children in the industrial world are also vulnerable to hunger (see "Hungry Children in the United States," pp. 95-96).

Only one or two percent of the world's children exhibit visible signs of malnutrition. But tens of millions of children under age five are chronically malnourished, prone to illness and poor development. In the developing world, many poor households run short of food between harvests, or amid drought and war.

Most malnourished children live in homes with adequate food. Specific problems such as low birthweight (which usually results from poor nutrition during pregnancy) and practices such as bottle-feeding in the absence of clean water or the income to afford enough formula contribute heavily to malnutrition. The main cause, however, is illness – especially diarrhea – that thrives in poor communities lacking clean water and sanitation. Chronic poor health saps children of nutrients.

When nourishment runs low, the body makes compromises. Virtually the only outward sign is sluggishness, as the body struggles to conserve energy. Undernourished children stand rather than run and play, sit rather than stand, lie instead of sit. To compensate for fewer nutrients, metabolic rates drop. Blood pressure sinks. If fat is low, the body borrows from reserves, depleting muscle and slowing or deforming bone growth.

Malnutrition invisibly amplifies the worst consequences of illness. Mildly malnourished children are twice as likely to die of disease, and moderately malnourished children are three times as likely. Malnutrition is a factor in one third of the 13 million annual deaths of children under five. Good nutrition, on the other hand, is excellent armor against disease.

Malnutrition strikes hardest in the last trimester of pregnancy and during the first year of life. Poorly nourished mothers tend to bear underweight babies – malnourished in the womb and likely to remain so in crucial early years. During infancy, tiny stomachs require constant feeding, brain development is nearing completion, and fledgling immune systems are weakest.

A child suffering malnutrition before her or his first birthday is likely to suffer below-normal growth even if nutrition improves thereafter. This affects physical and mental development, and means that children will never achieve their full potential to contribute to the life of their communities and nations.

Prevalence and Trends

The proportion of malnourished children under five in the developing world declined

A child suffering malnutrition before her or his first birthday is likely to suffer below-normal growth even if nutrition improves thereafter.

Hungry Children in the United States

by Marc J. Cohen

The United States could eliminate child hunger if the federal government fully funded social programs that are already in place and have demonstrated their effectiveness. Ironically, there is less information available about hunger among U.S. children than there is about child malnutrition in many developing countries. Bread for the World has advocated a U.S. national nutrition monitoring system, but this system is only now being designed and established.

Despite the limited data, researchers at Tufts University estimated in 1993 that 12 million U.S. children under 18 are hungry. Almost 4 million poor children suffer from iron deficiency anemia.

Over 37 million people, including 8 million children, lack health insurance, which contributes directly to nutrition problems by making children more susceptible to diseases such as measles. Also, low-income uninsured children are vulnerable to hunger because their families often must choose among food, medical care, shelter, clothing, utilities, or education. And, hungry children are two to three times more likely to experience health problems. The United States is the world's wealthiest nation, but 27 countries have a lower incidence of low birthweight babies and 20 have lower infant mortality rates.

Nearly 22 percent of U.S. children under 18 (14.6 million children) lived in poverty in 1992, at risk of hunger. This is double the child poverty rate of any other industrial country. Children are 40 percent of all poor people. Families with children make up 31 percent of the homeless population, extremely vulnerable to hunger, compared to 21 percent in the early 1980s.

Canada, Australia, and the United Kingdom also have high child poverty rates (about 10 percent). In the United Kingdom, the proportion of families living in poverty doubled between 1979 and 1986. France, Germany, the Netherlands, and Sweden have child poverty rates of 5 percent or less because of tax and child benefit policies.

The problem of full funding of U.S. government nutrition and child assistance programs is well illustrated by the Special Supplemental Food Program for Women, Infants, and Children (WIC). It provides nutritious food, health screening, and nutrition education to low-income, nutritionally vulnerable pregnant and nursing mothers

from 42 percent in 1975 to 34 percent in 1990. This is remarkable progress, but the number of malnourished children rose from 168 million to 184 million during the same period due to population growth.[2] For many of these children, the immediate cause is insufficient protein and calories.

Vitamin and mineral deficiencies also have a severe impact. Each year, the IQs of 1.2 million children of iodine deficient mothers are reduced by 10 points. At least 30,000 babies are stillborn, and over 120,000 are cretins – mentally retarded, physically stunted, deaf-mute, vision impaired, or paralyzed. The United Nations Children's Fund (UNICEF) reports:

Even when born normal, young children whose diets are low in iodine are held back by reduced intelligence, and live out their lives trapped in mental dullness and apathy. In this way the lack of iodine locks entire communities into poverty and underdevelopment, less able to learn in their childhood, less able to earn in their adulthood.[3]

Inadequate vitamin A causes progressive eye damage, eventually leading to blindness. In 1991, 14 million pre-school children suffered such damage. Every year, 250,000 to 500,000 preschool children go blind as a result; two-thirds die within a few months. Even mild vitamin A deficiency increases the risk of death from infections by 20 percent. About 190 million preschool children are at risk of vitamin A deficiency.

Iron deficiency anemia is the most common form of malnutrition in developing countries. It reduces school children's learning capabilities and increases susceptibility to infections and lead poisoning.

Overcoming Child Malnutrition

Complex biological and social processes determine nutritional status. Inadequate or unbalanced diets and disease are the immediate causes of malnutrition. Poor diets increase vulnerability to infection and its severity. At the same time, many diseases – especially childhood diseases such as measles – cause loss of appetite and ability to absorb nutrients.

Four conditions are necessary for adequate nutrition, that is, for sufficient dietary intake and the absence of disease:

- Access to an adequate quantity and quality of food to fulfill all nutritional requirements for all household members throughout the year (household food security);

- Adequate care of children and mothers;

- Access to basic health services; and

- A healthy environment.

Each is necessary, but by itself not sufficient. If all are fulfilled, children are likely to have satisfactory diets and health. Each condition depends on resource availability, control, and use. Communication (advocacy, information, education, and training) strongly influences resource use.

The importance of adequate maternal and child care for nutrition has only recently been fully recognized. Care involves breastfeeding and related feeding practices, food and personal hygiene, diagnosing illness, stimulating language and other cognitive capabilities, and providing emotional support. Family or community support also plays a vital role.

Needed health services include pre- and post-natal care, immunization, oral rehydration therapy (providing a mixture of water, sugar, and salt to prevent life-threat-

and children from birth to age five. According to Katrina Smith, a 27-year-old mother with two children enrolled in the program:

WIC helped me understand how to shop wisely. We learned how to select the cheapest and most nutritious foods. WIC taught me that buying in bulk allows my dollars to stretch, as well as clipping coupons to cut my overall food costs.

WIC spending is highly cost-effective because it reduces future federal health care expenditures. Yet 40 percent of those eligible to participate cannot for lack of government funding. Bread for the World made full funding of WIC its chief 1994 legislative priority.

Similarly, Head Start, which provides early childhood education and food to low-income children, and Job Corps, which trains low-income youth for employment, do not receive enough funds to enroll everyone eligible. Many schools choose not to participate in the School Lunch and Breakfast Programs, even though these play a critical role in meeting nutritional needs of many low-income children and facilitate learning.

A permanent solution to hunger in the United States will also require enhanced job training programs and a national commitment to full employment at wages that lift people out of poverty.

Until the appropriate policies are implemented, citizens must press to assure that the U.S. government keeps its promise to give children "first call." ∎

Dr. Marc J. Cohen is senior research associate at BFW Institute and editor of *Causes of Hunger*.

ening dehydration due to diarrhea), vitamin and mineral supplements, de-worming, family planning, and health education.

Finally, the most important features of a healthy environment are access to clean water and safe sewage systems, which allow control of diarrhea and other diseases.

Successful recent efforts to reduce child malnutrition have reflected an emerging new approach to development which recognizes poor people as key actors in poverty reduction, rather than passive aid recipients. This approach sees development

Photo: IAF

munity empowerment to create bottom-up demand for support from higher levels. Emphasis should be given to improving often neglected caring practices. These include breastfeeding and other feeding practices, hygiene practices, and cognitive stimulation. The role of women is critical, and actions should be environmentally sustainable.

- **Promote service delivery and capacity building** for empowerment. For example, distribution of vitamin A supplements through the health system should encompass training on how to grow and use vitamin A-rich foods. This should be done in combination with efforts to ensure access to land.

- **A nutrition information strategy** is necessary to make the other strategies work. Education and advocacy can encourage decision-makers at all levels to want and demand good information. When mothers understand the connection between nutrition and child development, they get involved in monitoring their children's growth. When decision-makers demand nutrition information, it becomes worthwhile to establish a nutrition surveillance system.

One example of these strategies in action is the UNICEF-financed health center in Yemessoa, Cameroon, Central Africa. Open 24 hours, it provides children with vaccinations daily, and has adequate supplies of affordable medicines for common ailments such as malaria and acute respiratory infections. Thanks to the prenatal care offered, the village virtually eliminated women's deaths from pregnancy and birth-related complications. More important, the community runs the facility. Comments Celestin Ngba, a Yemessoa resident, "Before our community took over the management of the center, the place was almost

> The proportion of malnourished children under five in the developing world declined from 42 percent in 1975 to 34 percent in 1990 . . . but the number of malnourished children rose from 168 million to 184 million during the same period due to population growth.

achieved through learning rather than blueprints, and encourages participation, decentralization, and effective communication. Four sets of strategies are associated with success and should be encouraged elsewhere:

- **Build consensus at all levels** on the causes of malnutrition. Internationally, the United Nations Subcommittee on Nutrition is facilitating this process. National nutrition policies should include salt iodization, regulation of the marketing of breastmilk substitutes, and universal access to health and education. Consensus building must seek increased awareness of malnutrition and its causes, and should make good nutrition good politics for leaders.

- **The "Triple A" strategy** is essential: strengthen the capacity of communities and their leaders to *assess* and *analyze* nutrition problems and design and implement affordable *actions*. People do not live at the national level, but in communities. Top-down nutrition policies should foster capacity building and com-

abandoned and there were never enough medicines." This sense of ownership is critical to sustaining the well-being of children and communities.

Keeping the Promise

The United Nations sponsored the World Summit for Children in 1990, an unprecedented gathering of leaders from developing and industrialized countries. Its declaration, signed by 157 heads of state and government, and the Convention on the Rights of the Child, ratified by 156 governments, form "social contracts" between the world's political leaders and its children. The goals, to be achieved by the year 2000, include:

- Halving of severe and moderate malnutrition among children under five;

- Reduction of low birthweight to less than 10 percent;

- A one-third reduction in iron deficiency anemia among women;

- Virtual elimination of vitamin A and iodine deficiency disorders;

- Making all families aware of the importance of supporting women in the task of exclusive breastfeeding for the first four to six months of a child's life (with breastfeeding continued well into the second year with appropriate complementary diet) and of meeting the special feeding needs of a young child through the vulnerable years;

- Institutionalization of growth monitoring; and

- Education on household food security.

The Summit goals represent a moral consensus supported by most religions and differing political ideologies. Political leaders and governments need to keep the promises of the Summit. This requires "a first call on resources for children." Countries are used to being compared for their economic development. Now the time has come to compare how they take care of their children.

Progress on Meeting the Summit's Goals

South Asia's rate of child malnutrition remains the world's highest, almost double that of sub-Saharan Africa, and South Asia is home to over half the developing world's undernourished children. But in Africa, unlike any other region, child malnutrition trends remained static or deteriorated during the 1980s. The picture is brighter in much of Southeast Asia, where child nutrition is improving rapidly because of effective public policies and considerable economic development.

Countries can be grouped according to their level of commitment to deal with child malnutrition. Fewer than 10 percent of the children are malnourished in such countries as Chile, Egypt, Swaziland, and Malaysia. Another group, including Thailand, Tanzania, and Zimbabwe, is on target to meet the World Summit for Children goal of reducing malnutrition due to inadequate protein and calories 50 percent by the year 2000. Some populous countries, such as Bangladesh, India, and China, have effective nutrition strategies, but lack resources for implementation. The fourth category is countries which have no clear strategy due to lack of national consensus on the causes of the problem, such as Ethiopia, Nigeria, and Nepal. Finally, some countries are unlikely to meet the goal because of war or civil strife, e.g., Angola, Haiti, Rwanda, and Sudan.

Large scale programs in both India and Africa have shown that the Summit's ambitious goal of halving child malnutrition is eminently feasible. Even in the midst of an economic crisis, Tanzania's community-based Iringa nutrition program has more than halved the rate of severe malnutrition in three years. The initial cost was $16 a child in 1984. Now it is $2.50 per child as the program goes nationwide.

Some progress has been made on vitamin and mineral deficiency goals. Many nations have begun to use child immunization systems to distribute vitamin A capsules, including Bangladesh, Brazil, India, Malawi, and the Philippines. The Indonesian government

recently reported that the Social Marketing of Vitamin A (SOMAVITA) project has increased nationwide consumption of capsules from 16 percent to 50 percent.[4]

At the urging of UNICEF and the World Health Organization, nearly 80 developing countries have banned the free or subsidized distribution of infant formula to new mothers in hospitals and maternity clinics. Exclusive breastfeeding of infants reduces illness and death and saves money.

Oral rehydration therapy (ORT) prevents more than a million children from dying of dehydration due to diarrheal disease each year; but more than three million children under age five still die annually from this condition.[5]

The Need for Public Involvement

Citizens must monitor progress and urge the commitment of resources to achieve the Summit goals. In countries such as the United States, which have not yet ratified the Convention on the Rights of the Child, citizen action is especially crucial. Gradually the information from these efforts will contribute to increasing global embarrassment for countries that have resources but avoid necessary political choices to achieve the goals. This will help make it good politics to ensure the rights of all children and bad politics to deny children their rights.

If the public in both developing and industrial countries insists that governments keep their promises, progress will continue. The future of humanity depends upon it. ∎

Dr. Urban Jonsson is director of UNICEF's South Asia Regional Office in Kathmandu, Nepal.

**Figure 7.1
The Causes of Child
Malnutrition –
A Conceptual
Framework**

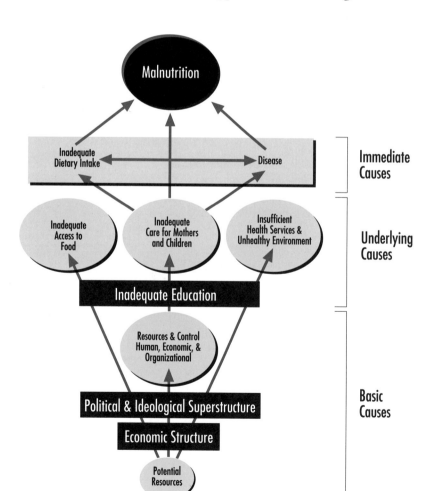

Part Two: Elderly People

by Jashinta D'Costa

Elderly people are disproportionately vulnerable to hunger and malnutrition in both industrial and developing countries. Two types of aging, "biological" and "sociogenic" (based on the role that society imposes on people as they age), interact to create the problems for elderly people. To end hunger among elderly people we must establish public policies that ensure their overall well-being. As we work for these policies, we must also remember that there is no substitute for family care.

Clotario Blest died a broken, forgotten old man. For years he had lived alone in a miserable boarding house. Just before his death, Franciscan priests found him and took him from the squalor of his room to the pristine quiet of their monastery. They tried to restore some weight to his 90-pound frame, but he had been neglected too long.[1]

Millions of the world's elderly people (those over 60 years old) live alone, overlooked by society. People live longer on average than in the past, but many elderly people are in poor physical or mental health and lack access to recreational and welfare facilities. They are disproportionately vulnerable to hunger and malnutrition in both industrial and developing countries.

In developing countries, numerous older people consume fewer calories than required for good health. Lack of social security programs contributes to their vulnerability.

Photo: Church World Service

- In Bangladesh, 85 percent of older workers consume less than 2,000 calories per day;

- In Latin America and the Caribbean, elderly people are less healthy than younger people and are at higher risk of illness, poverty, unemployment, and social isolation. Elderly men generally have better diets than women. One study documented mineral deficiencies and nutritional imbalances; another found prematurely aged people in Chile due to low income, deficient nutrition, poor environmental and sanitary conditions, and inadequate health care;[2] and

This elderly woman in the war-torn former Soviet territory of Nagorno-Karabakh was left without family and is cared for at an old people's home.

Vulnerability and Age

In developing countries, numerous older people consume fewer calories than required for good health.

- A study of elderly people in August Town, Jamaica, found that 51 percent of the females and 13 percent of the males were undernourished.[3]

Despite many sources of income in old age and the political influence of senior citizen organizations, hunger also persists among elderly people in the United States. Many low-income elderly people cannot afford an adequate diet or do not have access to stores with inexpensive and nutritious food. Many lack awareness of government assistance programs. Food insecurity is greatest among elderly minority people.

- Estimates of the proportion of elderly people in the United States with inadequate diets range from 8 percent to 16 percent (2.5 million to 4.9 million people);

- In a study of 10 industrial countries, the United States had the third highest elderly poverty rate following the United Kingdom and Israel;[4]

- Thirteen percent of aged people in the United States live below the poverty level of $6,729. The figure is 33 percent among older African Americans, compared to 11 percent for the elderly whites. Many elderly people who are not officially poor suffer from malnutrition;

- Elderly Hispanics have the highest rate of food insecurity, followed by African Americans; and

- One study suggests that 30 percent to 40 percent of elderly people in hospitals and nursing homes suffer from malnutrition.

The aging of the world's population is one of the most significant contemporary demographic changes. Worldwide, there are 513 million people aged 60 or over, accounting for 9 percent of global population, and the proportion is rising. Providing the care and support they need – including adequate food and opportunities to continue contributing to society – poses a growing challenge to individuals, families, and governments in rich and poor countries alike.

Global Perspective

The health and well-being of any age group depend in part on health, social, and educational policies. The nutritional status of elderly people also depends on cultural beliefs and practices, age, degree of social integration, extent of physical mobility, economic situation, and health. Both government and the family play important roles. The state can provide health care and social security, and the family offers crucial emotional support. Medical advances have increased longevity. But modernization has brought increases in average income and greater emphasis on productivity, which often leaves older people out of the mainstream:

> *In an industrialized society where self-sufficiency means survival, the older generation hopes to be independent and not to be a burden to their children. Other cultures that are close to the earth cycles regard aging as a natural process. Older is better. Maturity comes with age. The cycle of life moves from childhood, adolescence, adulthood, and finally to the maturity and wisdom of old age.[5]*

Economic development has also led to other social and cultural changes that create problems for elderly people. As a result of urbanization:

- The traditional extended family declines. This has often led to the abandonment of elderly people.

- Lifestyles change among both young and older people, as younger people move to cities and travel to work or school.

- Occupational mobility increases, sometimes placing parents and children in different social and cultural classes and creating a "generation gap."

- Industrial employment increases. This leads to a decline in agricultural employment and often entails a mandatory retirement age.

The decay of relationships, due mainly to geographical distance between family members, affects the mental health of elderly people who remain behind in the countryside. Urban elderly people likewise face increasing isolation:

Large cities throughout the world are becoming catchalls for many aged people who are homeless and unable to care for their own nutritional and health needs.[6]

For example, when Aboriginal Australians received citizenship rights in the late 1960s, this accelerated their urbanization, dependence on welfare, westernized diets, loss of hunter-gatherer skills, and increasingly sedentary lifestyles. They experienced increased incidence of diabetes and heart disease, and Aboriginal life expectancy decreased to 20 years less than that of whites. Elderly Aborigines receive weekly pension payments on Fridays. They consume most of their food during the weekend, and this binge eating causes nutritional imbalances.[7]

Inadequate policies and institutions also cause hunger. In the industrialized world, publicly-funded economic support systems are the main source of income for many elderly citizens. In most developed nations, there are also private pensions.

In the developing world, however, such systems are often rudimentary. Several

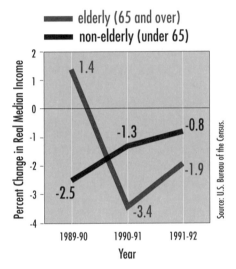

Figure 7.2
Change in Real Median Income of U.S. Elderly and Non-Elderly Households, 1989-1992

— elderly (65 and over)
— non-elderly (under 65)

Percent Change in Real Median Income

1.4
-1.3
-0.8
-2.5
-3.4
-1.9

1989-90   1990-91   1991-92
Year

Source: U.S. Bureau of the Census.

countries have some form of social security, but it is available to only a very small fraction of the population, and benefit levels are very low. In Africa, coverage is almost nonexistent, limited to wage-earners, who form a small portion of the labor force. Most Asian and Middle Eastern countries do not have coverage for agricultural workers, but India, Malaysia, and Turkey are exceptions.

Austerity programs in severely indebted developing countries have adversely affected elderly people. In Ghana, tighter government budgets still allow tax exemptions for child care but not for elder care.

War causes critical problems for elderly people, who often flee to refugee and displaced persons' camps or remain in their villages without the comfort of family or adequate food. Their less aggressive attitude and generally weaker physical condition restrain them from competing for food. Because of their marginal economic role, elderly people are sometimes left to fend for themselves when other family members are killed. This happened in Mozambique, where an elderly man reported, "The rebels did not take me because I'm too old."[8] Elderly people are sometimes left behind to starve slowly. Yet, it is elderly people who preserve traditional culture in times of war and social upheaval. They are the "national soul."[9]

Isolation often contributes to hunger among elderly people. They eat alone and cannot visit others easily. They may receive few, if any, visitors. In the United States, inadequate food intake is not always associated with insufficient money. Lack of motivation and cooking skills, as well as mental health problems, lead to malnutrition among elderly men, especially those who live and eat alone.

Public Policies

The solution to persistent hunger among elderly people lies in appropriate public policies to ensure their well-being. Two types of aging, "biological" and "sociogenic," acting together in varying degrees, depending on the circumstances, are responsible for the problems confronting aged people.[10] Policies cannot reverse biological aging, i.e., decreased visual, hearing, and physical capabilities. But policies can address sociogenic aging, the role that society imposes on people as they age. Prejudices contribute to sociogenic aging.

Policies cannot simply be replicated across countries. Effective policies must address cultural diversity, level of economic development, and resource availability. The success of any plan requires cooperative efforts of individuals, private institutions, and governments. Policies can secure and keep up the individual's spirit, transforming elderly people's despair into dignity.

On the basis of cultural heritage and economic conditions, governments of developing countries need to provide support to strengthen the family tie. Malaysia's government welfare program provides monthly cash assistance to families caring for older, needy relatives. To discourage the erosion of family values, the government ceased building old age institutions.

But as the number of childless elderly people increases, developing country governments need to establish institutional care. Such care is expensive, but will be necessary, given demographic trends.

Constructive policies can reverse the negative consequences of modernization: Taiwan has high rates of economic activity and prosperity among elderly people who work in agriculture and light industry.

Industrial countries have a large proportion of older people and a relatively small number of youth. This leads to greater costs for institutional care. Experts are suggesting more family care in these countries as well.

Social Security and Medicare have dramatically reduced poverty and hunger among the U.S. elderly population. Food stamps and the elderly feeding program also help reduce hunger. But this safety net needs to be strengthened. Social Security is threatened by the desire of some policy makers to reduce cost-of-living adjustments to shrink the federal budget deficit; if there is cost-cutting, low-income recipients should be protected. Funding for Senior Nutrition Programs has decreased. Inaccurate assumptions about poverty make many low-income seniors ineligible for government food programs. Small businesses, which employ nearly half of U.S. workers, provide pensions to only 20 percent of their employees.

Conclusion

Factors such as urbanization, modernization, and war all play key roles in the vulnerability of elderly people. Public policies can reduce their vulnerability.

And there is no substitute for family care to provide familiar surroundings, love and emotional ties, and a sense of belonging and feeling wanted. Despite the difficulties of keeping our "loving, caring relationships when [one has] the emotions of hunger, anger, and desperation," it is still possible to make a difference regarding our respect, love, and care for the elderly.[11]

On All Souls day, while I was lighting candles at my father's grave in Bangladesh, a feeble voice surprised me by asking, "Could you please give me a candle?" I turned to see a boy who was about 10 years old. Following his eyes, I saw a grave, lying dark in the middle of hundreds of illuminated graves. What has that little penniless boy taught us? Is it not love?

Dr. Souheil Odeh, after 11 years, finished his undergraduate and graduate studies and went back home, leaving his $4,000 per month U.S. engineering job behind to accept $700 a month in Jordan. The sense of responsibility for taking care of older parents who are in their late 70s, who took care of him throughout his life, moved his heart to join them in their time of greatest need. This unspoken rule needs to be pronounced in every heart and underlie public policies on aging. ∎

Jashinta D'Costa is a BFW Institute volunteer.

Photo: Catholic Charities

There is no substitute for family care.

Appendix

Table 1: Global Demographic Indicators

	Population (millions) 1994	Population (millions) 2010	Population annual growth rate 1990-92 (%)	Total Fertility rate 1992	Percent Age <15 1994	Percent Age 65+ 1994	Percent of population urbanized 1994	Life expectancy at birth (years)	Infant mortality rate (under 1) per 1,000 live births 1994	Under 5 mortality rate per 1,000 live births 1960	Under 5 mortality rate per 1,000 live births 1992	Maternal mortality rate per 100,000 live births 1980-91
Developing Countries												
Africa (sub-Saharan)												
Total	570.0	901.0	..	6.5	46	3	27	52	..	..	..	..
Angola	11.2	17.6	2.9	7.2	45	3	28	46	170	345	292	..
Benin	5.3	8.4	2.9	7.1	47	3	38	46	88	310	147	160
Botswana	1.4	2.1	3.1	5.2	48	3	26	62	45	170	58	250
Burkina Faso	10.1	15.5	2.6	6.5	48	4	21	48	101	318	150	810
Burundi	6.0	9.1	2.9	6.8	46	4	6	48	108	255	179	..
Cameroon	13.1	21.2	2.9	5.8	45	3	41	56	74	264	117	430
Cape Verde	0.4	0.6	..	4.4	44	5	44	68	40	164	61	..
Central African Republic	3.1	3.9	2.6	6.2	43	3	47	44	105	294	179	600
Chad	6.5	9.8	2.2	5.9	41	3	32	48	123	325	209	960
Comoros	0.5	0.9	..	7.1	48	3	28	56	..	..	..	..
Congo	2.4	3.2	2.9	6.3	44	3	41	49	82	220	110	900
Côte d'Ivoire	13.9	23.7	3.8	7.4	47	2	39	52	91	300	124	..
Djibouti	0.6	0.9	..	6.6	41	2	77	49	..	..	..	..
Equatorial Guinea	0.4	0.6	..	5.9	43	4	37	51	..	..	..	..
Eritrea	3.5	5.4	..	..	..	..	..	..	123	294	208	..
Ethiopia	55.2	89.0	2.6	7.0	49	3	15	52	123	294	208	560x
Gabon	1.1	1.4	3.6	5.2	33	6	46	54	95	287	158	190
Gambia	1.1	1.5	..	6.2	45	2	26	45	95	..	158	190
Ghana	16.9	26.6	3.3	6.1	45	3	34	56	103	215	170	1,000
Guinea	6.4	9.3	2.6	7.0	44	3	26	43	135	337	230	800
Guinea-Bissau	1.1	1.5	2.0	5.8	43	3	20	44	141	336	239	700x
Kenya	27.0	44.4	3.5	6.4	49	2	25	59	51	202	74	170x
Lesotho	1.9	2.8	2.6	4.8	41	4	19	61	108	204	156	..
Liberia	2.9	4.8	3.2	6.8	45	4	43	55	146	288	217	..
Madagascar	13.7	22.4	3.2	6.6	45	3	22	56	110	364	168	570
Malawi	9.5	14.7	4.3	7.6	48	3	17	44	143	365	226	400
Mali	9.1	15.0	3.0	7.1	46	4	22	45	122	400	220	2,000
Mauritania	2.3	3.5	2.7	6.5	44	4	39	48	118	321	206	..
Mauritius	1.1	1.3	1.1	2.0	30	5	39	69	20	84	24	99
Mozambique	15.8	25.4	1.7	6.5	44	3	27	47	167	331	287	300
Namibia	1.6	2.6	3.0	6.0	45	3	33	59	62	206	79	370x
Niger	8.8	14.3	3.3	7.1	49	3	15	47	191	320	320	700
Nigeria	98.1	162.0	3.2	6.6	45	3	16	54	114	204	191	800

	Population (millions) 1994	Population (millions) 2010	Population annual growth rate 1990-92 (%)	Total Fertility rate 1992	Percent Age <15 1994	Percent Age 65+ 1994	Percent of population urbanized 1994	Life expectancy at birth (years)	Infant mortality rate (under 1) per 1,000 live births 1994	Under 5 mortality rate per 1,000 live births 1960	Under 5 mortality rate per 1,000 live births 1992	Maternal mortality rate per 100,000 live births 1980-91
Rwanda	7.7	10.4	3.1	8.5	48	3	5	46	131	191	222	210
Senegal	8.2	12.4	2.8	6.2	47	3	39	49	90	303	145	600
Sierra Leone	4.6	6.9	2.5	6.5	45	3	32	43	144	385	249	450
Somalia	9.8	15.9	2.6	7.0	47	3	24	47	125	294	211	1,100
South Africa	41.2	58.4	2.5	4.2	39	4	57	65	53	126	70	84x
Sudan	28.2	43.0	3.0	6.2	46	2	23	53	100	292	166	550
Swaziland	0.8	1.3	..	5.0	47	3	23	56	..	..	..	..
Tanzania	29.8	48.4	3.4	6.8	47	3	21	51	111	249	176	340x
Togo	4.3	7.4	3.0	6.6	49	2	29	56	86	264	137	420
Uganda	19.8	30.7	2.9	7.3	47	3	11	42	111	218	185	300
Zaire	42.5	68.6	3.3	6.7	45	3	40	52	121	286	188	800
Zambia	9.1	13.9	3.4	6.5	48	2	49	44	113	220	202	150
Zimbabwe	11.2	16.8	3.3	5.5	48	3	27	56	60	181	86	..

South Asia

Afghanistan	17.8	34.7	1.4	6.9	46	4	18	42	165	360	257	640
Bangladesh	116.6	164.8	2.5	4.8	44	3	14	53	97	247	127	600
Bhutan	0.8	1.1	2.2	5.9	39	4	13	49	131	324	201	1,310
India	911.6	1,163.3	2.0	4.0	36	4	26	57	83	236	124	460
Nepal	22.1	32.3	2.7	5.6	44	3	8	51	90	279	128	830
Pakistan	126.4	191.1	3.2	6.3	44	3	28	60	95	221	137	500
Sri Lanka	17.9	21.0	1.5	2.5	35	4	22	73	15	130	19	80

East Asia and the Pacific

Burma (Myanmar)	45.4	59.2	2.1	4.3	36	4	25	59	83	237	113	460
Cambodia	10.3	15.7	2.5	4.5	44	3	13	49	117	217	184	500
China	1,192.0	1,376.1	1.5	2.3	28	6	28	70	35	209	43	95
Fiji	0.8	0.9	..	3.0	38	3	39	64	..	..	..	..
Hong Kong	5.8	6.3	1.2	1.4	21	9	..	78	6	52	7	6
Indonesia	199.7	250.3	2.0	3.2	37	4	31	60	71	216	111	450
Korea, N.	23.1	28.5	1.8	2.4	29	4	60	69	25	120	33	41
Korea, S.	44.5	49.7	1.2	1.7	24	5	74	71	8	124	9	26
Laos	4.7	7.2	2.8	6.7	45	4	19	51	98	233	145	300
Malaysia	19.5	26.6	2.6	3.7	36	4	51	71	14	105	19	59
Mongolia	2.4	3.5	2.7	4.7	44	4	57	65	61	185	80	140
Papua New Guinea	4.0	5.7	2.3	5.0	40	4	13	55	54	248	77	900
Philippines	68.7	89.3	2.4	4.0	39	4	44	64	46	102	60	100
Singapore	2.9	3.3	1.1	1.7	23	6	100	74	6	40	7	10
Solomon Islands	0.4	0.6	..	5.5	47	3	13	61	..	..	..	..
Thailand	59.4	68.8	1.5	2.3	29	5	19	69	27	146	33	50
Vietnam	73.1	91.7	2.2	4.0	39	5	21	65	37	219	49	120

Latin America and the Caribbean

Total	470.0	584.0	..	..	36	5	71	68	..	..	..	..
Argentina	33.9	39.9	1.3	2.8	30	9	86	71	22	68	24	140
Bolivia	8.2	11.4	2.5	4.7	42	4	58	61	80	252	118	600
Brazil	155.3	179.7	2.0	2.9	35	5	76	67	54	181	65	200

	Population (millions) 1994	Population (millions) 2010	Population annual growth rate 1990-92 (%)	Total Fertility rate 1992	Percent Age <15 1994	Percent Age 65+ 1994	Percent of population urbanized 1994	Life expectancy at birth (years)	Infant mortality rate (under 1) per 1,000 live births 1994	Under 5 mortality rate per 1,000 live births 1960	Under 5 mortality rate per 1,000 live births 1992	Maternal mortality rate per 100,000 live births 1980-91
Chile	14.0	17.4	1.7	2.7	31	6	85	72	15	138	18	67
Colombia	35.6	44.5	1.9	2.7	34	4	68	71	17	132	20	200
Costa Rica	3.2	4.4	2.8	3.2	36	5	44	76	14	112	16	36
Cuba	11.1	12.3	0.9	1.9	23	9	73	77	10	50	11	39
Dominican Republic	7.8	9.9	2.3	3.5	38	3	60	68	42	152	50	..
Ecuador	10.6	14.0	2.6	3.8	39	4	57	69	47	180	59	170
El Salvador	5.2	7.3	1.5	4.2	44	4	45	66	47	210	63	..
Guatemala	10.3	15.8	2.9	5.5	45	3	38	65	55	205	76	200
Guyana	0.8	1.0	1.1*	2.6	33	4	33	65	48	126	69	..
Haiti	7.0	9.8	1.9	4.9	40	4	31	46	87	270	133	340
Honduras	5.3	7.6	3.3	5.1	47	4	44	66	45	203	58	220
Jamaica	2.5	3.0	1.2	2.5	33	8	52	74	12	76	14	120
Mexico	91.8	118.5	2.3	3.3	38	4	71	70	28	141	33	110
Nicaragua	4.3	6.7	2.9	5.2	46	3	62	63	54	209	76	..
Panama	2.5	3.3	2.1	3.0	35	5	49	72	18	104	20	60
Paraguay	4.8	7.1	3.0	4.4	40	4	51	67	28	90	34	300
Peru	22.9	29.5	2.2	3.7	38	4	71	65	46	236	65	300
Suriname	0.4	0.5	..	2.8	41	4	70	69	..	..	..	..
Trinidad & Tobago	1.3	1.5	1.3	2.8	32	6	69	71	19	73	22	110
Uruguay	3.2	3.6	0.6	2.4	26	12	89	73	20	47	22	36
Venezuela	21.3	28.4	2.5	3.2	38	4	84	70	20	70	24	..

Middle East and North Africa

Algeria	27.9	38.2	2.8	5.0	44	4	50	67	60	243	72	140x
Bahrain	0.6	0.8	..	3.8	32	2	81	71	..	..	..	..
Cyprus	0.7	0.8	..	2.3	26	10	62	76	..	..	..	..
Egypt	58.9	80.7	2.5	4.2	40	4	45	62	43	258	55	270
Iran	61.2	100.4	3.8	6.1	47	4	57	65	44	233	58	120
Iraq	19.9	34.5	3.3	5.8	48	3	70	64	64	171	80	120
Jordan	4.2	6.6	3.2	5.8	41	3	70	67	25	149	30	48x
Kuwait	1.3	2.3	3.0	3.8	43	2	..	76	14	128	17	6
Lebanon	3.6	5.0	0.5	3.2	33	5	86	75	35	91	44	..
Libya	5.1	8.9	3.9	6.5	47	3	76	63	70	269	104	70x
Morocco	28.6	38.1	2.6	4.5	40	4	47	67	50	215	61	300x
Oman	1.9	3.4	4.2	6.8	36	3	12	71	24	300	31	..
Qatar	0.5	0.6	..	4.5	23	1	91	73	26	..	..	..
Saudi Arabia	18.0	30.5	4.4	6.5	43	2	79	70	35	292	40	41
Syria	14.0	24.2	3.5	6.3	48	3	51	66	34	201	40	140
Tunisia	8.7	11.3	2.3	3.6	37	5	59	68	32	244	38	70
Turkey	61.8	81.3	2.3	3.6	35	4	61	67	70	217	87	150
United Arab Emirates	1.7	2.9	4.2	4.6	32	1	83	72	18	240	22	..
Yemen	12.9	22.1	3.5	7.3	51	4	31	54	107	378	177	..

Industrial Countries

Albania	3.4	4.0	1.8	2.8	33	5	36	72	28	151	34	..
Australia	17.8	20.9	1.5	1.9	22	12	85	77	7	24	9	3
Austria	8.0	8.2	0.3	1.5	18	15	54	76	7	43	9	8

	Population (millions) 1994	Population (millions) 2010	Population annual growth rate 1990-92 (%)	Total Fertility rate 1992	Percent Age <15 1994	Percent Age 65+ 1994	Percent of population urbanized 1994	Life expectancy at birth (years)	Infant mortality rate (under 1) per 1,000 live births 1994	Under 5 mortality rate per 1,000 live births 1960	Under 5 mortality rate per 1,000 live births 1992	Maternal mortality rate per 100,000 live births 1980-91
Belgium	10.0	10.1	0.1	1.6	18	15	97	76	9	35	11	3
Bulgaria	8.4	8.4	0.1	1.9	20	14	67	72	16	70	20	9
Canada	29.1	33.4	1.1	1.8	21	12	77	77	7	33	8	5
Czech Republic	10.3	10.9	..	2.0	21	13	..	72	11	..	12	..
Denmark	5.2	5.3	0.1	1.7	17	16	85	75	7	25	8	3
Finland	5.1	5.2	0.4	1.8	19	14	80	75	6	28	7	11
Former Soviet Union												
Armenia	3.7	4.0	..	2.6	31	6	68	70	29	..	34	..
Azerbaijan	7.4	8.6	..	2.8	33	5	54	71	37	..	53	..
Belarus	10.3	10.7	..	2.0	23	11	67	71	20	..	23	..
Estonia	1.5	1.6	0.6	2.1	22	12	71	70	20	..	24	..
Georgia	5.5	6.1	..	2.3	25	9	56	73	25	..	29	..
Kazakhstan	17.1	18.6	..	3.0	31	6	58	69	43	..	50	..
Kyrgyzstan	4.5	5.6	..	4.0	38	5	37	69	49	..	60	..
Latvia	2.5	2.8	0.5	2.0	21	12	70	69	22	..	27	..
Lithuania	3.7	4.2	0.8	2.0	22	11	69	71	17	..	20	..
Moldova	4.4	4.6	..	2.6	28	8	48	69	31	..	36	..
Russian Federation	147.8	145.2	..	2.1	22	11	73	68	28	..	32	..
Tajikistan	5.9	8.7	..	5.4	43	3	31	69	65	..	85	..
Turkmenistan	4.1	5.3	..	4.6	40	4	45	66	72	..	91	..
Ukraine	51.5	49.7	..	2.0	21	12	68	69	21	..	25	..
Uzbekistan	22.1	29.9	..	4.4	41	4	40	69	56	..	68	..
France	58.0	58.8	0.5	1.8	20	15	74	77	7	34	9	9
Germany	81.2	78.2	0.2	1.5	16	15	85	76	7	40	8	5
Greece	10.4	10.9	0.5	1.5	19	14	58	77	8	64	9	5
Hungary	10.3	9.9	-0.2	1.8	19	14	63	69	15	57	16	15
Ireland	3.6	3.9	0.2	2.2	27	11	56	74	5	36	6	2
Israel	5.4	6.9	2.3	2.9	31	9	90	76	9	39	11	3
Italy	57.2	58.1	0.2	1.3	16	15	68	77	8	50	10	4
Japan	125.0	130.4	0.5	1.7	17	14	77	79	4	40	6	11
Netherlands	15.4	16.7	0.6	1.7	18	13	89	77	6	22	7	10
New Zealand	3.5	4.1	0.9	2.1	23	11	85	75	8	26	10	13
Norway	4.3	4.5	0.4	1.9	19	16	72	77	6	23	8	3
Poland	38.6	41.3	0.6	2.1	25	10	62	71	14	70	16	11
Portugal	9.9	10.3	0.1	1.5	20	13	34	74	11	112	13	10
Romania	22.7	23.0	0.4	2.2	22	11	54	70	23	82	28	72
Slovakia	5.3	5.9	..	..	25	10	57	71	12	..	14	..
Spain	39.2	40.7	0.3	1.4	19	14	78	77	8	57	9	5
Sweden	8.8	9.2	0.3	2.0	18	18	83	78	6	20	7	5
Switzerland	7.0	7.5	0.6	1.6	16	15	68	78	7	27	9	5
USA	260.8	300.4	1.0	2.0	22	13	75	76	9	30	10	8
United Kingdom	58.4	61.0	0.2	1.9	19	16	92	76	7	27	9	8
Yugoslavia (former)	10.5	11.6	0.6	1.9	23	10	47	72	19	113	22	27
World	**5,607**	**7,022**	..	**3.4**	**33**	**6**	**43**	**65**	..	..	..	..

Notes

* Growth rate for 1980-91.

X Indicates data that refer to years or periods other than those specified in the column heading, differ from the standard definition, or refer to only part of a country.

Table 2: Global Health, Nutrition, and Welfare Statistics

	Human Development Rank 1994	Mean years of schooling age 25+ Total 1992	Mean years of schooling Male 1992	Mean years of schooling Female 1992	% Infants with low birthweight 1985-90	% 1-year-olds Immunized 1992	Food Production per capita Index 1991 1979-81 = 100	Daily Calorie Supply as % of Requirements 1980-90	Annual Deforestation % 1981-90

Developing Countries
Africa (sub-Saharan)

Total	..	1.6	2.2	1.0	14	49	96	92	..
Angola	155	1.5	2.0	1.0	15	33	79	80	0.7
Benin	156	0.7	1.1	0.3	10	75	119	101	1.2
Botswana	87	2.5	2.6	2.5	8	75	68	100	0.5
Burkina Faso	172	0.2	0.3	0.2	12	46	119	95	0.7
Burundi	152	0.4	0.7	0.3	14	81	91	85	0.6
Cameroon	124	1.6	2.6	0.8	13	41	78	93	0.6
Cape Verde	122	2.2	3.2	1.3	..	94	..	125	0.0
Central African Republic	160	1.1	1.6	0.5	18	52	94	77	0.4
Chad	168	0.3	0.5	0.2	11	21	102	69	0.7
Comoros	141	1.0	1.2	0.8	13	34	..	90	..
Congo	123	2.1	3.1	1.1	15	75	92	107	0.2
Côte d'Ivoire	136	1.9	2.9	0.9	15	38	93	122	1.0
Djibouti	163	0.4	0.7	0.3	9	84	..	..	0.0
Equatorial Guinea	150	0.8	1.3	0.3	10	75	..	..	0.4
Ethiopia	161	1.1	1.5	0.7	10	14	86	71	0.3
Gabon	114	2.6	3.9	1.3	10	82	82	107	0.6
Gambia	166	0.6	0.9	0.2	10	88	90	103	0.8
Ghana	134	3.5	4.9	2.2	17	46	116	91	1.3
Guinea	173	0.9	1.5	0.3	11	55	90	100	1.1
Guinea-Bissau	164	0.4	0.7	0.1	12	73	..	97	0.7
Kenya	125	2.3	3.1	1.3	15	62	103	86	0.5
Lesotho	120	3.5	2.8	4.1	10	64	70	93	..
Liberia	144	2.1	3.3	0.8	..	44	66	97	0.5
Madagascar	131	2.2	2.6	1.7	10	34	86	93	0.8
Malawi	157	1.7	2.4	1.1	11	88	75	87	1.3
Mali	167	0.4	0.7	0.1	10	45	96	107	0.8
Mauritania	158	0.4	0.7	0.1	10	48	80	109	0.0
Mauritius	60	4.1	4.9	3.3	8	87	104	129	..
Mozambique	159	1.6	2.2	1.2	11	58	77	77	0.7
Namibia	127	1.7	..	..	14	71	..	..	0.3
Niger	169	0.2	0.4	0.2	20	28	78	98	0.0
Nigeria	139	1.2	1.7	0.5	17	43	123	93	0.7
Rwanda	153	1.1	1.5	0.5	16	86	84	80	0.2
Senegal	143	0.9	1.5	0.5	10	51	98	95	0.6
Sierra Leone	170	0.9	1.4	0.4	13	69	84	86	0.6
Somalia	165	0.3	0.5	0.2	..	24	78	81	0.4
South Africa	93	3.9	4.1	3.7	12	..	82	128	..
Sudan	151	0.8	1.0	0.5	15	69	80	83	1.0
Swaziland	117	3.8	4.1	3.4	7	92	85	105	..
Tanzania	148	2.0	2.8	1.3	16	87	78	91	1.2
Togo	145	1.6	2.4	0.8	32	51	95	99	1.4
Uganda	154	1.1	1.6	0.6	10	77	98	83	0.9
Zaire	140	1.6	2.4	0.8	10	40	94	97	0.6
Zambia	138	2.7	3.7	1.7	14	45	96	87	1.0
Zimbabwe	121	3.1	4.5	1.8	6	74	78	94	0.6

	Human Development Rank 1994	Mean years of schooling age 25+ Total 1992	Mean years of schooling Male 1992	Mean years of schooling Female 1992	% Infants with low birthweight 1985-90	% 1-year-olds Immunized 1992	Food Production per capita Index 1991 1979-81 = 100	Daily Calorie Supply as % of Requirements 1980-90	Annual Deforestation % 1981-90
South Asia									
Total	..	..	..	..	30	84	114	103	0.8
Afghanistan	171	0.9	1.6	0.2	19	35	71	76	..
Bangladesh	146	2.0	3.1	0.9	34	69	96	94	3.3
Bhutan	162	0.3	0.5	0.2	..	85	..	..	0.6
India	135	2.4	3.5	1.2	30	90	119	105	0.6
Nepal	149	2.1	3.2	1.0	26	73	127	103	1.0
Pakistan	132	1.9	2.9	0.7	30	81	106	101	2.9
Sri Lanka	90	7.2	8.0	6.3	22	88	90	99	1.3
East Asia and the Pacific									
Burma (Myanmar)	130	2.5	3.0	2.1	13	74	100	116	1.2
Cambodia	147	2.0	2.3	1.7	..	37	141	96	1.0
China	94	5.0	6.3	3.8	6	94	138	112	..
Fiji	59	5.1	5.6	4.6	18	96	..	108	..
Hong Kong	24	7.2	8.8	5.5	4	79	..	129	..
Indonesia	105	4.1	5.3	3.1	8	92	135	122	1.0
Korea, N.	101	6.0	7.4	4.6	..	96	104	123	..
Korea, S.	32	9.3	11.6	7.1	4	83	95	123	..
Laos	133	2.9	3.6	2.1	13	36	111	111	0.9
Malaysia	57	5.6	5.9	5.2	9	90	159	124	1.8
Mongolia	102	7.2	7.4	7.0	5	85	78	97	..
Papua New Guinea	129	1.0	1.3	0.7	23	76	..	116	0.3
Philippines	99	7.6	8.0	7.2	15	92	88	108	2.9
Singapore	43	4.0	4.8	3.2	7	90	..	144	0.0
Solomon Islands	126	1.0	1.2	0.8	20	77	..	84	..
Thailand	54	3.9	4.4	3.4	10	86	106	100	2.9
Vietnam	116	4.9	6.2	3.6	17	90	124	102	1.4
Latin America and the Caribbean									
Total	..	..	..	..	11	81	110	114	..
Argentina	37	9.2	9.0	9.5	6	87	95	130	..
Bolivia	113	4.0	5.0	3.0	9	82	124	83	1.1
Brazil	63	4.0	4.1	3.9	15	78	132	114	0.6
Chile	38	7.8	8.1	7.4	7	93	117	104	..
Colombia	50	7.5	7.3	7.7	17	80	111	104	0.6
Costa Rica	39	5.7	5.8	5.6	7	89	92	120	2.6
Cuba	89	8.0	7.9	8.1	7	95	96	137	0.9
Dominican Republic	96	4.3	4.6	4.0	14	59	95	100	2.5
Ecuador	74	5.6	5.8	5.3	10	83	115	106	1.7
El Salvador	112	4.2	4.4	4.0	8	66	100	102	2.1
Guatemala	108	4.1	4.4	3.8	10	62	88	101	1.6
Guyana	107	5.1	5.4	4.9	12	82	65	108	0.1
Haiti	137	1.7	2.0	1.3	15	30	84	94	3.9
Honduras	115	4.0	4.1	3.8	9	92	92	91	1.9
Jamaica	65	5.3	5.3	5.2	11	77	96	115	5.3
Mexico	52	4.9	5.0	4.8	5	92	96	132	1.2

Table 2, continued: Global Health, Nutrition, and Welfare Statistics

	Human Development Rank 1994	Mean years of schooling age 25+ Total 1992	Mean years of schooling Male 1992	Mean years of schooling Female 1992	% Infants with low birthweight 1985-90	% 1-year-olds Immunized 1992	Food Production per capita Index 1991 1979-81 = 100	Daily Calorie Supply as % of Requirements 1980-90	Annual Deforestation % 1981-90
Nicaragua	106	4.5	4.3	4.7	8	78	61	100	1.7
Panama	47	6.8	6.6	7.0	8	84	88	100	1.7
Paraguay	84	4.9	5.2	4.6	5	89	114	115	2.4
Peru	95	6.5	7.3	5.8	9	81	92	89	0.4
Suriname	85	4.2	4.3	4.0	12	77	..	..	0.1
Trinidad & Tobago	35	8.4	8.4	8.5	13	85	..	120	1.9
Uruguay	33	8.1	7.7	8.6	8	95	109	96	..
Venezuela	46	6.5	6.6	6.4	10	70	102	100	1.2

Middle East and North Africa

Algeria	109	2.8	4.8	0.9	9	89	107	118	..
Bahrain	58	4.3	5.2	3.6	4	92	..	..	..
Cyprus	26	7.0	7.6	6.5	5	85	100	..	0.1
Egypt	110	3.0	4.2	1.7	12	90	114	133	..
Iran	86	3.9	4.6	3.1	12	97	116	134	..
Iraq	100	5.0	5.9	4.0	15	82	68	133	..
Jordan	98	5.0	6.0	4.0	10	95	89	111	..
Kuwait	51	5.5	6.1	4.8	7	92	..	130	..
Lebanon	103	4.4	5.3	3.5	10	74	136	129	..
Libya	79	3.5	5.7	1.4	5	69	80	140	..
Morocco	111	3.0	4.4	1.6	9	87	140	131	..
Oman	92	0.9	1.4	0.3	8	97	..	..	..
Qatar	56	5.8	6.0	5.6	6	90	..	..	..
Saudi Arabia	67	3.9	6.3	1.6	7	90	..	120	..
Syria	73	4.2	5.2	3.1	8	89	77	126	..
Tunisia	81	2.1	3.1	1.2	7	89	113	137	..
Turkey	68	3.6	4.9	2.4	8	72	99	124	0.0
United Arab Emirates	62	5.6	5.6	5.7	6	89	..	151	..
Yemen	142	0.9	1.5	0.2	10	50	67	93	..

Industrial Countries

Albania	76	6.2	7.2	5.2	7x	87x	..	107	0.0
Australia	7	12.0	12.1	11.9	6x	86x	..	124	0.0
Austria	12	11.4	12.0	10.8	6x	60x	..	133	0.4
Belgium	13	11.2	11.2	11.2	6x	75x	..	149	0.3
Bulgaria	48	7.0	7.6	6.4	6x	97x	..	148	0.2
Canada	1	12.2	12.4	12.0	6x	85x	..	122	..
Czech Republic	27	9.2	9.8	8.6	..	97x	..	..	..
Denmark	15	11.0	11.1	10.9	6x	86x	..	135	0.2
Finland	16	10.9	11.0	10.8	4x	97x	..	113	0.0
Former Soviet Union									
Armenia	53	5.0	..	..	..	..	..	..	..
Azerbaijan	71	5.0	..	..	..	50x	..	..	..
Belarus	40	7.0	..	..	..	94x	..	..	0.5
Estonia	29	9.0	..	..	..	75x	..	..	..
Georgia	66	5.0	..	..	..	58x	..	..	..
Kazakhstan	61	5.0	..	..	..	90x	..	..	..

Table 2, continued: Global Health, Nutrition, and Welfare Statistics

	Human Development Rank 1994	Mean years of schooling age 25+ Total 1992	Mean years of schooling Male 1992	Mean years of schooling Female 1992	% Infants with low birthweight 1985-90	% 1-year-olds Immunized 1992	Food Production per capita Index 1991 1979-81 = 100	Daily Calorie Supply as % of Requirements 1980-90	Annual Deforestation % 1981-90
Kyrgyzstan	82	5.0	..	..	..	94x	..	..	..
Latvia	30	9.0	..	..	..	95x	..	..	..
Lithuania	28	9.0	..	..	..	89x	..	..	..
Moldova	75	6.0	..	..	..	92x	..	..	..
Russian Federation	34	9.0	..	..	..	83x	..	..	0.2*
Tajikistan	97	5.0	..	..	..	..	..	..	..
Turkmenistann	80	5.0	..	..	..	76x	..	..	..
Ukraine	45	6.0	..	..	..	90x	..	..	0.3
Uzbekistan	91	5.0	..	..	..	84x	..	..	..
France	6	12.0	11.9	12.1	5x	71x	..	143	0.1
Germany	11	11.6	12.2	11.1	..	80x	..	..	0.5
Greece	25	7.0	7.4	6.6	6x	76x	..	151	0.0
Hungary	31	9.8	9.7	9.9	9x	100x	..	137	0.5
Ireland	21	8.9	8.8	9.0	4x	78x	..	157	1.3
Israel	19	10.2	11.1	9.2	7x	88x	..	125	..
Italy	22	7.5	7.6	7.5	5x	50x	..	139	..
Japan	3	10.8	10.9	10.7	6x	66x	..	125	0.0
Netherlands	9	11.1	10.9	11.4	..	94x	..	114	0.3
New Zealand	18	10.7	10.5	10.9	6x	82x	..	131	..
Norway	5	12.1	12.2	11.9	4x	90x	..	120	..
Poland	49	8.2	8.5	7.8	..	94x	..	131	0.1
Portugal	42	6.4	7.3	5.6	5x	96x	..	136	0.5
Romania	72	7.1	7.5	6.7	7x	92x	..	116	0.0
Spain	23	6.9	7.1	6.6	4x	97x	..	141	0.0
Sweden	4	11.4	11.4	11.4	5x	95x	..	111	..
Switzerland	2	11.6	12.0	11.2	5x	83x	..	130	0.6
USA	8	12.4	12.3	12.5	7x	77x	..	138	0.1
United Kingdom	10	11.7	11.6	11.8	7x	89x	..	130	1.1
Yugoslavia (former)	..	..	..	..	..	76x	..	140	0.4
World	..	5.2	..	..	..	..	..	..	..

Notes

x Years outside range specified.

* USSR (former).

For definition of Human Development Index, see p. 51.

No data available for Eritrea.

Table 3: Global Economic Indicators

	GNP per Capita U.S. dollars 1992	GNP per Capita Real Growth rate (%) 1985-92	Real GDP per Capita (PPP $) 1991	Military Expenditure as % of education & health expenditure 1990-91	Total Debt $ US billions 1992	Debt Servicing as % of Exports 1992	Food as % of Exports 1992	Food as % of Imports 1992	Per Capita Energy Consumption (kg. of oil equiv.)	Food as % of Household Consumption 1980-85 1992

Developing Countries
Africa (sub-Saharan)

Total	530	-0.8*	..	43	194.3	..	..	..	258	..
Angola	b	..	1,000	208	9.6	7	..	13.5	..	..
Benin	410	-1.5	1,500	..	1.4	4	9.6	11.9	19	37
Botswana	2,790	8.1	4,690	22	0.6	..	3.6	4.6	395	25
Burkina Faso	290	0.9	666	30	1.1	..	9.4	13.0	16	..
Burundi	210	1.0	640	42	1.0	40	..	9.0	24	..
Cameroon	820	-6.7	2,400	48	6.6	16	9.0	15.1	77	24
Cape Verde	850	1.8	1,360	..	0.2	..	17.5	33.0	..	..
Central African Republic	410	-2.4	641	33	1.0	10	13.8	25.4	29	..
Chad	220	1.3	447	74	1.0	6	18.2	4.3	16	..
Comoros	510	-2.3	700	..	0.2	6	77.3	31.8	..	..
Congo	1,030	-3.0	2,800	37	4.8	11	0.8	22.3	131	37
Côte d'Ivoire	670	-5.7	1,510	14	18.0	31	39.9	18.2	125	39
Djibouti	b	..	1,000	..	0.2	4	37.1	32.5	..	..
Eqatorial Guinea	330	-0.3	700	..	0.3	5	8.3	19.6	..	..
Ethiopia	110	-2.0	370	190	4.4	14	7.2	61.9	21	49
Gabon	4,450	-2.1	3,498	51	3.8	17	2.2	11.2	784	..
Gambia	390	1.8	763	11	0.4	13	11.5	36.8	..	..
Ghana	450	1.2	930	12	4.3	27	30.2	40.5	96	50
Guinea	510	0.8	500	37	2.7	12	2.9	22.0	67	..
Guinea-Bissau	210	0.4	747	..	0.6	92	56.9	34.9	37	..
Kenya	330	0.6	1,350	24	6.4	25	10.4	12.1	92	38
Lesotho	590	0.8	1,500	48	0.5	6	8.7	18.4	..	..
Liberia	a	..	850	47	2.0	..	0.9	55.9	..	..
Madagascar	230	-1.7	710	37	4.4	21	30.3	13.9	38	59
Malawi	210	-0.3	800	24	1.7	24	8.1	14.7	40	30
Mali	300	-1.9	480	53	2.6	..	26.8	12.2	22	57
Mauritania	530	-0.1	962	40	2.3	..	9.6	60.9	108	..
Mauritius	2,700	6.3	7,178	4	1.1	8	29.8	11.1	385	24
Mozambique	60	-1.3	921	121	4.9	9	..	..	32	..
Namibia	1,610	1.1	2,381	23	..	..	9.6	8.3	..	..
Niger	300	-1.5	542	11	1.7	14	12.8	14.8	39	..
Nigeria	320	3.4	1,360	33	31.0	31	1.1	10.0	128	48
Rwanda	250	-2.8	680	25	1.0	..	0.4	12.6	28	29
Senegal	780	0.3	1,680	33	3.6	13	12.9	2.6	111	49
Sierra Leone	170	0.0	1,020	23	1.3	..	3.0	65.8	73	56
Somalia	a	0.0	759	200	2.5	..	2.3	27.7	7	..
South Africa	2,670	-1.3	3,885	41	..	..	5.0	6.7	2,487	34
Sudan	a	..	1,162	44	16.2	5	37.7	20.8	69	60
Swaziland	1,080	6.4	2,506	11	0.2	..	47.1	9.8	..	..
Tanzania	110	1.4	570	77	6.7	32	1.0	8.2	30	64
Togo	400	-1.5	738	39	1.4	7	8.2	13.2	46	..
Uganda	170	1.8	1,036	18	3.0	41	10.2	4.2	24	..
Zaire	a	..	469	71	10.9	..	0.5	21.0	..	..

	GNP per Capita U.S. dollars 1992	GNP per Capita Real Growth rate (%) 1985-92	Real GDP per Capita (PPP $) 1991	Military Expenditure as % of education & health expenditure 1990-91	Total Debt $ US billions 1992	Debt Servicing as % of Exports 1992	Food as % of Exports 1992	Food as % of Imports 1992	Per Capita Energy Consumption (kg. of oil equiv.)	Food as % of Household Consumption 1980-85 1992
Zambia	290	-2.1	1,010	63	7.0	29	2.6	10.6	158	36
Zimbabwe	570	-0.6	2,160	66	4.0	32	4.1	15.2	450	40
South Asia										
Total	310	3.0*	..	..	127.9	20.7	..	..	209	..
Afghanistan	a	..	700	..	..	..	21.3	13.9	..	..
Bangladesh	220	1.7	1,160	41	13.2	17	0.3	16.2	59	59
Bhutan	180	5.2	620	..	0.8	..	3.9	9.7	15	..
India	310	3.3	1,150	65	77.0	26	6.8	5.5	235	52
Nepal	170	2.1	1,130	35	1.8	12	18.9	8.6	20	57
Pakistan	410	1.7	1,970	125	24.1	23	8.5	10.3	223	37
Sri Lanka	540	2.2	2,650	107	6.4	13	4.8	11.3	101	43
East Asia and the Pacific										
Total	760	6.1*	..	..	320.2	..	..	..	593	..
Burma (Myanmar)	a	..	650	222	5.3	..	34.8	14.9	42	..
Cambodia	..	..	1,250	..	..	..	2.2	12.8	..	..
China	380	6.0	2,946	114	69.3	10	7.6	3.6	600	61
Fiji	2,010	2.6	4,858	37	0.3	9	23.2	12.9	..	..
Hong Kong	15,380	5.6	18,520	10		..	0.7	3.4	1,946	12
Indonesia	670	4.7	2,730	49	84.4	32	4.0	5.4	303	48
Korea, N.	b	..	1,750	..	..	..	12.7	11.5	..	..
Korea, S.	6,790	8.5	8,320	60	43.0	7	0.9	4.5	2,569	35
Laos	250	1.8	1,760	..	2.0	..	13.1	7.1	41	..
Malaysia	2,790	5.7	7,400	38	19.8	7	6.4	6.1	1,445	23
Mongolia	b	..	2,250	..	0.4	17	10.4	9.1	1,082	..
Papua New Guinea	950	-0.1	1,550	41	3.7	30	9.8	12.2	235	..
Philippines	770	1.9	2,440	41	32.5	28	11.9	5.6	302	51
Solomon Islands	710	2.7	2,113	..	0.1	..	23.9	14.0	..	..
Singapore	15,750	5.9	14,734	129		..	2.5	3.9	4,399	19
Thailand	1,840	8.3	5,270	71	39.4	..	12.3	1.8	614	30
Vietnam	a	..	1,250	..	..	..	16.2	4.7	..	..
Latin America and the Carribean										
Total	2,690	-0.2*	..	..	496.2	..	..	..	923	..
Argentina	6,050	0.5	5,120	51	67.6	35	42.4	4.3	1,351	35
Bolivia	680	1.0	2,170	57	4.2	39	8.9	10.4	255	33
Brazil	2,770	-0.7	5,240	23	121.1	24	13.3	8.7	681	35
Chile	2,730	6.1	7,060	68	19.4	21	14.8	4.7	837	29
Colombia	1,290	2.4	5,460	57	17.2	35	9.6	7.3	670	29
Costa Rica	2,000	2.6	5,100	5	4.0	21	41.9	7.2	566	33
Cuba	b	..	2,000	125	..	..	85.9	20.1	..	..
Dominican Republic	1,040	0.3	3,080	22	4.7	13	43.4	12.9	347	46
Ecuador	1,070	0.6	4,140	26	12.3	27	26.0	6.9	524	30
El Salvador	1,170	0.9	2,110	66	2.1	13	12.1	8.9	225	33
Guatemala	980	0.6	3,180	31	2.8	28	34.1	7.0	161	36
Guyana	330	-5.4	1,862	21	1.9	..	57.5	8.9	..	..

	GNP per Capita U.S. dollars 1992	GNP per Capita Real Growth rate (%) 1985-92	Real GDP per Capita (PPP $) 1991	Military Expenditure as % of education & health expenditure 1990-91	Total Debt $ US billions 1992	Debt Servicing as % of Exports 1992	Food as % of Exports 1992	Food as % of Imports 1992	Per Capita Energy Consumption (kg. of oil equiv.)	Food as % of Household Consumption 1980-85 1992
Haiti	..	-2.9	925	30	0.8	..	10.8	80.5	..	..
Honduras	580	0.5	1,820	92	3.6	35	28.7	6.8	175	39
Jamaica	1,340	2.9	3,670	8	4.3	25	17.2	12.9	1,075	36
Mexico	3,470	1.1	7,170	5	113.4	44	7.6	9.8	1,525	35
Nicaragua	410	-7.8	2,550	97	11.1	26	39.3	19.8	253	..
Panama	2,440	-1.2	4,910	34	6.5	31	32.4	8.5	520	38
Paraguay	1,340	1.0	3,420	42	1.8	41	33.8	4.6	209	30
Peru	950	-4.3	3,110	39	20.3	23	3.6	13.1	330	35
Suriname	3,700	-3.2	3,072	27	..	..	9.6	10.0	..	..
Trinidad & Tobago	3,940	-3.0	8,380	9	2.3	25	4.1	15.2	4,910	19
Uruguay	3,340	2.9	6,670	38	5.3	22	31.5	6.1	642	31
Venezuela	2,900	1.1	8,120	33	37.2	20	1.0	8.4	2,296	23

Middle East and North Africa

Total	1,950	-2.3*	..	..	189.0	..	..	..	1,109	..
Algeria	1,830	-2.0	2,870	11	26.4	72	0.3	26.0	988	..
Bahrain	..	-1.7	11,536	41	..	..	0.1	5.5	..	..
Cyprus	9,820	5.1	9,844	17	..	..	14.1	6.5	..	..
Egypt	630	0.8	3,600	52	40.0	15	9.8	24.6	586	49
Iran	2,190	-1.4	4,670	38	14.2	4	2.3	8.2	1,256	37
Iraq	b	..	3,500	271	..	..	1.9	51.4	..	..
Jordan	1,120	-7.0	2,895	138	8.0	20	12.8	19.4	813	35
Kuwait	d	..	13,126	88	..	..	**	7.3	..	..
Lebanon	b	..	2,500	..	1.8	7	23.0	14.1	..	..
Libya	c	..	7,000	71	..	..	**	10.6	..	..
Morocco	1,040	1.3	3,340	72	21.3	..	12.8	11.0	278	38
Oman	6,490	1.0	9,230	293	2.9	..	0.9	11.1	3,070	..
Qatar	16,240	-6.9	14,000	192	..	..	0.4	15.3	..	..
Saudi Arabia	7,940	1.3	10,850	151	..	..	1.0	12.7	4,463	..
Syria	..	0.0	5,220	373	16.5	..	12.2	17.1	823	..
Tunisia	1,740	2.1	4,690	31	8.5	20	7.1	6.2	567	37
Turkey	1,950	2.7	4,840	87	54.8	32	19.8	3.3	948	40
United Arab Emirates	22,220	0.0	17,000	44	..	..	2.0	8.4	14,631	..
Yemen	..	..	1,374	197	6.6	..	3.8	37.4	241	..

Industrial Countries

Albania	b	..	3,500	51	0.6	2	20.1	30.6	..	..
Australia	17,070	0.7	16,680	24	..	..	2.5	3.7	5,263	13
Austria	22,110	2.4	17,690	9	..	..	2.5	3.7	3,266	16
Belgium	20,880	2.8	17,510	20	..	..	..	..	5,100	15
Bulgaria	1,330	-3.6	4,813	29	12.2	7	10.3	0.4	2,422	..
Canada	20,320	0.3	19,320	15	..	..	6.5	4.6	7,912	11
Czech Republic	2,440	-5.3	..	..	..	..	..	..	3,873	..
Denmark	25,930	1.2	17,880	18	..	..	18.2	5.7	3,729	13
Finland	22,980	0.7	16,130	15	..	..	2.0	4.1	5,560	16
Former Soviet Union										
Armenia	780	-8.2	4,610	..	0.0	..	0.3	25.0	1,092	..

Table 3, continued: Global Economic Indicators

	GNP per Capita U.S. dollars 1992	GNP per Capita Real Growth rate (%) 1985-92	Real GDP per Capita (PPP $) 1991	Military Expenditure as % of education & health expenditure 1990-91	Total Debt $ US billions 1992	Debt Servicing as % of Exports 1992	Food as % of Exports 1992	Food as % of Imports 1992	Per Capita Energy Consumption (kg. of oil equiv.)	Food as % of Household Consumption 1980-85 1992
Azerbaijan	870	..	3,670	..	..	..	0.1	34.0	..	..
Belarus	2,910	..	6,850	..	0.2	..	..	..	4,154	..
Estonia	2,750	3.0	8,090	..	0.1	..	..	4.6	..	..
Georgia	850	..	3,670	..	0.1	..	..	..	..	..
Kazakhstan	1,680	..	4,490	..	0.0	..	53.7	24.9	4,722	..
Kyrgyzstan	810	2.3	3,280	..	0.0	..	..	..	1,148	..
Latvia	1,930	-3.6	7,540	..	0.1	..	..	..	..	..
Lithuania	1,310	-2.7	5,410	..	0.0	..	..	..	..	..
Moldova	1,260	-2.9	3,500	..	0.0	..	9.9	28.1	1,600	..
Russian Federation	2,680	..	6,930	132	..	..	0.3	14.2	5,665	..
Tajikistan	480	..	2,180	..	0.0	..	0.7	97.5	..	..
Turkmenistan	1,270	..	3,540	..	..	..	..	..	..	..
Ukraine	1,670	..	5,180	..	0.4	..	17.5	11.9	3,885	..
Uzbekistan	860	..	2,790	..	0.0	..	..	77.2	..	..
France	22,300	2.2	18,430	29	..	..	10.3	6.7	4,034	16
Germany	23,030	2.2	19,770	29	..	..	3.9	7.7	4,358	12
Greece	7,180	1.1	7,680	71	..	..	24.9	1.1	2,173	30
Hungary	3,010	-1.5	6,080	18	21.9	36	17.5	2.4	2,392	25
Ireland	12,100	5.0	11,430	12	..	..	20.7	7.9	2,881	22
Israel	13,230	2.3	13,460	106	..	..	6.5	5.3	2,367	21
Italy	20,510	2.3	17,040	21	..	..	5.5	9.1	2,755	19
Japan	28,220	4.0	19,390	12	..	..	0.2	8.8	3,586	17
Netherlands	20,590	2.1	16,820	22	..	..	16.0	9.4	4,560	13
New Zealand	12,060	-0.4	13,970	16	..	..	39.5	5.4	4,284	12
Norway	25,800	0.2	17,170	22	..	..	0.7	4.0	4,925	15
Poland	1,960	-1.9	4,500	30	48.5	9	6.8	8.8	2,407	29
Portugal	7,450	5.5	9,450	32	32.1	..	2.6	7.3	1,816	34
Romania	1,090	-5.5	3,500	25	3.5	11	7.3	11.5	1,958	..
Slovakia	1,920	-7.0	12,670	..	..	..	..	..	3,202	..
Spain	14,020	3.8	12,670	18	..	..	12.0	6.4	2,409	24
Sweden	26,780	0.4	17,490	16	..	..	1.4	4.6	5,395	13
Switzerland	36,230	1.1	21,780	14	..	..	12.6	4.2	3,694	17
United Kingdom	17,760	1.5	16,340	40	..	..	4.0	7.8	3,743	12
USA	23,120	1.1	22,130	46	..	..	7.1	3.2	7,662	10
Yugoslavia (former)	b	..	..	..	16.3	..	..	..	2,296	27
World	..	..	5,490	37	..	..	..	..	1,447	..

Notes

a GNP per capita estimated to be low-income ($675 or less).

b GNP per capita estimated to be lower-middle-income ($676-$2,695).

c GNP per capita estimated to be upper-middle-income ($2,696-$8,355).

d GNP per capita estimated to be high-income ($8,356 or more).

x Years outside of range specified.

Data for Eritrea, not yet disaggregated, are included in Ethiopia.

* Data for 1980-92.

** Negligible amount.

	% children <5 suffering from underweight 1990	% Severe underweight under 5 1980-92	% Wasting 12-23 months moderate and severe 1980-92	% Stunting 24-59 months moderate and severe 1980-92	% of population with access to health services 1985-92	% of population with access to safe water 1988-91 total	% of population with access to safe water 1988-91 urban	% of population with access to safe water 1988-91 rural	adult literacy rate 1990 total (%)	adult literacy rate 1990 male (%)	adult literacy rate 1990 female (%)
Africa (sub-Saharan)											
Total	26.0	9	12	49	56	43	75	35	51	63	40
Angola	35.3	..	..	..	30x	41	71	20	43	57	29
Benin	23.5	..	..	..	18	51	66	46	25	35	17
Botswana	26.8	..	..	..	89x	90	100	88	75	85	66
Burkina Faso	27.1	..	..	..	49x	68	44	72	20	31	10
Burundi	29.1	10x	10	60x	80	57	99	54	52	63	42
Cameroon	16.7	3x	2	51x	41	48	100	27	57	70	45
Cape Verde	18.8x	..	..	..	..	..	..	..	67	..	..
Central African Republic	31.9	..	..	..	45	24	19	26	40	55	26
Chad	30.6	..	..	..	30	57	25	70	33	46	20
Comoros	..	..	..	..	..	..	..	..	..	..	..
Congo	27.5	..	13	33	83	38	92	2	59	72	45
Côte d'Ivoire	12.3	2	17	20	30x	76	70	81	56	69	41
Djibouti	..	..	..	..	..	..	..	..	..	..	..
Equatorial Guinea	..	..	..	..	..	..	..	..	52	66	38
Ethiopia	39.8	16x	12x	63x	46	25	91	19	..	..	..
Gabon	15.1	..	..	..	90x	68	90	50	62	76	50
Gambia	17.1	..	..	..	..	..	..	27	30	43	18
Ghana	26.7	6	15	39	60	52	93	35	63	74	54
Guinea	24.0	..	..	..	75	53	87	56	27	39	15
Guinea-Bissau	23.4x	..	..	..	..	41	56	35	39	53	25
Kenya	17.4	3x	5x	32x	77	49	74	43	71	82	60
Lesotho	17.5	2	7	23	80	47	59	45	..	..	..
Liberia	20.1	..	..	..	39	50	93	22	42	53	31
Madagascar	38.1	8x	17	56x	65	23	55	9	81	90	74
Malawi	23.5	8	11	62	80	56x	97x	50x	..	..	..
Mali	21.6	9x	16	34x	35	41	53	38	36	46	27
Mauritania	15.7	..	18	65	45	66	67	65	35	48	22
Mauritius	17.0	..	16x	22x	100	96	100	92	80	85	75
Mozambique	46.8	..	..	..	39	22	44	17	34	46	21
Namibia	29.0	6	13	29	72	52	98	35	..	..	..
Niger	44.0	..	23x	38x	41	53	98	45	31	44	18
Nigeria	35.4	12	16	54	66	36	81	30	52	63	41
Rwanda	31.7	6x	9x	58x	80	66	75	62	52	67	39
Senegal	19.6	2	8	30	40	48	84	26	40	55	26
Sierra Leone	25.9	..	18	39	38	37	33	37	24	35	12
Somalia	38.8	..	..	..	80	27x	37	50	27	41	16
South Africa	43.0	..	..	..	..	..	..	..	..	..	..
Sudan	33.7	7x	13x	32x	51	48	55	43	28	45	13
Swaziland	8.8	..	..	..	..	..	..	..	..	..	..
Tanzania	24.2	7	10	58	76x	49	65	45	..	..	..
Togo	18.4	6x	10	37x	61	60	77	53	45	59	33
Uganda	25.5	5x	4x	51x	61x	33	60	30	51	65	37
Zaire	33.2	..	..	..	26	39	68	24	74	86	63
Zambia	26.0	6	10	47	75x	53	70	28	75	83	67
Zimbabwe	14.1	2	2	31	85	84	95	80	69	76	61

	% children <5 suffering from underweight 1990	% Severe underweight under 5 1980-92	% Wasting 12-23 months moderate and severe 1980-92	% Stunting 24-59 months moderate and severe 1980-92	% of population with access to health services 1985-92	% of population with access to safe water 1988-91 total	% of population with access to safe water 1988-91 urban	% of population with access to safe water 1988-91 rural	adult literacy rate 1990 total (%)	adult literacy rate 1990 male (%)	adult literacy rate 1990 female (%)
South Asia											
Total	62.0	25	19	64	52	80	85	78	48	..	..
Afghanistan	40.3	..	..	..	29	23	40	19	32	48	15
Bangladesh	65.8	27	28	65	45	84	82	81	37	49	23
Bhutan	..	..	4x	56x	65	34	60	30	41	55	26
India	63.1	27x	..	65x	..	85	87	85	50	64	35
Nepal	50.5	..	..	..	..	42	67	39	27	39	14
Pakistan	41.6	14	11	60	55	56	80	45	36	49	22
Sri Lanka	42.0	2x	21x	39x	93x	60	80	55	89	94	85
East Asia and the Pacific											
Total	26.0	..	..	..	87	68	83	63	..	..	..
Burma (Myanmar)	33.0	9x	..	..	48	32	37	..	82	90	72
Cambodia	37.7	..	..	..	53	36	65	33	38	52	24
China	21.0	3x	8x	41x	90	72	87	68	80	92	68
Fiji	..	..	..	..	..	..	..	..	..	..	..
Hong Kong	..	..	..	..	99x	100	100	96	..	..	..
Indonesia	38.0	..	..	..	80	51	68	43	84	91	77
Korea,N.	..	..	..	..	0	..	..	..	..	..	..
Korea,S.	..	..	..	..	100	97	97	96	97	99	95
Laos	34.0	..	20	44	67	36	54	33	..	..	..
Malaysia	17.6	..	..	..	..	78	96	66	80	89	72
Mongolia	..	..	2x	29x	95	80	100	58	..	..	..
Papua New Guinea	36.0	..	..	..	96	33	94	20	65	82	48
Philippines	33.5	5	14	45	75	82	85	79	90	90	90
Singapore	..	..	..	..	100	100	100	..	..	..	..
Solomon Islands	..	..	..	..	..	..	..	..	..	..	..
Thailand	13.0	4x	10	28x	90	77	87	72	94	96	92
Vietnam	41.9	14	12x	49x	91	24	39	21	89	93	84
Latin America and the Caribbean											
Total	12.0	2	4	23	74	78	87	55	89	..	..
Argentina	1.2	..	..	..	71	65	73	17	96	97	96
Bolivia	11.4	3x	2	51x	63	52	77	27	79	86	72
Brazil	7.1	1	3	16	..	87	95	61	82	84	81
Chile	2.0	0x	1	10x	97	86	100	..	94	95	94
Colombia	10.1	2x	5	18x	60	86	87	82	87	88	86
Costa Rica	8.1	..	3	8	80x	93	100	86	93	93	93
Cuba	8.4	..	1x	..	98	98	100	91	95	96	94
Dominican Republic	12.0	2	1	22	80	67	82	45	84	86	83
Ecuador	13.0	0	4	39	88	55	63	43	87	89	85
El Salvador	19.4	..	3	36	56	47	85	19	75	80	70
Guatemala	25.0	8x	3	68x	34	62	92	43	56	65	48
Guyana	18.0	..	..	..	..	..	..	..	97	99	96
Haiti	24.4	3x	17x	51x	50	39	55	33	55	61	49
Honduras	19.8	4	2x	34x	66	77	98	63	75	78	73
Jamaica	7.2	1	6	7	90	100	100	100	99	99	99

	% children <5 suffering from underweight 1990	% Severe underweight under 5 1980-92	% Wasting 12-23 months moderate and severe 1980-92	% Stunting 24-59 months moderate and severe 1980-92	% of population with access to health services 1985-92	% of population with access to safe water 1988-91 total	% of population with access to safe water 1988-91 urban	% of population with access to safe water 1988-91 rural	adult literacy rate 1990 total (%)	adult literacy rate 1990 male (%)	adult literacy rate 1990 female (%)
Mexico	13.9	..	6x	22x	78	76	81	68	89	91	86
Nicaragua	18.7	11	0	22	83	54	76	21	..	..	..
Panama	11.0	..	7	24	80x	83	100	66	90	90	90
Paraguay	4.2	1	0	17	61	35	50	24	91	93	89
Peru	13.1	2	3	46	75x	56	77	10	86	93	80
Suriname	..	..	..	..	..	..	..	..	96	96	96
Trinidad & Tobago	9.0	0x	5	4x	99	97	99	91	..	..	..
Uruguay	7.0	2x	..	16x	82	75	85	5	97	98	97
Venezuela	5.9	..	4	7	..	89	89	89	89	88	91

Middle East and North Africa

	% children <5 suffering from underweight 1990	% Severe underweight under 5 1980-92	% Wasting 12-23 months moderate and severe 1980-92	% Stunting 24-59 months moderate and severe 1980-92	% of population with access to health services 1985-92	% of population with access to safe water 1988-91 total	% of population with access to safe water 1988-91 urban	% of population with access to safe water 1988-91 rural	adult literacy rate 1990 total (%)	adult literacy rate 1990 male (%)	adult literacy rate 1990 female (%)
Total	14.0	..	8	31	78	77	94	61	..	..	..
Algeria	12.3	..	7	18	88	68x	85x	55x	61	74	49
Bahrain	..	..	..	..	..	..	..	..	79	84	71
Cyprus	7.5	..	..	..	..	..	..	..	..	..	..
Egypt	10.0	3	4	32	..	90	95	86	50	66	35
Iran	39.0	..	..	..	80	89	100	75	56	67	45
Iraq	11.9	2	..	..	93	77	93	41	62	73	51
Jordan	12.7	1	3	21	97	99	100	97	82	91	72
Kuwait	5.0	..	2	14	100	..	100	..	74	78	68
Lebanon	8.9	..	..	..	95	92	95	85	81	89	74
Libya	4.0	..	..	..	..	97	100	80	66	78	52
Morocco	12.0	4x	x	34x	70	56	100	18	52	64	40
Oman	..	5	11	22	95	84	91	77	..	..	..
Qatar	..	..	..	..	..	..	..	..	..	..	..
Saudi Arabia	12.6	..	..	..	97	95	100	74	64	76	50
Syria	12.5	..	..	..	83	74	90	58	67	82	53
Tunisia	8.9	2x	4	23x	90x	99	100	99	68	77	59
Turkey	10.5	..	..	..	..	78x	95x	63x	82	91	72
United Arab Emirates	7.0	..	..	..	99	95	..	..	..	..	..
Yemen	19.1	4	17	49	38	36	61	30	41	56	28

Notes

x Years outside range specified.

No data available for Eritrea.

Table 5: United States Poverty Trends

	1970	1980	1982	1984	1985	1986	1987	1988	1989	1990	1991	1992
Population in millions	205.1	227.8	232.5	237.0	239.3	241.6	243.9	246.3	248.3	248.7	252.2	255.1
Total poverty rate	12.6	13.0	15.0	14.4	14.0	13.6	13.4	13.1	12.8	13.5	14.2	14.5
White poverty rate	9.9	10.2	12.0	11.5	11.4	11.0	10.4	10.1	10.0	10.7	11.3	11.6
Black poverty rate	33.5	32.5	35.6	33.8	31.1	31.1	32.6	31.6	30.7	31.9	32.7	33.3
Hispanic poverty rate	..	25.7	29.9	28.4	29.0	27.3	28.1	26.8	26.2	28.1	28.7	29.3
Elderly poverty rate	24.6	15.7	14.6	12.4	12.6	12.4	12.5	12.0	11.4	12.2	12.4	12.9
Total child poverty rate	15.1	18.3	21.9	21.5	20.7	20.5	20.5	19.7	19.6	20.6	21.1	21.9
White child poverty rate	..	13.9	17.0	16.7	16.2	16.1	15.4	14.6	14.8	15.9	16.1	16.9
Black child poverty rate	..	42.3	47.6	46.6	43.6	43.1	45.6	44.2	43.7	44.8	45.6	46.6
Hispanic child poverty rate	..	33.2	39.5	39.2	40.3	37.7	39.6	37.9	36.2	38.4	39.8	39.9
Poverty rate of people in female-headed households	38.1	36.7	40.6	38.4	37.6	38.3	38.3	37.2	32.2	33.4	39.7	38.5
Percent of federal budget spent on food assistance	0.5	2.4	2.1	2.1	2.0	1.9	1.9	1.9	1.9	1.9	2.0	2.3
Total infant mortality rate	20.0	12.6	11.5	10.8	10.6	10.4	10.1	10.0	9.7	9.1	8.9	8.5
White infant mortality rate	17.8	11.0	10.1	9.4	9.3	8.9	8.6	8.5	8.5	7.7	7.3	..
Black infant mortality rate	32.6	21.4	19.6	18.4	18.2	18.0	17.9	17.6	17.6	17.0	17.6	..
Unemployment rate	4.9	7.1	9.7	7.5	7.2	7.0	6.2	5.5	5.3	5.5	6.7	7.4

Household income distribution (per quintile in percentages)

	1970	1980	1982	1984	1985	1986	1987	1988	1989	1990	1991	1992
Lowest	..	5.0	4.5	4.4	4.4	4.3	4.3	4.4	3.8	3.9	3.8	3.8
Second	..	11.6	11.0	10.7	10.8	10.8	10.6	10.7	9.5	9.6	9.6	9.4
Middle	..	17.3	16.9	16.7	16.7	16.7	16.6	16.7	15.8	15.9	15.9	15.8
Fourth	..	24.5	24.2	24.1	24.1	24.2	24.1	24.2	24	24	24.2	24.2
Highest	..	41.5	43.5	44.2	44.1	44.2	44.4	44.1	46.8	46.6	46.5	46.9

Table 6: United States – State Poverty Conditions

	Populations in millions July 1993	% Population in Poverty 1992	Unemployment Rate April 1994**	AFDC and Food Stamp Benefits as % of Poverty Level, 4 person Family, 1993	Infant Mortality Rate 1993	% of Children Under 12 Hungry, 1991	% of Population all ages Hungry, 1991
Alabama	4.19	17.1	5.8	47.2	9.9	17.0	15.8
Alaska	.60	10.0	8.3	92.7	7.5	8.3	9.9
Arizona	3.94	15.1	5.6	63.6	7.0	12.1	12.4
Arkansas	2.42	17.4	5.1	51.6	9.5	18.4	14.5
California	31.21	15.8	9.6	82.7	6.7	13.1	13.2
Colorado	3.57	10.6	5.4	64.4	7.5	9.9	8.7
Connecticut	3.28	9.4	4.9	85.5	7.5*	7.8	7.2
Delaware	.70	7.6	5.5	63.0	8.3	10.6	6.3
District of Columbia	.58	20.3	7.3	68.4	18.5	17.1	15.6
Florida	13.68	15.3	7.4	60.4	8.7	13.2	12.9
Georgia	6.92	17.8	5.6	58.5	10.1	13.1	14.4
Hawaii	1.17	11.0	5.6	98.1	6.7	10.8	6.4
Idaho	1.10	15.0	4.7	61.5	7.5	15.6	11.6
Illinois	11.70	15.3	5.5	63.8	10.3	13.9	11.3
Indiana	5.71	11.7	4.9	59.4	9.3	12.0	13.2

Table 6 continued: United States – State Poverty Conditions

	Populations in millions July 1993	% Population in Poverty 1992	Unemployment Rate April 1994**	AFDC and Food Stamp Benefits as % of Poverty Level, 4 person Family, 1993	Infant Mortality Rate 1993	% of Children Under 12 Hungry, 1991	% of Population all ages Hungry, 1991
Iowa	2.81	11.3	3.6	68.1	6.9	14.7	8.0
Kansas	2.53	11.0	5.9	70.1	8.2	10.5	10.3
Kentucky	3.79	19.7	4.9	54.8	8.8	14.3	15.8
Louisiana	4.30	24.2	8.4	50.5	9.8	15.9	15.9
Maine	1.24	13.4	6.4	72.5	6.6	11.2	11.8
Maryland	4.97	11.6	5.4	66.7	9.4	7.9	7.6
Massachusetts	6.01	10.0	6.1	75.9	5.6	9.3	9.2
Michigan	9.48	13.5	5.7	73.0	9.3	13.3	11.8
Minnesota	4.52	12.8	4.2	75.5	7.3	9.8	10.8
Mississippi	2.64	24.5	7.2	43.0	11.9	18.9	19.9
Missouri	5.23	15.6	5.0	59.2	8.5	12.7	12.4
Montana	.84	13.7	5.2	67.4	7.9	14.7	12.9
Nebraska	1.61	10.3	3.1	64.6	8.8	13.2	8.0
Nevada	1.39	14.4	5.2	63.0	6.6	12.9	9.6
New Hampshire	1.13	8.6	4.6	72.8	4.8	5.8	6.1
New Jersey	7.88	10.0	7.2	68.4	8.0	10.0	8.1
New Mexico	1.62	21.0	5.1	64.3	9.3	17.2	18.8
New York	18.20	15.3	8.2	85.1	8.5	14.6	12.8
North Carolina	6.95	15.7	3.9	55.8	10.3	12.4	12.2
North Dakota	.64	11.9	3.8	68.4	7.1	12.8	12.2
Ohio	11.09	12.4	6.3	64.2	8.8	11.7	11.2
Oklahoma	3.23	18.4	6.5	62.7	9.2	13.5	14.2
Oregon	3.03	11.3	5.9	75.2	6.7	11.3	11.3
Pennsylvania	12.05	11.7	6.6	69.2	8.7	12.3	9.2
Rhode Island	1.00	12.0	6.2	79.8	8.5	12.2	8.7
South Carolina	3.64	18.9	7.0	51.0	9.4	15.0	13.7
South Dakota	.72	14.8	2.8	66.3	10.5	13.4	11.7
Tennessee	5.10	17.0	4.7	49.9	9.9	14.7	13.0
Texas	18.03	17.8	6.3	49.4	7.6	13.6	14.7
Utah	1.86	9.3	3.5	67.4	6.0	11.3	10.8
Vermont	.58	10.4	4.0	82.5	4.9	10.0	10.6
Virginia	6.50	9.4	5.1	63.2	9.7*	9.7	8.3
Washington	5.26	11.0	5.9	79.3	6.9	10.7	8.0
West Virginia	1.82	22.3	8.9	57.1	9.3	18.3	15.0
Wisconsin	5.04	10.8	4.7	75.3	8.0	11.4	8.3
Wyoming	.47	10.3	6.7	62.0	8.1	10.2	8.3

Notes

* 1991.
** Preliminary data

Sources for Tables

TABLE 1: Column 1 - Population Reference Bureau, Inc., *World Population Data Sheet 1994* (Washington: Population Reference Bureau, 1994); hereafter *"WPDS."*

2 - *Ibid.*

3 - UNICEF, *The State of the World's Children 1994* (New York: Oxford University Press, 1994); hereafter *"SWC."*

4 - United Nations Development Program, *Human Development Report 1994* (New York: Oxford University Press, 1994); hereafter *"HDR."*

5 - *WPDS.*

6 - *Ibid.*

7 - *Ibid.*

8 - *Ibid.*

9 - *SWC.*

10 - *Ibid.*

11 - *Ibid.*

12 - *Ibid.*

TABLE 2: Column 1 - *HDR.*

2 - *Ibid.*

3 - *Ibid.*

4 - *Ibid.*

5 - For developing countries, *Ibid.* For industrial countries and the newly independent states of the former Soviet Union, *SWC* (1990 data).

6 - For developing countries, *HDR.* For industrial countries and former Soviet Union (measles only), *SWC* (1990-1992 data).

7 - *HDR.*

8 - For developing countries, *HDR.* For industrial countries and former Soviet Union, *SWC.*

9 - World Resources Institute, *World Resources 1994-1995* (New York: Oxford University Press, 1994).

TABLE 3: Column 1 - World Bank, *World Development Report 1994* (New York: Oxford University Press, 1994) (for regional aggregate data) and *The World Bank Atlas 1994* (Washington: World Bank, 1994).

2 - *World Development Report 1994.*

3 - *HDR.*

4 - *Ibid.*

5 - World Bank, *World Debt Tables 1993-94* (Washington: World Bank 1993).

6 - *Ibid.*

7 - Based on data provided by the Food and Agriculture Organization of the UN.

8 - Based on FAO data.

9 - *World Development Report 1994.*

10 - *SWC.*

TABLE 4: Column 1 - U.N. Administrative Committee on Coordination/Subcommittee on Nutrition, *Second Report on the World Nutrition Situation, Vol.II: Country Trends, Methods, and Statistics* (Geneva: ACC/SCN, 1993).

2 - *SWC.*

3 - *Ibid.*

4 - *Ibid.*

5 - *Ibid.*

6 - *Ibid.*

7 - *Ibid.*

8 - *Ibid.*

9 - *HDR.*

10 - *Ibid.*

11 - *Ibid.*

TABLE 5: - Except as noted, data from U.S. Bureau of the Census. Percent of federal budget spent on food assistance from U.S. Department of Agriculture. Unemployment rate from U.S. Department of Labor. Infant mortality data from National Center for Health Statistics.

TABLE 6: Column 1 - U.S. Bureau of the Census.

2 - U.S. Bureau of the Census.

3 - U.S. Department of Labor.

4 - *Kids Count Data Book 1994* (Washington: Center for the Study of Social Policy, 1994).

5 - National Center for Health Statistics, *Monthly Vital Statistics Report* 42:12 (May 1994).

6 - Food Research and Action Center, Community Childhood Hunger Identification Project (1991 data).

7 - Center on Hunger, Poverty, and Nutrition Policy, Tufts University (1991 data).

ACC/SCN	U.N. Administrative Committee on Coordination/ Subcommittee on Nutrition
AFDC	Aid to Families with Dependent Children
AIDS	Acquired Immune Deficiency Syndrome
BFW	Bread For The World
EU	European Union
FAO	Food and Agriculture Organization of the U.N.
GATT	General Agreement on Tariffs and Trade
HDI	Human Development Index
IFAD	U.N. International Fund for Agricultural Development
IFI	International Financial Institution
NGO	Nongovernmental Organization
OPEC	Organization of Petroleum Exporting Countries
U.N.	United Nations
UNDP	U.N. Development Program
UNHCR	U.N. High Commissioner for Refugees
UNICEF	U.N. Children's Fund
U.S.	United States
WIC	Special Supplemental Food Program for Women, Infants, and Children

Anemia – A condition in which the hemoglobin concentration (the number of red blood cells) is lower than normal as a result of a deficiency of one or more essential nutrients, such as iron, or due to disease.

Apartheid – The legally-enforced system of racial segregation and discrimination against blacks and others of colored descent in South Africa.

Caste – An exclusive social or occupational class or group; in Hinduism, distinct hereditary social classes.

Child mortality rate – The annual number of deaths of children between one and five years of age per 1,000 live births.

Cretinism – Physical and mental retardation due to iodine deficiency.

Daily calorie requirement – The average number of calories needed to sustain normal levels of activity and health, taking into account age, sex, body weight, and climate; roughly 2,350 calories per person per day.

Debt service – The sum of repayments of principal and payments of interest on debt.

Desertification – The change of arable land into a desert, either from natural causes or human activity.

Developing countries – Countries in which most people have a low economic standard of living. Also known as the "Third World," the "South," and the "less developed countries."

Ethnicity – A system of categorizing communities according to culture, custom, race, language, religion, and other social distinctions.

Fallow – To leave land uncultivated for one or more seasons.

Famine – A situation of extreme scarcity of food, potentially leading to widespread starvation.

Fertility rate – The number of children born by a woman during her lifetime, a measure of long-term population changes.

Food security – Assured access for every person, primarily by production or purchase, to enough nutritious food to sustain productive human life.

Foreign exchange – Currency acceptable for use in international trade, such as U.S. dollars. The value of one currency in terms of another is the *exchange rate*.

Goiter – Enlargement of the thyroid gland (causing a swelling in the front of the neck) due to iodine deficiency.

Green revolution – A term used to describe technological changes in agricultural production methods since World War II. The technologies rely on the use of improved seeds, known as high-yielding varieties, chemical fertilizers, and pesticides.

Gross domestic product (GDP) – The value of all goods and services produced within a nation during a specified period, usually a year.

Gross national product (GNP) – The value of all goods and services produced by a country's citizens, wherever they are located.

Hunger – A condition in which people lack the basic food intake to provide them with the energy and nutrients for fully productive, active, and healthy lives.

Industrial countries – Countries in which most people have a high economic standard of living (though there are often significant poverty populations). Also called "developed countries" or the "North."

Infant mortality rate (IMR) – The annual number of deaths of infants under one year of age per 1,000 live births.

Inflation – An increase in overall prices, which leads to a decrease in purchasing power.

Informal sector or economy – Small-scale manufacture and trade in goods and services, generally not recognized in official plans, policies, and statistics.

International Monetary Fund (IMF) – An international organization which makes loans to countries which have foreign exchange and monetary problems. These loans are conditioned upon the willingness of the borrowing country to adopt IMF-approved economic policies.

Low birthweight infants – Babies born weighing 2,500 grams (five pounds, eight ounces) or less, who are especially vulnerable to illness and death during the first month of life.

Malnutrition – Failure to achieve nutrient requirements, which can impair physical and/or mental health. Malnutrition may result from consuming too little food or a shortage or imbalance of key nutrients, e.g., micronutrient deficiencies or excess consumption of refined sugar and fat.

Micronutrients – Vitamins, major minerals, and trace elements needed for a healthy and balanced diet.

Morbidity – The proportion of sickness or of a specific disease in a geographic locality.

Patriarchy – Systems of social and cultural organization characterized by male dominance.

Poverty line – An official measure of poverty defined by national governments. In the United States, it is based on ability to afford the U.S. Department of Agriculture's "Thrifty Food Plan," which provides a less-than-adequate diet.

Purchasing Power Parity (PPP) – An estimate of the U.S. dollars required to purchase comparable goods in different countries.

Recession – A period in which a country's GDP declines in two or more consecutive three-month periods; a period of reduced economic activity that is less severe than a full fledged economic crisis ("depression").

Sovereignty – Supreme independent political authority, generally residing in national governments.

Structural adjustment program (SAP) – Economic policy changes, often imposed upon an indebted country by its lenders as a condition for future loans, intended to stimulate economic growth. These generally involve reducing the role of government in the economy and increasing exports.

Stunting – Failure to grow to normal height caused by chronic undernutrition during the formative years of childhood.

Sustainability – Society's ability to shape its economic and social systems so as to maintain both natural resources and human life.

Underemployment – The situation of not being fully employed year round.

Under five mortality rate – The annual number of deaths of children under five years of age per 1,000 live births.

Undernutrition – A form of mild, chronic, or acute malnutrition which is characterized by inadequate intake of food energy (measured by calories), usually due to eating too little. Stunting, wasting, and being underweight are common forms of undernutrition.

Underweight – A condition in which a person is seriously below normal weight for her/his age.

Unemployment – The state of being without work, usually applied to those not working involuntarily.

Uprooted people – People displaced against their will from their communities and means of survival, including refugees who flee their homelands, people displaced within their own countries, and people living in "refugee-like" circumstances who are not legally recognized as refugees.

Vulnerability to hunger – Individuals, households, communities, or nations who have enough to eat most of the time, but whose poverty makes them especially susceptible to changes in the economy, climate, or political conditions.

Wasting – A condition in which a person is seriously below the normal weight for her/his height due to acute undernutrition.

World Bank – An intergovernmental agency which makes long-term loans to the governments of developing nations.

Notes and Bibliography

Introduction

1. The Bellagio Declaration, issued by 23 hunger experts from 14 countries in 1989, sets specific, feasible targets for reducing world hunger by the year 2000: eliminate deaths by famine, cut malnutrition in half for mothers and small children, eradicate iodine and vitamin A deficiencies, and end hunger in half the poorest households. The Medford Declaration, issued in 1991 and endorsed by thousands of organizations representing millions of people, focuses on hunger in the United States. It calls for full funding of U.S. government food programs, economic self-reliance through market-based employment and training programs, child care, and tax incentives which reward work.

2. U.S. Bureau of the Census, *Statistical Abstract of the United States: 1993* (Washington: U.S. Government Printing Office, 1993).

3. "The Entertainment Economy, *Business Week*, March 14, 1994, p. 60.

4. Christopher Lasch, *The True and Only Heaven: Progress and Its Critics* (New York: W.W. Norton, 1991), p. 516.

5. Andrew Bard Schmookler, *The Illusion of Choice: How the Market Economy Shapes Our Destiny* (Albany: State University of New York Press, 1993), pp. 12-13.

6. World Bank, *World Development Report 1994* (New York: Oxford University Press, 1994).

Overview of World Hunger

1. FAO, *World Food Supplies and the Prevalence of Hunger* (Rome: FAO, 1992), p. 8.

2. Africa in this table equals sub-Saharan Africa elsewhere (except inclusion of Algeria and non-inclusion of Somalia). Eastern Mediterranean includes all of Near East and North Africa (except Algeria) and countries such as Afghanistan, Iran, Pakistan, and Somalia. Americas includes the United States and Canada. Asia includes all of Asia (except for some countries that are included in Eastern Mediterranean) as well as Australia, New Zealand, and Japan.

3. Shlomo Reutlinger, "Addressing Hunger: An Historical Perspective of International Initiatives," Background Paper Prepared for the World Bank Conference on Overcoming Global Hunger, The American University, Washington, DC, November 29-December 1, 1993, p. 9.

4. South Asia consists of Afghanistan, Bangladesh, India, Iran, Nepal, Pakistan, and Sri Lanka. Southeast Asia includes Indonesia, Cambodia, Laos, Malaysia, Burma (Myanmar), Papua New Guinea, the Philippines, Thailand, and Vietnam.

5. Center on Hunger, Poverty, and Nutrition Policy at Tufts University. These figures have been challenged. The most commonly used method of estimating hunger (inability to afford sufficient food to meet the nutritional needs of a household) is through interviews, in which randomly selected people are asked whether they know someone who at some time in the past year did not have enough to eat.

6. Barry Davidson, Canadian Association of Food Banks, personal communication, April 1994.

7. Bob Evans, National Anti-Poverty Organization, personal communication, April 1994.

**Additional Sources –
Developing Countries:**

ACC/SCN. *First Report on the World Nutrition Situation.* Geneva:ACC/SCN, 1987.

ACC/SCN. *Second Report on the World Nutrition Situation, Volume I: Global and Regional Results.* Geneva: ACC/SCN, 1992.

ACC/SCN. *Second Report on the World Nutrition Situation, Volume II: Country Trends, Methods, and Statistics.* Geneva: ACC/SCN, 1993.

Avery, Dennis T. *Global Food Progress 1991.* Indianapolis: Hudson Institute, 1991.

Chen, Robert S., ed. *The Hunger Report: 1990.* Providence: Alan Shawn Feinstein World Hunger Program, 1990.

Chen, Robert S. and Pitt, M. M. *Estimating the Prevalence of World Hunger: A Review of Methods and Data.* Providence: Alan Shawn Feinstein World Hunger Program, 1991.

Cohen, Marc J. and Hoehn, Richard A., eds. *Hunger 1992: Ideas that Work, Second Annual Report on the State of World Hunger.* Washington: Bread for the World Institute, 1991.

FAO. *Production Yearbook, 1992.* Rome: FAO, 1993.

_____. *Foodcrops and Shortages* No. 3 (May/June 1994). Rome: FAO, 1994.

FAO and World Health Organization. *Nutrition and Development: A Global Assessment.* Rome: FAO and WHO, 1992.

_____. *World Declaration and Plan of Action for Nutrition.* Rome: FAO and WHO, 1992.

_____. *Preventing Specific Micronutrient Deficiencies.* ICN Theme Paper No 6. Rome: FAO and WHO, 1992.

Field, John O. "From Food Security to Food Insecurity: The Case of Iraq, 1990-91." *GeoJournal* 30:2 (1993).

Kates, Robert *et. al. The Hunger Report: 1988.* Providence: Alan Shawn Feinstein World Hunger Program, 1988.

_____. *The Hunger Report: Update 1989.* Providence: Alan Shawn Feinstein World Hunger Program, 1989.

Lipton, Michael. *The Poor and the Poorest.* Washington: World Bank, 1988.

Lipton, Michael and Maxwell, S. *The New Poverty Agenda: an Overview.* Institute for Development Studies Discussion Paper No. 306. Sussex: IDS, 1992.

Marek, T. *Ending Malnutrition: Why Increasing Income is not Enough.* AFTPN. Washington D.C.: World Bank, 1992.

Maxwell, S. and Frankenberger, T. *Household Food Security: Concepts, Indicators, Measurements.* New York: UNICEF/IFAD, 1992.

Millman, Sara R. *et al. The Hunger Report: Update 1991.* Providence: Alan Shawn Feinstein World Hunger Program, 1991.

Millman, Sara R. and Chen, Robert S. *Measurement of Hunger: Defining Thresholds.* Providence: Alan Shawn Feinstein World Hunger Program, 1991.

Psacharopoulos, G. *et al. Poverty and Income Distribution in Latin America: The Story of the 1980s.* Latin America Regional Study Report No. 27. Washington D.C.: World Bank, 1993.

Sen, Amartya. *Poverty and Famines.* Oxford: Pergamon Press for the International Labor Organization, 1981.

_____. *Hunger and Entitlements: Research for Action.* Helsinki: World Institute for Development Economics Research, United Nations University, 1987.

Serageldin, Ismail. "More than 700 Million People Suffer from Hunger and Malnutrition." *World Bank News,* November 18, 1993, pp. 2-6.

Svedberg, P. *Poverty and Undernutrition in Sub-Saharan Africa: Theory, Evidence, Policy.* Monograph Series No. 19. Helsinki: Institute for International Economic Studies, 1991.

United Nations. *The World's Women: 1970-1990, Trends and Statistics.* New York: United Nations, 1991.

U.S. Committee for Refugees. *World Refugee Survey 1994.* Washington: Immigration and Refugee Services of America, 1994.

Uvin, P. "Regime, Surplus, and Self-Interest: The International Politics of Food Aid." *International Studies Quarterly* 36:2 (1992).

_____. *The International Organization of Hunger.* London: Kegan Paul, 1994.

_____. "The State of World Hunger." In *The Hunger Report: 1993,* pp. 1-42. Edited by Peter Uvin. Langhorne, PA: Gordon and Breach for the Alan Shawn Feinstein World Hunger Program, 1994.

Walters, Harry. "An Issues Paper." Background Paper Prepared for the World Bank Conference on Overcoming Global Hunger, The American University, Washington, DC, November 29-December 1, 1993.

World Food Council. *The Global State of Hunger and Malnutrition: 1992 Report.* Rome: WFC, 1992.

World Food Program. *1993 Food Aid Review.* Rome: WFP, 1993.

World Health Organization. *National Strategies for Overcoming Micronutrient Malnutrition.* Geneva: WHO, 1991.

_____. *Health for All Database.* Geneva: WHO, 1992.

Western Europe:
Baldwin, Geoffrey. "Farewell to Europe's Welfare State." *Toward Freedom,* October 1993, pp. 4-5.

European Federation of National Organizations Working with the Homeless (FEANTA). Brochure. Brussels: FEANTA, 1993.

Rowen, Hobart. "Europe in the Mire of Joblessness." *The Washington Post,* January 20, 1994.

Snyder, A. Cecilia. "Western Europe." In *Hunger 1994: Transforming the Politics of Hunger,* pp. 157-160. Edited by Marc J. Cohen. Silver Spring, MD: Bread for the World Institute, 1993.

United States:
Billingsley, Andrew. *Climbing Jacob's Ladder: The Enduring Legacy of African-American Families.* New York: Simon and Schuster, 1993.

"Can We End Poverty U.S.A.?" *Hunger Notes* 19:2 (Fall 1993).

Cohen, Barbara E. and Burt, Martha R. *Eliminating Hunger: Food Security for the 1990s.* Urban Institute Project Report. Washington: The Urban Institute, 1989.

"Food Stamp Rolls Fell to 27.7 Million, Says FNS." *Nutrition Week,* July 8, 1994, p. 8.

Midgley, Jane. *The Women's Budget, 4th Edition.* Philadelphia: The Jane Addams Peace Association, 1991.

Phillips, Kevin. *The Politics of Rich and Poor.* New York: Random House, 1990.

Second Harvest. *Update,* Winter 1994.

Snyder, A. Cecilia. "Hunger Facts." Bread for the World Background Paper No. 124, February 1994.

Thurow, Lester. *Book World, The Washington Post,* October 31, 1993.

Canada:
Centre for International Statistics on Economic and Social Welfare. *Countdown 93: Campaign 2000 Child Poverty Indicator Report.* Ottawa: Canadian Council for Social Development, 1993.

National Anti-Poverty Organization and Charter Committee on Poverty Issues. *Canada's Second Report on the Implementation of the International Covenant of Economic, Social, and Cultural Rights, Articles 10-15.* Geneva: Committee on Economic, Social, and Cultural Rights, 1993.

Statistics Canada. *Income Distributions by Size in Canada 1992.* Ottawa: Statistics Canada, 1993.

Former Soviet Union, Central and Eastern Europe:
De Souza, Michele; Lundell, Mark R.; and Lamb, Jason M. "Price Reform and the Consumer in Central and Eastern Europe." *FoodReview* (United States Department of Agriculture, Economic Research Service) 16:3 (September-December 1993): 17-22.

Feshbach, Murray and Friendly, Alfred, Jr. *Ecocide in the U.S.S.R.: Health and Nature Under Siege.* New York: Basic Books, 1992.

Hockstader, Lee. "Where Rich Land Makes Poor Farmers." *The Washington Post,* April 18, 1994.

Lane, Charles. "Wounds of War: Srebrenica's Children." *Newsweek,* May 3, 1993, p.48.

Lenfant, C. and Ernst, N. "Daily Dietary Fat and Total Food-Energy Intakes – Third National Health and Nutrition Examination Survey, Phase 1, 1989-91." *Morbidity and Mortality Weekly Report* (National Institutes of Health), February 25, 1994, pp. 116-125.

Organization for Economic Co-operation and Development, Directorate for Food, Agriculture, and Fisheries, Committee for Agriculture, Ad Hoc Group on East/West Economic Relations in Agriculture. Reports on Agriculture in the Former Soviet Union and Central and Eastern Europe. 1994

Power, Samantha. "US Says Hindering Bosnia Aid Falls Under War Crime Probe." *Boston Globe,* January 8, 1994.

Randal, Jonathan C. "Serbs Heed Threat, Shift Heavy Guns." *The Washington Post,* April 25, 1994.

Sedik, David J. "Russian Price Reform Eliminates Shortages, Alters Meat Consumption." *FoodReview* 16:3 (September-December 1993): 12-16.

Traynor, Ian. "I estimate that 20 to 30 people are dying of starvation everyday." *Guardian,* March 15, 1993.

Powerlessness and Politics

1. Solon L. Barraclough, *An End to Hunger? The Social Origins of Food Strategies* (London and Atlantic Highlands, NJ: Zed Press for the United Nations Institute on Social Development and the South Centre, 1991), p. 120.

2. Betsy Hartmann and James Boyce, *Needless Hunger: Voices from a Bangladesh Village* (San Francisco: Institute for Food and Development Policy, 1979).

3. Quoted in Richard Critchfield, *Villages* (Garden City, NY: Anchor Press/Doubleday, 1981), p. 20.

4. Paul P. Streeten, "Hunger," Boston University Institute for Economic Development Discussion Paper Series, No. 4, December 1989, p. 14.

5. United Nations Fund for Population Activities, *The State of World Population 1993* (New York: UNFPA, 1993), p. 11.

6. Rehman Sobhan, "The Politics of Hunger and Entitlements," in Jean Drèze and Amartya Sen, eds., *The Political Economy of Hunger, Volume I: Entitlements and Well-Being* (Oxford: Clarendon Press, 1990), p. 94.

7. Jean Drèze and Amartya Sen, *Hunger and Public Action* (Oxford: Clarendon Press, 1989), pp. 277-278.

8. Frances Fox Piven and Richard Cloward, *Why Americans Don't Vote* (New York: Pantheon, 1988), pp. xi, 17-18, 199.

9. Hartmann and Boyce, p. 8; see also Barraclough, pp. 180-182.

10. "World Declaration on Nutrition," Paragraph 1, p.1, in *International Conference on Nutrition: World Declaration and Plan of Action for Nutrition* (Rome: FAO and WHO, 1992).

11. *Ibid.,* Paragraph 12, p. 3.

12. David C. Korten, *Getting to the 21st Century: Voluntary Action and the Global Agenda* (West Hartford, CT: Kumarian, 1990), pp. 10-11.

13. Richard W. Franke and Barbara H. Chasin, "Kerala: Radical Reform as Development in an Indian State," Food First Development Report No. 6 (October 1989); Drèze and Sen, *Hunger and Public Action Public Action,* pp. 222-223, 251-252, 277-278; Barraclough, pp. 119-120.

14. Cornelia Nkomo, ORAP Division Head, personal interview, Washington, DC, February 25 and March 22, 1994; United Nations Development Program, *Human Development Report 1993* (New York: Oxford University Press, 1993), p. 97; Bill Rau, *From Feast to Famine: Official Cures and Grassroots Remedies to Africa's Food Crisis* (London: Zed, 1991), pp. 174, 192.

15. Jane Pryer and Nigel Crook, *Cities of Hunger: Urban Malnutrition in Developing Countries* (Oxford: Oxfam, 1988), pp. 66-82.

16. *Ibid.,* p. 81.

17. Information provided by ROCC and World Hunger Year's "Reinvesting in America" project.

18. "The Great Tablecloth," cited in *World Hunger: Awareness, Affinity, Action* (Washington: The Congressional Hunger Center, 1993), p. 27.

Additional Sources:
Andrews, Margaret S. and Clancy, Katherine L. "The Political Economy of the Food Stamp Program in the United States." In *The Political Economy of Food and Nutrition Policies,* pp. 61-78. Edited by Per Pinstrup-Andersen. Baltimore and London: The Johns Hopkins University Press for the International Food Policy Research Institute, 1993.

Avery, William P., ed. *World Agriculture and the GATT.* Boulder, CO: Lynne Rienner, 1993.

Barry, Tom. *Central America Inside Out.* New York: Grove Weidenfeld, 1991.

Bread for the World Institute. *Hunger 1990: A Report on the State of World Hunger.* Washington: Bread for the World Institute, 1990.

Byron, William J., S.J. "On the Protection and Promotion of the Right to Food." In *Science, Ethics, and Food,* pp. 14-30. Edited by Brian W.J. LeMay. Washington: Smithsonian Institution Press, 1988.

Cohen, Marc J., ed. *Hunger 1994: Transforming the Politics of Hunger, Fourth Annual Report on the State of World Hunger.* Silver Spring, MD: Bread for the World Institute, 1993.

The Courier: Africa-Caribbean-Pacific-European Union No. 143 (January-February 1994).

Field, John O. "From Nutrition Planning to Nutrition Management: The Politics of Action." In *The Political Economy of Food and Nutrition Policies,* pp. 225-235.

Foster, Phillips. *The World Food Problem: Tackling the Causes of Undernutrition in the Third World.* Boulder: Lynne Rienner, 1992.

Fowler, Robert Booth and Orenstein, Jeffrey R. *Contemporary Issues in Political Theory.* New York: Wiley, 1977.

Goodno, James B. *The Philippines: Land of Broken Promises.* London and Atlantic Highlands, NJ: Zed, 1991.

Hopkins, Raymond F. "Nutrition-Related Policy Research: A Political Science Perspective on the Role of Economic and Political Factors." In *The Political Economy of Food and Nutrition Policies,* pp. 206-222.

Horner, Simon. "*1993 Human Development Report:* '90 Percent of the World's People Lack Control Over their Own Lives.'" *The Courier: Africa-Caribbean-Pacific-European Community* No. 140 (July-August 1993): 86-88.

Indivisible Human Rights: The Relationship of Political and Civil Rights to Survival, Subsistence, and Poverty. New York: Human Rights Watch, September 1992.

International Fund for Agricultural Development. *The State of World Rural Poverty: An Inquiry into Its Causes and Consequences.* New York: New York University Press, 1992.

Johnson, Clifford M. *et al. Child Poverty in America.* Washington: Children's Defense Fund, 1991.

Jonsson, Urban. "Integrating Political and Economic Factors within Nutrition-Related Policy Research: An Economic Perspective." In *The Political Economy of Food and Nutrition Policies,* pp.193-205.

_____. "The Socio-Economic Causes of Hunger." In *Food as a Human Right,* pp. 22-36. Edited by Asbjorn Eide *et al.* Tokyo: The United Nations University, 1984.

Judd, Frank. "Fair's Fair: Democracy, Social Justice, Sustainable Development, and International Synergy." *Development: Journal of the Society for International Development* (1992:3): 6.

Kutzner, Patricia L. *World Hunger: A Reference Handbook.* Santa Barbara, CA: ABC-Clio, 1991.

Lindbloom, Eric N. *Building on Basics: A Report on the Global Education Crisis and U.S. Foreign Aid to Basic Education.* Washington: RESULTS Educational Fund, 1990.

Massignon, Nicole. "The Urban Explosion in the Third World." *OECD Observer,* June/July 1993, pp. 18, 20-21.

Matthews, David. *Politics for People: Finding a Responsible Public Voice.* Urbana: University of Illinois Press, 1994.

McAfee, Kathy. *Storm Signals: Structural Adjustment and Development Alternatives in the Caribbean.* Boston: South End, 1991.

Nzongola-Ntalaja, ed. *The Crisis in Zaire: Myths and Realities.* Trenton, NJ: Africa World Press, 1986.

Pinstrup-Andersen, Per. "Integrating Political and Economic Considerations in Programs and Policies to Improve Nutrition: Lessons Learned." In *The Political Economy of Food and Nutrition Policies,* pp. 225-235.

Poleman, Thomas T. "World Hunger: Extent, Causes, and Cures." In *The Role of Markets in the World Food Economy,* pp. 41-75. Edited by D. Gale Johnson and G. Edward Schuh. Boulder: Westview, 1983.

Ram, N. "An Independent Press and Anti-Hunger Strategies: The Indian Experience." In *The Political Economy of Hunger, Vol. I,* pp. 146-190. Edited by Drèze and Sen.

Tussie, Diana. "Trading in Fear? U.S. Hegemony and the Open World Economy in Perspective." In *The New International Political Economy,* pp. 79-95. Edited by Craig N. Murphy and Roger Tooze. Boulder: Lynne Rienner, 1991.

Wallerstein, Immanuel. *The Modern World System: Capitalist Agriculture and the Origins of the European World Economy.* New York and London: Academic Press, 1974.

_____. "The Rise and Future Demise of the World Capitalist System: Concepts for Comparative Analysis." *Comparative Studies in Society and History* XVI:4 (October 1974): 387-415.

Webb, Patrick and von Braun, Joachim. "Ending Hunger Soon: Concepts and Priorities." Background Paper Prepared by the International Food Policy Research Institute for the World Bank Conference on Overcoming Global Hunger, The American University, Washington, DC, November 29-December 1, 1993.

World Bank. *World Development Report 1990: Poverty.* New York: Oxford University Press, 1990.

Wright, Robin and McManus, Doyle. *Flashpoints: Promise and Peril in a New World.* New York: Alfred A. Knopf, 1991.

Power, Hunger, and the World Bank

1. G.K. Helleiner, *Debt Relief for Africa: A Call for Urgent Action on Human Development,* UNICEF Staff Working Papers No. 11 (New York: UNICEF, 1993).

2. World Bank, *Annual Report 1993* (Washington: World Bank, 1993), p. 31.

3. United Nations Development Program, *Human Development Report 1994* (New York: Oxford University Press, 1994), p. 64.

4. Development Assistance Committee, *Development Cooperation, 1993 Report* (Paris: Organization for Economic Cooperation and Development, 1993), p. 188; this figure excludes lending by the World Bank's concessional arm, the International Development Association.

The Right to Food

1. Philip Alston, "International Law and the Human Right to Food," in Philip Alston and Katarina Tomasevski, eds., *The Right to Food* (Dordrecht: Martinus Nijhoff for the Netherlands Institute of Human Rights, 1984).

2. Katarina Tomasevski, ed., *The Right to Food: Guide Through Applicable International Law* (Dordrecht: Martinus Nijhoff, 1987); Centre for Human Rights, *Right to Adequate Food as a Human Right* (New York: United Nations, 1989), p. 19.

3. For further information, contact: Food Security Treaty Campaign, 3501 La Entrada, Santa Barbara, CA 93105, Tel. (805) 563-2193.

Violence and Militarism

1. H.A. Bulhan, *Frantz Fanon and the Psychology of Violence* (New York: Plenum, 1985); J. Salmi, *Violence and Democratic Society* (London: Zed, 1993).

2. United Nations Development Program, *Human Development Report 1994* (New York: Oxford University Press, 1994).

3. *Ibid.*

4. *Ibid.*

5. *Ibid.*; U.S. Committee for Refugees, *World Refugee Survey 1994* (Washington: Immigration and Refugee Services of America, 1994).

6. *Ibid.*, p. 42.

7. John. P. Lederach, "Mediating Conflict," *Journal of Peace Research* 28:1 (1991).

8. Frances Stewart, "War and Development," Development Studies Working Papers No. 56 (Oxford: International Development Center, 1993).

9. Larry Minear *et al.*, *Humanitarianism Under Siege: A Critical Review of Operation Lifeline Sudan* (Trenton: Red Sea Press and Washington: Bread for the World Institute, 1991).

10. Cornell West lecture, African American Studies Program, Smithsonian Institution, April 1994.

11. Walter Wink, *Engaging the Powers: Discernment and Resistance in a World of Domination* (Minneapolis: Fortress Press, 1992), p. 214.

Additional Sources:

Arora, Vivek and Bayoumi, Tamim. "Reductions in World Military Expenditure: Who Stands to Gain?" *Finance and Development*, March, 1994.

Beckmann, David. "Sober Prospects and Christian Hope." In *Friday Morning Reflections at the World Bank*, pp. 17-35. Edited by David Beckmann. Cabin John, MD: Seven Locks, 1991.

Chelliah, U.B.P. "War Breeds Hunger: Feeding the Victims." *Forum for Applied Research and Public Policy*, Winter 1993.

Drèze, Jean and Sen, Amartya. *Hunger and Public Action* (Oxford: Clarendon, 1989).

"The Economics of Crime." *Business Week*, October 13, 1993, p. 72.

Fox, Thomas J. "Hungry Eat Guns, Not Bread." *National Catholic Reporter*, December 1993.

Giddens, Anthony. *The Nation-State and Violence.* Los Angeles: University of California Press, 1985.

Gil, D.G. *Unravelling Social Policy: Theory, Analysis, and Political Action Towards Social Equality.* Rochester, VT: Schenkman, 1990.

"Guns at Home." *The Washington Post*, October 12, 1993.

Kaplan, Robert D. "The Coming Anarchy." *Atlantic Monthly*, February 1994.

Lewey, Guenter. *Peace and Revolution: The Moral Crisis of American Pacifism.* Ann Arbor, MI: Books on Demand, 1988.

"Matters of Scale." *Worldwatch*, March/April 1994.

Neibuhr, Gustav. "Religion and War." *The Washington Post*, December 12, 1993.

Sojourners, February-March and December 1991; February-March and July 1992; February-March, April, and September-October 1993.

The State of World Conflict Report. Atlanta: Carter Center, 1993.

UNICEF. *Annual Reports, 1990-1993.* New York: UNICEF, 1990-1993.

Poverty in a Global Economy

1. Ismail Serageldin, *Development Partners: Aid and Cooperation in the 1990s* (Stockholm: Swedish International Development Authority, 1993).

2. World Bank, *World Development Report 1993* (New York: Oxford University Press, 1993); United Nations Development Program, *Human Development Report 1993* (New York: Oxford University Press, 1993).

3. Nancy Birdsall and Richard Sabot, "Inequality and Growth Reconsidered," Draft Paper Presented at American Economic Association Annual Meeting, January 1994; Sylvia Nasas, "Economics of Equality: A New View," *The New York Times*, January 8, 1994.

4. International Monetary Fund, *Government Finance Statistics Yearbook: 1993* (Washington: IMF, 1993).

5. Edward B. Fiske, *Basic Education: Building Block for Global Development* (Washington: Academy for Educational Development, 1993).

6. Peter G. Peterson, *Facing Up: How to Rescue the Economy from Crushing Debt and Restore the American Dream* (New York: Simon and Schuster, 1993), pp. 320 ff.

7. *Ibid.*

8. U.S. Bureau of the Census, "Poverty in the United States: 1992," *Current Population Reports: Consumer Income*, Series P60-185 (Washington: U.S. Government Printing Office, 1993).

Population, Consumption, and Environment

1. Population Reference Bureau, Washington D.C., telephone inquiry, June 10, 1994; World Resources Institute, *World Resources 1994-1995* (New York: Oxford University Press, 1994), pp. 27 ff; "Developing World will Claim Huge Share of Population Growth," *Christian Science Monitor*, April 29, 1994.

2. UNICEF, *The State of the World's Children 1993* (New York: Oxford University Press, 1993).

3. Jessica Matthews, "Population Control That Works", *The Washington Post*, April 1, 1994.

4. "On Investing in Women," *The Newsletter From the International Center for Economic Growth*, January 1994, p. 6.

5. Lawrence Summers "Investing in All the People," *The Pakistan Development Review* 31:4 Part 1 (Winter 1992): 380.

6. Family Health International, "Breastfeeding as a Family Planning Method," *Lancet*, November 19, 1988, pp.1204-1205; "Use of Lactational Amenorrhoea Method During First Six Months After Childbirth Can Increase Child Spacing," *BFHI News,* January/February 1994, p.6.

7. Wellstart International, "Breastfeeding is Remarkable," *Expanded Promotion of Breastfeeding*, 1992, p.1.

8. *Ibid.*, pp. 14, 19.

9. UNICEF, *The State of the World's Children, 1994,* (New York: Oxford University Press, 1994), p.24.

10. World Resources Institute, *A Guide to the Global Environment* (Washington: WRI, 1994), p.5.

11. Lester R. Brown *et al.*, *State of the World 1993* (New York: W. W. Norton, 1993).

12. *Ibid.*, p. 27.

13. *Ibid.*, p. 50.

14. Lester R. Brown, Hal Kane, and Ed Ayres, *Vital Signs 1993* (New York: W. W. Norton and Washington: Worldwatch Institute, 1993), pp. 40, 42.

15. B. Larson, "Fertilizers to Support Agricultural Development in sub-Saharan Africa: What is Needed and Why," Center for Economic Policy Studies Discussion Paper No. 13 (Arlington, VA: Winrock International, 1993); Montague Yudelman *et al.*, *Feeding 10 Billion People in 2050: The Key Role of the CGIAR's International Agricultural Research Centers* (Washington: Action Group on Food Security, 1994); Jessica Matthews, "Malthus's Warning," *The Washington Post*, June 7, 1994.

16. Dennis Avery, "The Organic Farming Threat to People and Wildlife," Hudson Briefing Paper Number 162 (Indianapolis: Hudson Institute, 1994); Julian L. Simon, *The Ultimate Resource* (Princeton: Princeton University Press, 1981).

17. Paul Harrison, *The Greening of Africa* (London: Paladin Grafton Books, 1987).

18. Durning, Alan B., "Poverty and the Environment: Reversing the Downward Spiral," Worldwatch Paper No. 92 (Washington: Worldwatch Institute), p. 27; see also *Understanding the Presbyterian Hunger Program* (Louisville, KY: Presbyterian Hunger Program, no date).

19. Durning, pp. 41-42.

20. World Bank, *World Development Report 1992* (New York: Oxford University Press, 1992), p. 49.

21. *Ibid.*, p.109.

22. Wendell Berry "Out of Your Car, Off Your Horse," *The Atlantic*, February 1991, pp. 62-63.

Racism and Ethnocentrism: International

Barry, Tom. *Roots of Rebellion: Land and Hunger in Central America.* Boston: South End, 1987.

Bello, Walden. *Dark Victory.* London: Pluto, 1994.

"Crisis Aid in Indonesian Famine." *Christian Science Monitor*, October 31, 1979.

Drèze, Jean and Sen, Amartya, eds. *The Political Economy of Hunger, Volume III: Endemic Hunger.* Oxford: Clarendon Press, 1991.

DuBois, W.E.Burghardt. *The Souls of Black Folk.* Chicago: McClurg, 1922.

Fanon, Frantz. *Black Skin, White Masks.* New York: Grove Weidenfeld, 1967.

Gajanayoke, Indra; Caldwell, John C.; and Caldwell, Pat. "Why is Health Relatively Poor on Sri Lanka's Tea Estates?" *Social Science Medicine* 32:7 (1991).

Gamini, Gabriella and Chaudhary, Vivek. "Sri Lankan Villagers Flee Ethnic Attacks in East." *Christian Science Monitor*, August 21, 1990.

"Government on East Timor: Malnutrition, not Starvation." *The Southeast Asia Record*, November 9-15, 1979.

Harris, Marvin. *Patterns of Race in the Americas*. New York: Walker, 1964.

"Horror on Our Doorstep." *The Melbourne Age*, November 1, 1979.

Jordan, Winthrop D. *White Over Black: American Attitudes Toward the Negro, 1550-1812*. Baltimore: Penguin, 1969.

Middle East Watch/Physicians for Human Rights. *The Anfal Campaign in Iraqi Kurdistan: The Destruction of Koreme*. New York: Human Rights Watch, 1993.

Moberg, Mark A. "Marketing Policy and the Loss of Food Self-Sufficiency in Rural Belize." *Human Organization* 50:1 (1991).

"Notes on the Current Situation in East Timor." Parliament of Australia, Foreign Affairs Group, April 6, 1979.

Patterson, Orlando. *Freedom Volume I: Freedom in the Making of Western Culture*. New York: Basic Books, 1991.

"Timorese Battle Famine." *The Washington Post*, November 15, 1979.

Twose, Nigel and Pogrund, Benjamin. *War Wounds: Development Costs of Conflict in Southern Sudan – Sudanese People Report on their War*. London: Panos, 1988.

West, Cornel. *Race Matters*. New York: Vintage Books, 1994.

Racism and Ethnocentrism: The United States

1. Michael Harrington, *The Other America: Poverty in the United States* (NY: Macmillan, 1962).

2. Food Research and Action Center, *Hunger in the United States* (Washington: FRAC, 1993).

3. Billy J. Tidwell, ed., *The State of Black America 1994* (New York: National Urban League, 1994) and *The State of Black America 1993* (New York: National Urban League, 1993).

4. U.S. Bureau of the Census, "Poverty in the United States: 1992," *Current Population Reports: Consumer Income*, Series P60-185 (Washington: U.S. Government Printing Office, 1993), pp. x-xi.

5. National Council of La Raza, *State of Hispanic America 1993* (Washington: NCLR, 1993).

6. U.S. Food and Nutrition Service, "Characteristics of Food Stamp Households: Summer 1992," Advance Report, October 26, 1993, Table 3, p.7.

7. Bread for the World, *A Child Is Waiting: 1994 Offering of Letters Kit* (Silver Spring, MD: BFW, 1994), p.7.

8. William Julius Wilson, *The Declining Significance of Race: Blacks and Changing American Institutions, Second Edition* (Chicago: University of Chicago Press, 1980), p. 1.

9. Richard A. Hoehn, "Religious Communities Respond to Hunger," in Marc J. Cohen, ed., *Hunger 1994: Transforming the Politics of Hunger* (Silver Spring, MD: Bread for the World Institute, 1993), p. 38.

10. Billy J. Tidwell, *Playing to Win: A Marshall Plan for America* (New York: National Urban League, 1991).

Native Americans

1. U.S. Bureau of the Census, *We, the . . . First Americans* (Washington: U.S. Government Printing Office, 1993) p. 6; "Poverty in Arizona: A People's Perspective," *Arizona Human Services*, April/May 1994, p. 19.

2. Dee Brown, *Bury My Heart at Wounded Knee* (New York: Random House, 1970).

Gender Discrimination

1. Seema Singh Chauhan, *Options for a Better Life for Young Women: The Prerana-CEDPA Partnership*, (Washington: Center for Economic Development and Population Activities, 1990), p.1.

2. Elizabeth Mathiot (Moen), "Work and Leisure Time Use: The Household Survey," *Hunger Notes* 18:3-4 (Winter/Spring 1993): 33; see also p. 32.

3. United Nations, *The World's Women: Trends and Statistics, 1970-1990* (New York: United Nations, 1991), p. 4.

4. Susan Okie, "Where Choosing a Good Mate is the Will of God," *The Washington Post*, February 15, 1993.

5. "Health Care and the Refugee Family," *Refugees*, no.95 (1994): 26.

6. Information on PEP provided by the Academy for Educational Development.

Additional Sources:

Accion International. *Bolivia Background Paper*. Cambridge, MA: Accion International, 1993.

"Bolivia: The Poverty of Progress." *Report on the Americas* 25:1 (July 1991): 20-21.

Capeling-Alakija, Sharon. "The Bibingka Principle: Women Between the Fires." *Harvard International Review*, Fall 1993, p. 35.

Cash, Nathaniel. "Bolivia's Vice President, First Indian in High Office, Waits for Change." *The New York Times*, September 19, 1993.

Cowan, Ruth. *Pro Mujer: Programs for Women in Bolivia*. Brochure. New York: Pro Mujer, 1994.

Ferris, Elizabeth G. "Women in Uprooted Families." *Development: Journal of SID* (1993:4): 31-33.

"Help For Single-Parent Refugee Families." *Refugees*, no.95 (1994): 21.

International Fund for Agricultural Development. *Women: The Roots of Rural Development*. Rome: IFAD, 1989.

Jacobson, Jodi L. "Gender Bias: Road-block to Sustainable Development." Worldwatch Paper No. 110. Washington: Worldwatch Institute, 1992.

Martin, Susan Forbes. *Refugees, Women, and Development*. London: Zed, 1992.

New Options for International Basic Education. Washington: Academy for Educational Development, 1993.

O'Grady, Barbara. *Teaching Communities to Educate Girls in Balochistan*. Washington: Academy for Educational Development, 1994.

Snyder, Margaret. "Women: The Key to Ending Hunger." The Hunger Project Papers No. 8, August 1990.

U.N. Department of Public Information. *Conference to Set Women's Agenda into Next Century* New York: UNDPI, 1993.

Wali, Sima. "Uprooted Women and Hunger." In *Hunger 1993: Uprooted People*, pp. 54-59. Edited by Marc J. Cohen. Washington: Bread for the World Institute, 1992.

Vulnerability and Age: Children

1. This section is adapted from UNICEF, *The State of the World's Children 1994* (New York: Oxford University Press, 1994), p. 16.

2. These data are based on the numbers and percentage of children under five with lower-than-expected weights for their age. Such a measure does not distinguish between chronic and acute malnutrition, nor between inadequate consumption of calories and protein on the one hand and lack of vitamins and minerals on the other.

3. UNICEF, p. 26.

4. Information on SOMAVITA provided by Academy for Educational Development (AED).

5. ORT information provided by AED.

Additional sources:

Bread for the World. *A Child is Waiting: 1994 Offering of Letters Kit*. Silver Spring, MD: Bread for the World, 1994.

Crocker, D. "Toward Development Ethics." *World Development* 19:5 (1991): 457-483.

Goulet, D. "Tasks and Methods in Development Ethics." *Cross Currents* 38:2 (1988).

Kates, R.W. "Statement to the US House of Representatives, Committee on Agriculture, Subcommittee on Foreign Agriculture and Hunger." April 29, 1993.

Koniz-Booher, Peggy, ed. *Communication Strategies to Support Infant and Young Child Nutrition: Proceedings of an International Conference*. Washington: Academy for Educational Development, 1992.

Micronutrients: Increasing Survival, Learning, and Economic Productivity – A Report on the USAID Micronutrient Program. Washington: Academy for Educational Development, 1993.

Parlato, Margaret; Green, Cynthia; and Fishman, Claudia. *Communicating to Improve Nutrition Behavior: The Challenge of Motivating the Audience to Act*. Washington: Academy for Educational Development, 1992.

Results and Realities: A Decade of Experience in Communication for Child Survival. Washington: Academy for Educational Development, 1992.

Seidel, Renata, ed. *Notes from the Field in Communication for Child Survival*. Washington: Academy for Educational Development, 1993.

Uccelani, Valerie and Vella, Jane. *Learning to Listen to Mothers: Strengthening Communication for Nutrition and Growth Promotion*. Washington: Academy for Educational Development, 1993.

UNICEF. *The Progress of Nations 1993*. New York: UNICEF, 1993.

_____. *The State of the World's Children 1991*. New York: Oxford University Press, 1991.

Vulnerability and Age: Elderly People

1. Clif Cartland, "The Burden of Age," *World Vision*, June-July 1991, p. 12.

2. Sergio Valiente, "Diet and Malnutrition in Chilean Elderly," Paper Presented in Round Table on "Nutrition and Malnutrition in the Elderly," XIV World Congress of Gerontology, Acapulco, Mexico, June 19-23, 1989.

3. Elizabeth Mesfin *et al.*, "Nutritional Status, Socioeconomic Environment, and Lifestyle of the Elderly in Au-gust Town, Kingston, Jamaica," in Pan American Health Organization and American Association of Retired Persons, *Midlife and Older Women in Latin America and the Caribbean* (Washington: PAHO, 1989).

4. John Codler *et al.*, "Inequality Among Children and Elderly in Ten Modern Nations: The United States in an International Context," Papers Presented at the Hundred and First Annual Meeting of the American Economic Association, New York, December 28-30, 1988.

5. John Rich, M. M., "Growing Old Gracefully," *Maryknoll*, March 1994, p. 7; see also p. 10.

6. *Ibid.*

7. Mark Wahlqvist *et al.*, "An Anthropological Approach to the Study of Food and Health in an Indigenous Population," *Food and Nutrition Bulletin* 13:2 (June 1991): 145-149.

8. Ansah Ruth Ayisi, "Family Values," *Africa Report*, January-February, 1993, p. 66.

9. United Nations, *Portraits of Age* (video), April 1994.

10. Cesar Chelala, *Health of the Elderly: A Concern for All*, Communicating for Health Series No. 2 (Washington: PAHO, 1992), p. 1.

11. UNICEF. "A Year to Renew the Family," *First Call for Children*, January-March, 1994, p.1.

Additional Sources:

Brody, Jane E. "Personal Health." *The New York Times*, February 8, 1990.

Burt, Martha R. *Hunger Among the Elderly: Local and National Comparisons*. Washington: Urban Institute, 1993.

Davies, Michael. "Older Populations, Aging Individuals and Health for All." *Health Forum* 10 (1989): 299-320.

Edwards, S.J. *Nutrition in the Middle and Later Years*. Boston: John Wright, PSG, Inc., 1983.

Haessig, Carolyn J. "Factors Influencing Food Intake of ELDERHOSTEL Participants: 1956 and 1981. *Journal of Nutrition for the Elderly* (1984): 13-26.

Heisel, Marsel A. "Aging in the Context of Population Policies in Developing Countries." *Population Bulletin of the United Nations* 17 (1984): 58.

Ibrahim, M. *Tradition and Modern Development in Bangladesh Society*. Dhaka: Bangladesh Association for the Aged, 1985.

Kendig, Mall L. *et al.*, eds. *Family Support for the Elderly: The International Experience*. Geneva: World Health Organization, 1992.

Oyog, Angeline. "The Future is Grey." *Populi*, December 1992/January 1993, pp. 4-5.

Telephone interview with Dr. Nevin Scrimshaw, Emeritus Professor of Nutrition, Massachusetts Institute of Technology, May 1994.

Tout, Ken. *Aging in Developing Countries*. New York: HelpAge International, 1989.

U.S. Bureau of the Census, Center for International Research, 1993 Database (unpublished).

Sponsors

Bread for the World Institute seeks to inform, educate, nurture, and motivate concerned citizens for action on policies which affect hungry people. Based on policy analysis and consultation with poor people, it develops educational resources and activities including its annual report on the state of world hunger, policy briefs, and study guides, together with workshops, seminars, briefings, and an anti-hunger leadership development program. Contributions to the Institute are tax-deductible. It works closely with Bread for the World, a Christian citizens' movement of 44,000 members, who advocate specific policy changes to help overcome hunger in the United States and overseas.

> 1100 Wayne Ave., Suite 1000
> Silver Spring, MD 20910
> Ph. (301) 608-2400
> Fx. (301) 608-2401

BROT für die Welt is an association of German Protestant churches which seeks to overcome poverty and hunger in developing countries, as an expression of their Christian faith and convictions, by funding programs of relief and development. Founded in 1959, BROT has funded more than 15,000 programs in over 100 nations in Africa, Latin America, and Asia. For nearly 35 years the emphases of the programs which BROT funds has shifted from relief to development and empowerment. BROT's programs of education in Germany are intended to lead to changes – in understanding and lifestyle at the personal level, and to policy changes at the national, European Union, and international levels.

> Stafflenbergstrasse 76, Postfach 10 11 42
> D-70010 Stuttgart, Germany
> Ph. 07 11-2159-0
> Fx. 07 11-2159-368

CARE is the world's largest relief and development organization not affiliated with a government or religion. Each year, CARE reaches more than 25 million people in over 40 nations in Africa, Asia, and Latin America. The organization's work began in 1946, when its famous CARE packages helped Europe recover from World War II. Today, CARE improves health care and the environment, helps subsistence farmers and small business owners produce more goods, addresses population concerns, and reaches disaster victims with emergency assistance. The scope of CARE's work is broad, but its vision focuses on a single concept – helping people help themselves.

> 151 Ellis Street
> Atlanta, GA 30303
> Ph. (404) 681-2552
> Fx. (404) 577-6271

Christian Children's Fund is the largest independent childcare agency in the world, providing assistance to more than half a million children and their families in 40 countries and the United States. An international, not-for-profit, nonsectarian agency, free of political associations, Christian Children's Fund provides education, medical care, food, clothing, and shelter to children around the world. Services are provided based on need and without regard to sex, race, creed, or religion. Christian Children's Fund recently began new programs in Central and Eastern Europe and the Middle East.

> 2821 Emerywood Parkway, PO Box 26227
> Richmond, VA 23261-6227
> Ph. (804) 756-2700
> Fx. (804) 756-2718

LCMS World Relief (Lutheran Church – Missouri Synod) provides relief and development funding for domestic and international projects. Based under the Synod's Department of Human Care Ministries, LCMS World Relief provides domestic grants for Lutheran congregations and social ministry organizations as well as other groups with Lutheran involvement which are engaged in ministries of human care. Domestic support is also provided to Inter-Lutheran Disaster Response and Lutheran Immigration and Refugee Service. International relief and development assistance is channeled through the Synod's mission stations and partner churches as well as Lutheran World Relief.

> 1333 So. Kirkwood Road
> St. Louis, MO 63122-7295
> Ph. (800) 248-1930, ext. 1392
> Fx. (314) 965-0541

Lutheran World Relief, founded in 1945, acts in behalf of Lutheran Churches in the U.S.A. LWR is an overseas relief and development agency which responds quickly to disasters and humanitarian crises and supports more than 160 long-range development projects in over 35 countries throughout Africa, Asia, the Middle East, and Latin America. Through an Office on Development Policy in Washington D.C., LWR also monitors legislation on foreign aid and development and serves as an advocate for public policies which address the root causes of hunger, injustice, and poverty.

> 390 Park Avenue South
> New York, NY 10016
> Ph. (212) 532-6350
> Fx. (212) 213-6081

For twenty-five years, the **Presbyterian Hunger Program** has provided a channel for congregations to respond to hunger in the United States and around the world. With a commitment to the ecumenical sharing of human and financial resources, the program provides support for programs of direct food relief, sustainable development, and public policy advocacy. A network of 100 Hunger Action Enablers leads the Presbyterian Church (USA) in the study of hunger issues, engagement with communities of need, advocacy for just public policies, and the movement toward simpler corporate and personal lifestyles.

> 100 Witherspoon Street
> Louisville, KY 40202-1396
> Ph. (502) 569-5832
> Fx. (502) 569-5018

Share Our Strength (SOS) works to alleviate and prevent hunger by distributing grants, educating the public, and creating community outreach programs in the United States and throughout the world. SOS is one of the nation's largest private, nonprofit sources of funds for hunger relief, and mobilizes thousand of volunteers to contribute their skills and resources to its programs. Founded in 1984 to organize the food industry on behalf of hunger relief groups, SOS's network of volunteers now includes more than 6,000 chefs, restaurateurs, writers, artists, photographers, and creative professionals from a variety of fields. Since its inception, SOS has raised over $15 million for distribution to more than 600 hunger relief and community development organizations in the U.S., Canada, and in developing countries. Beneficiaries include: direct food assistance programs (food banks, prepared and perishable food rescue programs), long-term approaches to hunger relief (nutrition education, microenterprise development), and international community development agencies. Some of Share Our Strength's programs include: Share Our Strength's Taste of the Nation, presented by American Express; Operation Frontline; Writers Harvest: The National Reading; Share Our Strength's Book Projects; and SOS Market Booths.

> 1511 K Street, N.W., Suite 940
> Washington, DC 20005
> Ph. (202) 393-2925
> Fx. (202) 347-5868

Shield-Ayers Foundation

The **United Methodist Committee on Relief** (UMCOR) was formed in 1940 in response to the suffering of people during World War II. It was a "voice of conscience" expressing the concern of the church for the disrupted and devastated lives churned out by the war. UMCOR has expanded its ministry into more than 80 countries to minister with compassion to persons in need, through programs and services which provide immediate relief and long-term attention to the root causes of their need. Focusing on refugee, hunger, and disaster ministries, the work of UMCOR, a program department of the General Board of Global Ministries of the United Methodist Church, is carried out through direct services and a worldwide network of national and international church agencies which cooperate in the task of alleviating human suffering.

> 475 Riverside Drive, Room 1374
> New York, NY 10115
> Ph. (212) 870-3816 (800) 841-1235
> Fx. (212) 870-3624

The **United Nations Children's Fund** (UNICEF) for more than 40 years has supported countries to improve and expand their services for children, to help establish priorities, and to reach the neediest children. UNICEF promotes the well-being of children throughout their formative years in 127 countries and territories. Almost all UNICEF resources are invested in the poorest developing countries, with the greatest share supporting children up to age five. UNICEF support is provided for emergencies and for longer-term programs in such areas as health, water supply and sanitation, nutrition, and education. UNICEF is an integral, yet semi-autonomous part of the U.N. system. It is also unique among U.N. organizations in that it relies entirely on voluntary public and government contributions.

> 3 United Nations Plaza
> New York, NY 10017-4414
> Ph. (212) 326-7035
> Fx. (212) 888-7465

World Vision, founded in 1950, is a Christian humanitarian aid organization carrying out relief and development activities in 94 countries, including the United States. The U.S. national support office is headquartered in Los Angeles, and national support offices in 16 other countries raise funds for transforming the lives of the poor in Africa, Asia, Latin America, and Eastern Europe. Meeting the health care, educational, vocational, and nutritional needs of children and their families is the focal point of programs leading to the long-term sustainable development of communities. Through 6,243 projects, worldwide, World Vision affirms the right of every child to education, good nutrition, health care, and spiritual nurture. More than 1 million children are sponsored through World Vision donors from industrialized nations.

> 919 West Huntington Drive
> Monrovia, CA 91016
> Ph. (818) 357-7979
> Fx. (818) 303-7651

Cosponsors

The **Academy for Educational Development** (AED), founded in 1961, is an independent, nonprofit service organization committed to addressing human development needs in the United States and throughout the world. Under contracts and grants, the Academy operates programs in collaboration with policy leaders; nongovernmental and community-based organizations; governmental agencies; international multilateral and bilateral funders; and schools, colleges, and universities. In partnership with its clients, the Academy seeks to meet today's social, economic, and environmental challenges through education and human resource development; to apply state-of-the-art education, training, research, technology, management, behavioral analysis, and social marketing techniques to solve problems; and to improve knowledge and skills throughout the world as the most effective means for stimulating growth, reducing poverty, and promoting democratic and humanitarian ideals. The Academy for Educational Development is registered with the U.S. Agency for International Development as a private voluntary organization. The Academy is exempt from federal income taxes under Section 501 (c)(3) of the Internal Revenue Code. Contributions to the Academy are tax deductible.

> 1875 Connecticut Avenue, N.W.
> Washington, D.C. 20009-1202
> Ph. (202) 884-8000
> Fx. (202) 884-8400
> Internet: ADMINDC@AED.ORG

Christian Reformed World Relief Committee (CRWRC) is the relief and development agency of the Christian Reformed Church in North America, with offices in Grand Rapids, Michigan, and Burlington, Ontario, Canada. CRWRC was begun in 1962 to respond to the needs of Korean war victims, Cuban refugees, and victims of natural disasters in North America. Today, it focuses on helping the poorest of the poor meet their own needs through community development in more than 30 countries around the world. Through cooperative efforts with national Christian churches and organizations, CRWRC staff enables more than 75,000 families to free themselves from material and spiritual poverty. CRWRC also helps strengthen churches and community organizations.

> 2850 Kalamazoo Ave., S.E.
> Grand Rapids. MI 49560-0600
> Ph. (616) 247-5875
> Fx. (616) 246-0806

Church World Service (CWS) is a global relief, development, and refugee assistance ministry of the 32 Protestant and Orthodox communities that work together through the National Council of Churches. Founded in 1946, CWS works in partnership with local church organizations in more than 70 countries worldwide, supporting sustainable self-help development of people which respects the environment, meets emergency needs, and addresses root causes of poverty and powerlessness. Within the United States, CWS resettles refugees, assists communities in responding to disasters, advocates for justice in U.S. policies which relate to global issues, provides educational resources, and offers opportunities for communities to join a people-to-people network of global and local caring through participation in a CROP walk.

> 475 Riverside Drive, Suite 678
> New York, NY 10115-0050
> Ph. (212) 870-2257
> Fx. (212)870-2055

CODEL (Coordination in Development) is a membership association of Catholic, Protestant, and Orthodox organizations that respond globally to our Lord's invitation, "Whatever you do to the least of mine, you do unto me," through environmentally sustainable socioeconomic development. The purpose of CODEL throughout the developing world is to support training and other development activities identified by people of all faiths who have limited opportunities to participate in economic, social, environmental, and political decisions that affect their lives. CODEL supports these activities wherever that support fosters ecumenical collaboration and Christian unity. CODEL also seeks to inform and awaken the consciousness of the people of the U.S. to human needs.

> 475 Riverside Drive, Suite 1842
> New York, NY 10115-0050
> Ph. (212) 870-3000
> Fx. (212) 870-3545

EuronAid is a European association of nongovernmental organizations which facilitates dialogue with the Commission of the European Union. EuronAid cooperates with the Commission in programming and procuring food aid for the NGOs, then arranges and accounts for delivery to Third World NGOs for distribution. In recent years, triangular operations (purchases within Third World nations) have accounted for half of EuronAid's food aid, which meets both emergency and development purposes. EuronAid assimilates the experiences of NGOs involved in food aid and employs this knowledge in its dialogue with the Commission and the European Parliament to achieve improved management of food aid. EuronAid was created in 1980 by major European NGOs in cooperation with the Commission of the European Union. The association has at present 26 member agencies, and services an additional 50 European NGOs on a regular basis.

> PO Box 12
> NL-2501 CA Den Haag
> The Netherlands
> Ph. 31 70 330 57 57
> Fx. 31 70 364 17 01

Freedom from Hunger, founded in 1946 as Meals for Millions, launches innovative programs to eliminate chronic hunger – providing resources and information that empower the poorest families and communities to help themselves. The *Credit with Education* program in developing countries on four continents supports self-help groups of women by providing cash, credit, and nonformal adult education. *Credit* enables participants to increase their income-earning and savings opportunities so they can buy or grow more and better food. *Education* enhances their money management and offers knowledge and motivation to improve their health, nutrition, and family planning practices. In the United States, Freedom from Hunger helps existing health and human service programs work more effectively with low-income communities to improve family health and nutrition.

> 1644 DaVinci Court
> Davis, CA 95617
> Ph. (916) 758-6200
> Fx. (916) 758-6241

Hunger Action – United Church of Christ. For almost 20 years the Hunger Action program has been overseeing the hunger ministries of the United Church of Christ. Working with local congregations, regional and national offices, the Hunger Action program offers a holistic approach, providing educational and worship resources, making grants to organizations seeking to address systemic causes of hunger and poverty, and coordinating efforts of advocacy and public policy.

> 700 Prospect Avenue
> Cleveland, OH 44115
> Ph. (216) 736-3290
> Fx. (216) 736-3293

MAZON: A Jewish Response to Hunger has granted more than $8 million since 1986 to nonprofit organizations confronting hunger in the United States and abroad. MAZON (the Hebrew word for "food") awards grants principally to programs working to prevent and alleviate hunger in the United States. Grantees include emergency and direct food assistance programs, food banks, multi-service organizations, anti-hunger advocacy/education and research projects and international hunger-relief and agricultural development programs in Israel and impoverished countries. Although responsive to organizations serving impoverished Jews, in keeping with the best of Jewish tradition, MAZON responds to all who are in need.

> 2940 Westwood Blvd., Suite 7
> Los Angeles, CA 90064-4120
> Ph. (310) 470-7769
> Fx. (310) 470-6736

Mennonite Central Committee (MCC), founded in 1920, is an agency of the Mennonite and Brethren in Christ churches in North America, and seeks to demonstrate God's love through committed women and men who work among people suffering from poverty, conflict, oppression, and natural disaster. MCC serves as a channel for interchange between churches and community groups where it works around the world and North American churches. MCC strives for peace, justice, and dignity of all people by sharing experiences, resources, and faith. MCC's priorities include disaster relief and refugee assistance, rural and agricultural development, job creation (SELFHELP Crafts), health, and education.

> 21 South 12th Street
> Akron, PA 17501-0500
> Ph. (717) 859-1151
> Fx. (717) 859-2171

Save the Children Federation/U.S. helps make lasting, positive differences in the lives of disadvantaged children in the United States and 35 countries overseas. Programs are guided by a set of principles known as CBIRD – community-based integrated rural development. This approach includes community participation in identifying goals and implementing projects. The CBIRD approach relies on nonformal educational techniques – transferring skills and encouraging self-help and the maximum use of available resources. In SC's international programs, the four key development sectors are: primary health; environmentally sound sustainable agriculture; productivity, especially through small-scale enterprises; and education. Save the Children also supports refugee assistance programs in Africa, Asia, and the Middle East, and provides disaster relief.

> 54 Wilton Road
> Westport, CT 06880
> Ph. (203) 221-4000
> Fx. (203) 221-4123

Second Harvest is a network of 185 affiliated food banks in the United States which provide food to the hungry through nearly 50,000 social service agencies. As the largest charitable source of food in the United States, the Second Harvest network annually distributes more than 500 million pounds of donated food and grocery products.

The Second Harvest mission is to:

- Feed the hungry by soliciting and judiciously distributing marketable but surplus food and grocery products to a nationwide network of food banks;

- Develop, certify, and support Second Harvest food banks that channel food and grocery products to local nonprofit charities that provide services to the needy;

- Serve as a liaison between food banks and donors; and

- Educate the public about the nature of, and solutions to, the problems of hunger.

> 116 South Michigan Avenue, Suite 4
> Chicago, IL 60603-6001
> Ph. (312) 263-2303
> Fx. (312) 263-5626

The Trull Foundation (and predecessor B.W. Trull Foundation) has been interested in educational, religious, cultural, and social programs since 1948. Current priorities include concern for:

1. The needs of the Palacios, Texas area where the Foundation has its roots;

2. Pre-adolescents, and opportunities to direct lives away from child abuse, neglect, and hunger, towards an adolescence of good mental and physical growth; and

3. Mexican-Americans in South Texas, to help them "catch up," hurdle a language barrier, a poverty barrier, and system which has consistently kept them poor, uneducated, and unrepresented.

> 404 Fourth St.
> Palacios, TX 77465
> Ph. (512) 972-5241

The **United Nations Development Programme** (UNDP) is the world's largest multilateral development grant organization. Funded by voluntary contributions from governments totalling about US $1 billion yearly, it serves more than 170 developing countries and territories. To carry out its programs, UNDP draws upon developing countries' capacities, as well as the expertise of specialized U.N. agencies and nongovernmental organizations. People are at the center of all UNDP activities, which aim to build developing countries' capacities for sustainable human development. The emphasis is on poverty alleviation and grassroots development; environmental protection and regeneration; job creation; and the advancement of women. Close cooperation is maintained with other U.N. agencies. UNDP administers the U.N. Development Fund for Women and several other special purpose funds. With the World Bank and U.N. Environment Program, it manages the Global Environment Facility. At the country level, the head of the UNDP office is usually responsible for coordinating all U.N.-supported development activities.

One United Nations Plaza
New York, NY 10017
Ph. (212) 906-5000
Fx. (212) 826-2057

Winrock International is a leader in sustainable agricultural, rural development, and environmental programs that help people increase food production and stimulate economic growth, without threatening natural resources. Projects provide technical assistance, human resource development, policy and institutional improvement. Winrock works in the United States, Asia, Africa, the Middle East, Latin America, the Caribbean, Eastern Europe, and the former Soviet Union. Projects are funded by grants, contracts, and contributions from public and private sources. Operations are headquartered outside Little Rock, Arkansas, on the mountain-top farm of the late Winthrop Rockefeller. Regional offices are located in Arlington, Virginia; Manila, the Philippines; and Abidjan, Côte d'Ivoire.

Route 3, Box 376
Morrilton, AR 72110-9537
Ph. (501) 727-5435
Fx. (501) 727-5242

World Relief is the relief and development arm of the National Association of Evangelicals in the United States. Since 1944, World Relief has provided both immediate and long-term assistance to people who suffer from poverty, disease, hunger, and war. Working with groups in Asia, Latin America, Africa, the Middle East, and the United States, World Relief supports programs focused on disaster relief, refugee assistance, income generation, and health.

PO Box WRC
Wheaton, IL 60189
Ph. (708) 665-0235
Fx. (708) 653-8023